To our children, John and Marie

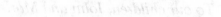

ACKNOWLEDGMENTS

The authors are indebted to Michael C. Braswell, Ph.D., Department of Criminal Justice, East Tennessee State University, and to Susan Braswell for the editorial assistance they provided in the preparation of this text.

ABOUT THE AUTHORS

William G. Archambeault is an Associate Professor of Criminal Justice, Louisiana State University at Baton Rouge. He holds a Ph.D. in Criminology from Florida State University, and Master and Bachelor degrees in Criminology from Indiana State University. He is the author or co-author of numerous publications in the areas of criminal justice organizational management and comparative criminal justice. He is also the co-author of a text on correctional supervisory management and a text on microcomputer applications in criminal justice.

Betty J. Archambeault is a Curriculum Specialist and computer science instructor at Catholic High School in Baton Rouge, a private college preparatory school. She holds a Ph.D. in Education from Louisiana State University, and Master and Bachelor degrees in English Education from Indiana State University. She has nineteen years of teaching experience at the elementary, secondary and college levels. She is the author of several articles on communication and readability issues as related to criminal justice management and the applications of computer-assisted instruction. She is also the co-author of a text on correctional supervisory management and a text on microcomputer applications in criminal justice.

PREFACE

Computers in Criminal Justice Administration and Management: Introduction to Emerging Issues and Applications, Second Edition, provides a learning foundation for understanding the increasing use of computers in criminal justice and explores the implication of an emerging *information dependent society*. Presented in this text is an introduction to computers as management tools with emphasis on microcomputer applications in the administration of American police, court, corrections, and juvenile organizations. As in the first edition, particular focus is given to data base management, information networking, computer assisted writing (CAW), computer assisted instruction (CAI) and computer related criminal justice issues. In addition, this edition includes a separate chapter on the rapidly developing area of computer assisted monitoring of offenders (CAMO).

Every attempt has been made to keep discussions current with evolving technology. However, the reader should understand that "current technology" changes every six to ten months, and major advances occur in cycles of three to four years as manufacturers introduce new or improved products to the marketplace. Examples of hardware and software illustrate fixed points in an ever-transforming world of "new and improved" computer technology. It is important to understand examples in terms of emerging trends.

This text has been written in a "user friendly format," which presumes that a reader has a basic awareness of computers and management. While its focus is on criminal justice organizational management, the technology discussed, suggestions made, products (hardware and software) described, and information presented make this text applicable to a wide range of interests. The agency head or department manager who is faced with the purchase of a small computer system will find the hardware-software commentary throughout the text to be of value. The researcher, fiscal officer, or planner involved in data base management, inventory control, or statistical analysis will find Chapter 2 of interest. The scholar, student, or others interested in professional writing will find the discussions on computer assisted writing (CAW) or word processing in Chapter 3 to be helpful. The teacher, corrections worker, or agency trainer will find discussions of computer assisted instruction (CAI) in Chapter 4 to be of use in selecting courseware. Discussion on computer assisted monitoring of offenders (CAMO) will be of interest to a wide variety of readers, especially to agencies considering the adoption of CAMO. Finally, the last chapter on emerging issues will be of interest to anyone interested in computers and criminal justice.

This text contains a Preface, Table of Contents, six chapters, Cumulative Bibliography, Glossary of Selected Terms, and Index. Each chapter begins with a Chapter Preview and Study Questions and concludes with Review Questions. The Cumulative Bibliography includes references cited in the chapters and recommends additional sources of information. The Glossary lists and defines terms used in the text. The Index provides quick reference to the topics discussed.

Table of Contents

Chapter 1

COMPUTERS IN CRIMINAL JUSTICE: AN OVERVIEW

CHAPTER PREVIEW

This chapter presents a basic introduction to computers, computer terminology, computer languages, the history of computer development, concepts of organizational management, and the applications of computers in the administration of criminal justice agencies and institutions. It serves as a foundation for later chapters. This chapter assumes that the reader has a basic awareness of computers. For readers who want more detailed information, supplemental sources are suggested in the Cumulative Bibliography at the end of the text.

Advances in computer technology, particularly in the area of microcomputers and minicomputers, have revolutionized many concepts of organizational management, altered the value of information, and affected the flow of information within organizations. Computer technology has changed, and will continue to change the nature of American society, the processes of government, and the disposition of justice itself. This chapter describes a variety of computer hardware and uses specific products as illustrations. While every attempt has been made to present examples of current technology, the life expectancy of the label "current" is less than a year, and major developments in technology occur every three to four years. As a result, some product information may not be current by the time this text is in print. Nevertheless, it is important to understand the general trends in computer technology and the potential of various trends for the future of criminal justice.

Several limitations of the book need to be expressed here. First, while a number of different types of computers are discussed, emphasis is placed on microcomputer technology as related to criminal justice management. Microcomputers are the first computers which most people encounter and are the most widely used category of computers found in organizations today.

Second, most decisions and examples of hardware and software are limited to IBM compatible products. This is because IBM, as discussed later in this chapter, is recognized as an industry standard. IBM and IBM clones account for approximately 75-80% of the professional microcomputers in use in American business related organizations today. Although IBM is losing much of its market share to its clones, particularly to a group of companies which will be referred to later as "the gang of nine," and although other brands, especially the Apple MacIntosh, are also challenging IBM's dominance, IBM standards continue to dominate the microcomputer industry.

Third, at the time of this revision, the OS/2 operating system, which is discussed later in this chapter, had been recently released. Most examples of IBM compatible software are limited to PC/MS-DOS 3.3 (and earlier) based versions.

STUDY QUESTIONS

The following study questions may be used as a guide to reading Chapter 1. Key terms and concepts related to these questions are printed in italics throughout the chapter.

1.   What are the significant historical events in the development of modern computers?

2.   What is the information society?

3.   How is the information society affecting criminal justice organizations?

4.   What elements should be considered when evaluating computers for possible purchase?

CRIMINAL JUSTICE ORGANIZATIONAL MANAGEMENT: THE MICROCOMPUTER INTERFACE WITH AN INFORMATION SOCIETY

An organization exists whenever two or more people come together to work toward some common goal. To ensure that the organizations they manage achieve their assigned tasks, administrators must perform a complex variety of tasks. One organization characterized by a unique complexity of management tasks is the American criminal justice system. All components of the American criminal justice system, the police, the courts, the correctional system and juvenile justice, consist of various agencies, bureaus or departments; each is an organization. The structure and processes involved in directing, controlling and administering these agencies, bureaus or departments is organizational management. By definition, criminal justice organizational management includes the interrelated administrative processes of organizing, planning, communicating, staffing, training, budgeting, directing and controlling (Archambeault and Archambeault, 1982:40-65). These processes are not the primary focus of this text and are not discussed in their entirety. For the purpose of this text, it is sufficient to note that all management processes share one common characteristic; success is dependent on the collection, analysis, storage and retrieval of information.

America and other industrialized societies are in the midst of an information technology revolution. Information technology has become a source of enormous power; those who control the flow of information control economic, industrial, political and social institutions. The potential for misuse of this power has suggested to some writers that America is experiencing the rise of a computer state, in which the government has the ability to monitor every electronic transaction of individuals, including credit card use, checks and telephone calls. Others argue that in a free society access to information is guaranteed, and information technology will lead to greater expression of individual freedoms.

Like other American organizations, criminal justice has become increasingly information dependent. In order to function, these organizations are dependent upon the rapid and accurate processing of massive volumes of information. The diverse and often conflict ridden criminal justice organization of the 1980s struggles to cope with the demands of a rapidly changing society and interdependent world economy. Unlike business and industry, which have also become increasingly information dependent, criminal justice agencies face additional problems. New computer technologies create new opportunities for computer crime. The task of defining, presenting, control-

ling and investigating crimes associated with computer hardware and software falls squarely in the realm of criminal justice organizations. Thus, for
criminal justice, computer technology has become both a management survival tool and a new source of problems.

Computer technology, particularly the microcomputer, has revolutionized communication and information processing. America is in the process
of evolving from an industrial society to what Naisbitt (1982) calls an informational society, in which information itself and the speed of its delivery are
major economic factors. The result is a society in which we "now mass- produce information the way we used to mass-produce cars." As Drucker, a futurist commentator notes, "The productivity of knowledge has already become the key to productivity, competitive strength, and economic achievement. Knowledge has already become the primary industry, the industry that
supplies the economy the essential and central resources of production"
(Naisbitt, 1982:17).

The information society is now an American economic, political and social reality in which individual and organizational survival is dependent on the
ability to access information. As telecommunication continues to improve,
both the rate of change and the degree of individual and organizational dependency on information will increase. The extent of change is unforesee-
able. Electronic delivery of mail will be commonplace. Projections by the
Office of Technology Assessment show that the volume of first class mail,
measured in millions of pieces, will drop from 75 in 1985 to 55 by the year
2000. Shopping, business and financial transactions between individuals and
organizations will be accomplished electronically. Education and training
will employ computer assisted programs which will interact with video display
terminals combining real life circumstances and simulation. Medical doctors
will routinely consult a computerized expert system for a second opinion.
Computer literacy will become as fundamental in American society as the
ability to read. Employers will insist on computer literacy for all employees.
The demand for computer system designers and engineers will be high, although the need for general programmers may decrease because software
programs will be easily modified by the user. By the 1990s, computer literacy
will become a basic job requirement for employment in criminal justice, especially in policework. Robots, which are essentially computers with mobil-
ity, will be employed extensively in police and corrections work, as well as in
schools and homes.

Accelerated technological advances in information assimilation and delivery, and the concomitant pressures on human organizations, are today
forcing a major change in organizational management structures. Traditional
concepts of bureaucratic management will be discarded and replaced with
new systems and concepts. (See, e.g. Naisbitt, 1982; Ouchi, 1982; Athos and

Pascale, 1982). Changes are also being forced on the criminal justice organization. (See, e.g. Archambeault, 1982; Archambeault and Weirman, 1983; Archambeault and Fenwick, 1983).

Advances in large centralized computer systems have assisted in the administration of some criminal justice organizations since the late 1960s. However, until recently, the cost of equipment and the high level of employee education and the amount of sophisticated training necessary to make use of this technology limited the application of these computer systems to only the largest agencies and institutions. Furthermore, software incompatibility, or the inability of programs developed for one type of computer in one agency to run on another agency's computer, hindered or prevented the exchange of information between agencies. The advent of the microprocessor and microchip and the resulting miniaturization of computer hardware has reduced the size and price of computers so that some microcomputers today are smaller and less expensive than a high-quality electric typewriter. Yet, these microcomputers offer accessibility to worldwide information systems through a standard telephone modem. Microcomputers have changed forever the management processes of American police, courts, corrections and juvenile justice. New technological advancements will continue to change these organizations. A review of the historical development of the modern computer provides a basis for understanding contemporary computers and some of the problems computer users may experience.

THE DEVELOPMENT OF COMPUTERS: AN HISTORICAL PERSPECTIVE

A *computer* by definition is "a device capable of accepting information, applying prescribed processes to the information, and supplying the results of these processes" (Sippl, 1985:89). When literally applied, the term computer would seem to include all electronic devices containing microchips with logic circuits ranging from "computer-like" toys (e.g. video arcade games, Speak'N Spell) to personal computers to the large state-of-the-art mainframe computers (e.g. IBM 3081, UNIVAC 1100). While the widespread use of computers is a phenomenon of the twentieth century, efforts to create computer devices have a long history. This section traces the development of modern computers and man's hesitant, and often suspicious, acceptance of them.

Pre-Twentieth Century Devices

The history of computers is the history of mankind's attempt to dupli-
cate and expand human intelligence through mechanical, electrical and electronic means. The origins of present day computers can be traced back to
the abacus, a primitive device capable of rapid mathematical computations in
the hands of a skilled user. The abacus is known to have existed in India,
China and Japan as early as 3500 B.C., and in Europe as early as 1000 B.C.
In the early 1600s, John Napier designed a multiplication tool, called Napier's
Bones, which consisted of a series of rods with numbers printed on them.
The user slid the rods up and down, matching the numbers, to complete
multiplication and division problems. This led to the invention of the slide
rule in the mid-1600s (Hopper and Mandell, 1987).

In 1642, Blaise Pascal, a French philosopher and mathematician, designed and built a mechanical device capable of adding and subtracting.
Based on an intricate system of eight rotating gears contained within a rect-
angular box approximately eighteen inches long, the device was so delicately
balanced that it required frequent adjustments to maintain accuracy. Pascal
designed the device with the hope that it would assist his father, a tax official,
and other clerks as they added long columns of numbers. Although his father
appreciated the calculating device, the tax clerks refused to use the machine
because they believed it might eliminate their jobs (Hopper and Mandell,
1987; Stern and Stern, 1983).

Working independently of Pascal, a Prussian mathematician, Gottfried
Liebniz, designed a mechanical device in 1671 capable of adding, subtracting,
multiplying and dividing. Liebniz spent several years perfecting his machine,
which like Pascal's device, was based on a series of gears. Viewed essentially
as a curiosity in Europe, Liebniz sent copies of the device to the Emperor of
China and Peter the Great of Russia in 1694. Although the machine had
potential, the lack of precisely made gears caused it to prove unreliable
(Graham, 1986).

The profit motive encouraged Joseph Jacquard, a Frenchman, to create
a device which foreshadowed early computer cards. The Jacquard family had
amassed a small fortune selling intricately woven silk fabric which they purchased from peasant weavers working in cottage industries. Recognizing that
certain fabric patterns were more popular with customers, Jacquard wanted
to ensure that the French weavers would all produce the most popular patterns. In 1801, he invented a card-like device which could be attached to the
loom. The cards had holes punched in them which were arranged in a certain pattern. As the loom was operated, the holes in the cards controlled the
pattern by allowing wire hooks to drop through the holes and grasp the
thread. Where there were no holes, there was no contact between the wire

hooks and the thread. In reality, these cards functioned as a program, automatically directing the operation of the loom. The device met resistance from the cottage industry weavers who feared unemployment. To protest Jacquard's device, the French weavers wedged their wooden shoes (sabots) into the looms. The practice occurred so often that the French began to call the protesting weavers "saboteurs." Despite the protests, by 1812, Jacquard's device was used on over 11,000 looms in France alone (Stern and Stern, 1983).

The beginning of the Industrial Revolution in the eighteenth century created a wide spread need for reliable calculating devices. The father of the modern computer, Charles Babbage, was a prolific inventor. His inventions included the skeleton key, the locomotive cow catcher and the speedometer (Graham, 1986; Stern and Stern, 1983). In 1822, Babbage worked with John Herschel, an astronomer, to devise a machine capable of accurately calculating astronomical tables used in navigation. The result was the Difference Engine, which despite its name, calculated tables based on repeated additions (Graham, 1986). Recognizing the value of the invention, the British government provided Babbage a grant equivalent to $7000 to perfect the machine (Stern and Stern, 1983).

After only a short period of time, Babbage abandoned his original invention to begin work on a more ambitious project, the Analytical Engine. This steam powered machine had several components similar to twentieth century computers, including an arithmetic/logic unit to manipulate data, a control unit to perform stored instructions, an input unit which received instructions and data on punched cards, and an output unit which produced results (Hopper and Mandell, 1987; Graham, 1986). Because Babbage continuously changed plans and appeared to make little progress, the British government discontinued funding for the Analytical Engine in 1827.

Although the Analytical Engine was never perfected, it received attention from several sources and papers describing the machine that were circulated among mathematicians throughout Europe. The first program written to demonstrate the capabilities of the machine was authored by Countess Augusta Ada Lovelace. Daughter of the English poet, Lord Byron, Lovelace had been educated as a mathematician, which was unusual for an aristocratic nineteenth century British female. In 1842, she read a paper, written in French, describing Babbage's Analytical Machine. With Babbage's permission, she translated the paper into English, added her own notes, and included a demonstration program. In addition, she later invented the programming "loop," a now common programming technique. Because of her contributions, she is recognized as the first programmer (Graham, 1986; Hopper and Mandell, 1987).

The concept of punched cards suggested by Jacquard, Babbage and Lovelace was further developed by Herman Hollerith, a statistician employed by the U.S. Census Bureau. In order to reduce the time needed to tabulate census data, in 1884, Hollerith invented a machine to read and sort data from punched cards. Hollerith's cards were the exact size of an 1880 U.S. dollar bill and contained 12 rows of 80 columns for encoding data concerning an individual's birth date, sex and citizenship. Hollerith's cards remained the standard for recording data for computer use until the 1970s when video display terminals became common. After leaving the Census Bureau, Hollerith established a company to produce and market the punched card data processing equipment; this company later merged with several competitors and became IBM. Hollerith's equipment received its first widespread use in the 1890 Census. His inventions were so successful that census data was processed in two and a half years compared to the seven and a half years needed to process data from the 1880 census, despite a 13 million increase in population (Stern and Stern, 1983; Hopper and Mandell, 1987; Graham, 1986).

Twentieth Century Electro-Mechanical Devices

In 1936, Konrad Zuse, a German engineer, developed plans for a series of computers. Working first with mechanical designs, then electro-mechanical devices, he prepared preliminary diagrams and plans for an electronic computer which would utilize data recorded in binary code. Lacking government support, he was unable to obtain the necessary components to construct a working model. As a consequence, his plans were never fully developed (Graham, 1986).

In the 1930s the German government applied a digital engine, called the Enigma, to the ciphering of coded messages. This machine was originally developed by a Dutchman for the purpose of encoding business transactions (see, e.g. Brown, 1976) but was adapted by the German military to send messages during World War II. Enigma employed a rotor cipher, similar in principle to piano rolls with punched holes, which could be removed and changed. An electrical impulse was passed through the rotor cipher and a crude binary code, consisting of a hole or no hole, was used to send and receive coded messages. Both the transmitter and the receiver of the message needed identical cylinders. Breaking the code without a rotor was deemed "impossible" because of infinite numerical combinations.

A number of secret projects were undertaken by the British in World War II to decipher intercepted enemy messages written in various codes (Stern and Stern, 1983). One of these was the breaking of the Enigma code. In 1938, British military intelligence discovered that a Polish Jew, forced to leave Germany and then living in France, was a mathematician who had worked as an engineer in the factory where the Enigma was constructed. After traveling to Britain, he worked in cooperation with British experts and was able to reconstruct the Enigma from memory. This information was used by British engineers who had been working on their own digital engine, called a Turing machine. These designs were combined and the end product, known as the Bomb, was a punched tape reader capable of deciphering all transmissions from the German High Command. The Germans did not learn until the end of the war that their Enigma code had been broken.

The Bomb was perhaps the earliest form of a crude basic computer. As with all technological developments it presented ethical and moral problems from the start. On November 14, 1940, the Germans bombed the city of Coventry. Hundreds of civilians were killed, thousands were wounded, and most of the town was damaged or destroyed. Although Churchill's government had 48 hours warning because they had intercepted and deciphered coded transmissions from the German High Command, the British took no steps to warn the people of Coventry for fear the Germans would learn Enigma had been compromised. The moral dilemmas of the computer age had begun, and they continue even today.

The war effort in the United States contributed the next major development in modern computing when, in 1944, Howard Aiken completed a project, begun in 1939, which involved IBM, the U.S. War Department and Harvard University. The result of the project was the development of the first electromechanical automatic calculator, called Mark I. It was used to calculate weapon trajectories for the U.S. Navy until the end of the war. The Mark I used electric current to represent numbers; since electric current is either on or off, Aiken used the binary number system to convey data and instructions to the machine (Hopper and Mandell, 1987).

Programmers working on Mark I have the distinction of coining the term "bug" as related to computers. Working in August in a large room with open windows, Mark I suddenly stopped calculations in the middle of a program. Assuming that an electrical short had occurred in one of the many circuits which comprised the computer, Grace Hopper, a Navy officer assigned to the project, began checking all electrical connections. She found that a moth had been caught between two small moving parts of the computer. From then on, whenever the computer stopped, the programmers said that they had to "debug" the computer.

Twentieth Century Vacuum Tube and Electronic Computers

The switch to electronic computers and vacuum tube technology occurred in 1946 when J. Presper Eckert and John Mauchly, working at the University of Pennsylvania, completed ENIAC (Electronic Numerical Integrator and Calculator). Beginning in 1943 and working under contract with the U.S. Army, Eckert and Mauchly were charged with the task of developing a machine capable of computing range tables for artillery weapons. The resulting device contained 18,000 vacuum tubes, 30 control panels, weighed over 60,000 pounds, and completely filled a large room (Stern and Stern, 1983). Although much faster in completing complex calculations than Mark I, ENIAC had several problems. The numerous vacuum tubes frequently overheated, broke and had to be replaced, and locating broken or cracked tubes proved to be a very time consuming task. Additionally, all operating instructions had to be entered prior to each calculation using a series of hand set switches contained on each of the thirty control panels. In the mid-1940s, John Von Neumann simplified the problem of entering operating instructions by inventing the stored-program concept. Von Neumann's concept was incorporated in EDVAC, another computer developed by Eckert and Mauchly, and EDSAC, a similar computer developed at Cambridge University in England (Hopper and Mandell, 1987).

After World War II ended, developments in computer technology occurred at a rapid rate. Many of these developments were due to totally new technologies created to solve problems of older computers. Consequently, it is common practice to discuss these changes in terms of generations. Below is a brief description of each computer generation, including the more significant developments.

First Generation: 1951-1958

These early computers, often called mainframes, were very large in physical size, expensive to build, expensive to maintain, expensive to operate and generally unreliable due to delicately balanced operating systems. Their primary component was vacuum tubes. Most used punched cards, based on Hollerith's design, to enter data and instructions. Revolving magnetic drums were used to store information inside the computer in machine language (binary code). Symbolic languages were developed to overcome the difficulty of programming in binary code. Language translator programs were developed by Grace Hopper, Rear Admiral of the U.S. Navy, to translate the symbolic language programs into machine readable language (Hopper and Mandell, 1987).

The speed of operation for First Generation computers was measured in milliseconds (thousandths of a second). Two thousand instructions could be completed per second; the average cost of computing each function was five dollars (Stern and Stern, 1983).

Second Generation: 1959-1964

Several hardware advances led to the development of Second Generation computers. Transistors replaced vacuum tubes and eliminated over-heating problems. Magnetic-cores replaced magnetic-drums as internal memory units which resulted in faster processing speeds. Magnetic tapes and magnetic-disks, patterned after those used for sound recordings during World War II, were developed for external data storage. High-level programming languages, like COBOL and FORTRAN, were developed making programming easier (Hopper and Mandell, 1987; Graham, 1986).

The speed of operation for Second Generation computers was measured in microseconds (millionths of a second). One million instructions could be completed in one second; the average cost of completing each function was fifty cents (Stern and Stern, 1983).

Third Generation: 1965-1971

The development of integrated circuits on silicon chips by Jack S. Kelby of Texas Instruments, replaced transistors and further reduced the physical size of computers. For several years the IBM System/360 series of computers dominated the field. The software industry began to emerge, and prepared programs for payroll, billing and related functions were introduced. Microcomputers, smaller and less costly than mainframes were developed, although they were not yet generally available. Remote terminals, located at some distance from the main computer, but linked electronically to it, were introduced (Hopper and Mandell, 1987).

The speed of operation for Third Generation computers was measured in nanoseconds (billionths of a second). Ten million instructions could be performed in a second, and the average cost of each function was five cents (Stern and Stern, 1983).

Fourth Generation: 1972-Present

The development of large-scale integrated circuits eliminated the need for magnetic-cores and further improved the time needed to process data. Microprocessors, originally developed by Ted Hoff of Intel Corporation, led to the development of microcomputers. First marketed as "build it yourself" plans, the detailed designs for home microcomputers were instantly popular, surprising most industry analysts. It is doubtful that many of these "build it yourself" computers were ever constructed due to a shortage of the necessary parts. Both the experienced computer user and the novice became customers when the computer industry responded to consumer demands and marketed the first ready to use microcomputers in the late 1970s. The software industry continued to expand and develop new products. One significant software development, which also further strengthened the demand for microcomputers, was VisiCalc. Introduced in 1979, VisiCalc was the first electronic spreadsheet for microcomputers. Very-large-scale integrated circuits were developed allowing further miniaturization and the development of powerful minicomputers. Very-large-scale integrated circuits also contributed to a decrease in overall size, reduction of costs, and improvement of speed of operation (Hopper and Mandell, 1987; Graham, 1986).

Operational speed for Fourth Generation computers is measured in picoseconds (trillionths of a second). One hundred million to one billion instructions can be performed in a second; the average cost per function is less than one cent (Stern and Stern, 1983).

A recent development of Fourth Generation computers is the supercomputer, developed by Seymour Cray of Cray Research. These machines, called the Cray-1, Cray-2 and Cray X-MP, are used for lengthy and complex mathematical problems necessary for weather forecasting, aircraft design, energy conservation, nuclear research, cryptography and nuclear reactor safety analysis.

Another fourth generation development is the expert system. Some specialists suggest that expert system computers are transitional machines which will lead to the next generation (Hopper and Mandell, 1987). Expert systems are computers programmed to imitate an expert in a particular field of study. Based on data entered into the computer, an expert system is able to draw conclusions and suggest possible alternatives based on the information encoded into the permanent memory of the computer. Expert systems have great value for specialists as a means of reviewing and checking their own evaluation of the problem being analyzed. The most common use for expert systems today is in the field of medicine.

Fifth Generation: Future

In 1982, Japan's Ministry of Industrial Trade and Administration announced the beginning of a project to develop fifth generation computers. Similar projects were soon started in the United States and other countries. The nature and design of Fifth Generation computers is unclear at this point. One anticipated advancement for Fifth Generation computers is the use of parallel processing which would enable thousands of operations to be performed at the same time.

The most significant advancement predicted for this generation of computers is a change in the logic circuitry which has been traditionally based on the binary code. The logic circuitry of Fifth Generation computers is expected to imitate human thought, not the binary code. This advancement would make possible the development of artificially intelligent computers capable of imitating the reasoning and decision patterns of humans (Graham, 1986).

Fifth Generation developments, such as artificial intelligence will lead to what is called Fifth Generation languages. These may make it possible to input commands and receive output using the native language of the user, without the need to utilize a programming language. Artificial intelligence and Fifth Generation languages may make it possible to access data bases written in different computer languages and using different logic systems which are currently incompatible. These may also make it possible for a much larger range of people to use computers than ever before. Finally, Fifth Generation computer technology will continue to propel the progression of microcomputer technology and accelerate potential applications. To appreciate how far microcomputers have developed in less than two decades, consider the following brief history of microcomputers.

Evolution of Microcomputers

Computers are in a process of evolution. Fourth Generation technology miniaturized equipment size and created a whole new genre of computers: the microcomputer or personal computers. For the first time in man's recorded history, electronic information processing machines became available to the average person. What had been the tools and toys of a few hundred mathematicians and scientists became available to millions.

The first microcomputers which appeared in the early 1970s were not very powerful by today's standards. Early consumer products offered as little as 4K of RAM memory, lacked a true operating system, and had little software. By the late 1970s and early 1980s hundreds of different companies and thousands of products entered the microcomputer market. When micro-computers first hit the consumer market, most manufacturers used their own operating systems and produced their own software; incapatibility was pur-poseful. Gradually, C/P.M. (Control Program for Microcomputers) became somewhat of a standard, except for innovative leaders like Apple Computer and Atari who continue in their own directions even today. Many of the ad-vanced systems of this period were C/P.M.80 based, 8-bit computers with 48 to 64 K of RAM memory. These machines were capable of word processing, filing, and accounting functions. However, hardware and software designs limited the usefulness of these machines. In addition, there was a major problem of incompatibility among different machines, since many manufac-turers purposely designed their systems to run only their own software.

The early 1980s saw the introduction of a more powerful microproces-sor, an 8 bit 8086/8 based machine, and a new operating system, *MS-DOS*. IBM introduced its own version, PC-DOS, which gradually came to dominate the microcomputer market. Rivals such as Apple and Wang continued to de-velop their own processors and software. By the mid-1980s hundreds of companies which had attempted to market their own computers and different operating systems had gone out of business or stopped competing in the mi-cro market. With a few exceptions, notably Apple, surviving companies mar-keted products which were IBM clones, capable of running most IBM soft-ware. IBM equipment and software became a de facto industry standard. It was not that IBM made the best machines or the fastest, other manufacturers produced higher quality and faster machines, but IBM was a stable manu-facturer in the industry and the greatest volume of business related software was IBM compatible. Another reason American business organizations turned to IBM PC/MS-DOS equipment was that the 8086/8 machine was superior to other products in handling spreadsheets. C/P.M. machines were fine for word processing, but were very slow in processing the numerical cal-culations necessary to use spreadsheets. Similarly, Apple products (Apple II, III, Lisa) were also judged inferior. Hence, Apple, which had been initially accepted by many businesses, lost ground to IBM. By the mid-1980s IBM compatible machines accounted for more than three-fourths of microcom-puters used by American business organizations. For example, in 1985 IBM sales accounted for approximately 46% of all business related microcomputer sales, IBM compatible clones accounted for another 30%, Apple about 15%, and all others about 3%. More importantly, competition among clone man-ufacturers had become so keen that for each six month period from 1980-1986 the price of equipment dropped, while standard options and power in-creased. It was a buyer's market. A marginal degree of standardization in the market helped to create a classification system of microcomputers, based on IBM's line of equipment. For example, the following definitions might have been applied until the early part of 1987.

BASIC PC   referred to an 8086/8 machine, usually with two floppy drives (5 1/4 inch), 128 to 512 K RAM, and monitor.

XT   referred to an 8086/8 machine, usually with one floppy (5 1/4 inch) drive and one hard disk (internal 15 - 20 Mb) drive, 128 to 640 K of RAM and monitor.

AT   referred to an 80286 16 bit machine, with one 1.2 Mb floppy (5 1/4 inch) drive, one 360 K floppy (5 1/4 inch) drive, one internal hard disk (20 - 40 Mb), 640 to 750 RAM, and monitor

RT   referred to an 80386 32 bit machine, with one 1.2 Mb floppy (5 1/4 inch) drive, one 360 K floppy drive (5 1/4 inch), 640 - 1Mb of RAM and monitor, also available with the IBM RISC processor which is essentially a minicomputer level microprocessor and which is used for highly specialized applications. RISC stands for Reduced Instructional Systems Computer, meaning that it is not intended for a wide range of different types of instructions.

By the late-1980s, still more powerful microprocessors were introduced, including the 16-bit 80268 chip and the 32-bit 80386 and M68000, M68020, M68030 chips. An even more powerful chip, the 80486 chip is due to be marketed around 1989 or 1990. These are the basis of a significantly more powerful type of microcomputer, sometimes referred to as "super-micros" which will dominate the market for years to come.

However, a major defeat for the champions of standardization and compatibility occurred in mid-1987 when IBM introduced a whole new line of computers, called the PS/2 (Personal System 2) Models 25 through 80, leaked the planned release of a Model 90 and announced the end of production of the PC line. This new line of computers may become the standard or they may not. All models except 30-286 use the new micro-channel bus architecture. The following describes the PS/2 line.

Model 25,30   8086 machines, with 640K RAM, 3.5 mini disk drives, operating at 8 Mhz. Model 30 has the option of a 20 Mb hard disk drive, the Model 25 does not. Model 25 is designed for students and does not have the expansion potential of the Model 30. These are reported to be about twice as fast as the earlier PC and XT models.

Model 30-286   80286 machine with 512K (Expandable to 16 Mb) RAM, 20 Mb hard disk, 10 Mhz., with 3 1/2-inch drive. This model uses the standard AT Bus.

Model 50,60   80286 machines, with 1 to 15Mb RAM, 3 1/2 mini disk drives, operating at 10 Mhz. Model 50 has option of 20-60Mb hard disk drive, while Model 60 has options of 44Mb, 70Mb, or 115Mb hard disk drives with a maximum of 185Mb expansion possible. These models replace various versions of the AT line and offer a processing speed of from 3 to 4 times that of earlier AT models.

Model 70, 80   80386 machines, with 2 to 16Mb RAM, 3.5 mini disk drives, operating at 16-25 Mhz., has option of 44 to 120 Mb hard disk drives with a maximum of 230Mb expansion possible. The machine appears to be replacing both upline ATs and downlined RTs. It is designed to compete at the lower end of the mini-computer market.

Model 90   80386 machine, dual RISC processor, 20-25 Mhz., yet to be released in full configuration, designed to compete in minicomputer market for highly specialized limited applications.

While there were some design improvements, particularly in terms of ease of repair and more efficient operating speeds, IBM's decision to introduce these new computers was undoubtedly motivated by a desire to regain its early 1980 market position when it controlled nearly 60% of the market. To combat the popularity of less expensive clones, IBM introduced a 3 1/2 inch hard cover minidisk, which combined the features of a floppy and the protection of a cartridge. Earlier 5 1/4 inch disk drives were not available options, forcing buyers to either use the new IBM systems or be denied access to improvements.

In addition, a new operating system, *OS/2*, was introduced late in 1987, making these new systems incompatible with older systems without expensive additions and modifications. OS/2, which was previously referred to during beta testing as "PC-DOS 5.0", is intended to replace and make obsolete past versions of PC/MS-DOS. It is designed to allow microcomputers to employ true multitasking or multiprogramming capabilities and to access memory up to 15-16Mb. OS/2 is designed to run exclusively on 80826 and 80836 micro-processors, hence, it will not run on past generations of 8086/8 microproces-sors. Owners of IBM PCs, XTs or compatibles will be forced to buy new equipment unless third party vendors introduce upgrades. See detailed dis-cussion of OS/2 in Illustration 2.

While IBM standards have changed, it is unclear whether the market standards for microcomputers will change accordingly; only time will tell. Another rival company, COMPAQ, perhaps the most well known of the IBM clones, now claims to be the industry standard, not IBM. At the same time Apple, which nearly went under during the early 1980s because of its mar-keting strategies, has introduced new products which offer greatly increased computing power combined with a mouse-driven, user friendly operating system.

The cliche which states that the only unchanging fact is the inevitability of change, is the best way to characterize microcomputer evolution. Since the 1970s the microcomputer has become increasingly more powerful and comparatively less expensive, and has been used more extensively by a greater number of people. Some personal computers, such as the IBM PS/2, Models 80 and 90, have become as powerful as minicomputers and some mainframe computers of only a few year ago. There exists a great diversity and a wide range of available options exist among microcomputers. To pro-vide a framework for understanding these differences as well as differences between minicomputers and mainframes, the following typology is provided.

COMPUTER TYPOLOGY:
A BASIC UNDERSTANDING OF DIFFERENCES

For the purposes of this text, computers are classified into seven cate-gories: 1) Electronic Toys, 2) Game or Home Use Microcomputers, 3) Indi-vidual Use Microcomputers, 4) Professional Application Microcomputers: Single User/Function Systems, 5) Professional Application Microcomputers: Multiple User/Function Systems, 6) Minicomputers, and 7) Mainframe Computers. Each category is depicted in Figure 1-1 and discussed below.

The category *Electronic Toy* refers to a large class of electronic devices which use microchips or microprocessors and are capable of limited memory. Game programs are electronically imprinted onto microchips. This is the same technology which has produced arcade games such as Pac-Man or Space Invaders; when the power is connected, the program runs. Examples of this class would include electronic learning devices such as Speak and Spell, Speak and Math, and Little Professor, made by Texas Instruments.

Game machines include Atari 2600, 5200 and 7800, Coleco-Vision, Intel-vision, Odyssey 2, Nintendo and others. These devices generally do not have RAM memory or data storage capabilities, although conversion kits for Atari systems, and others, can make these "computer-like." The value of these devices is principally entertainment, although the learning machines of Texas Instruments have some educational value. In criminal justice management these types of devices have little value, except for entertainment or basic educational skills drill. At the opposite end of the continuum is the *Mainframe Computer*. Generally, these are the huge computers run by major corporations, universities and divisions of government, although there are mid-sized mainframes which are no larger than some minicomputers of the 1970s. Mainframe computers are at the extreme end of the computer spectrum and are true multi-user and multi-function machines, meaning that they may be able to service hundreds of different users and to run many different types of programs at the same time. Computers such as the IBM 3033, 4331, 370, 3081, UNIVAC 1100, Hewlett-Packard 1000, 3000, Data General C-150, 350 and Honeywell 2015, 3200, 6000 are capable of hundreds of billions of bytes of RAM and storage.

COMPUTER CLASSIFICATION CONTINUUM

T	Game & Home	Individual	Professional:	Professional:	M	M F
O	Use Micro-	Use Micro-	Single User /	Multi-User /	I	A R
Y	Computers	Computers	Function Micro-	Function Micro-	N	I A
S			Computers	Computers	I	N M
						E

ENTERTAINMENT VALUE	PROFESSIONAL APPLICATIONS
HOME USE	AGENCY USE
LOW COST	HIGH COST
NON-EXPANDABLE MEMORY	EXPANDABLE MEMORY
NON-EXPANDABLE STORAGE	EXPANDABLE STORAGE
SINGLE TASKING	MULTI-TASKING

FIGURE 1-1

Mainframe computers may cost millions to purchase, hundreds of thousands to operate, and may require armies of programmers and technicians to maintain. They are capable of operating complex tasks which extend from coordinating national defense to operating robotic assembly lines in auto plants. Their application in criminal justice is detailed in Chapter 2. A mainframe computer ordinarily uses a dumb terminal to access the immense memory of the computer via telephone line connections or satellite. Some terminals permit limited operations to be performed at the terminal itself; however, most require the communications protocol or link between the terminal and the mainframe CPU to be activated before operations can be executed. Hence, effective use of the computer is inhibited by problems with phone lines and limited by the competency level of the user. Problems and limitations associated with mainframe usage led to the development of smart terminal stations which were capable of limited memory and operations without constant interaction with the main computer. This led, eventually, to the development of microcomputers.

Between the extremes of Electronic Toys and Mainframe Computers are found the Microcomputers and Minicomputers which are the primary focus of this text. *Minicomputers* are scaled down mainframes which are essentially multi-user computers which can perform beyond the level of professional microcomputers. *Microcomputers*, also referred to by the generic term *personal computer* or *PC*, are computers designed for individual use or a small number of users. Both the micro and mini are complete computer systems; they contain all the components of a computer, including memory, storage and input and output devices. These small computer systems represent a broad range of computer technology and capabilities. The categories described below classify small computer systems on the basis of five criteria.

1) *Usable Memory* -- Microcomputers are rated here according to actual usable memory or *RAM* (random access memory). Computer memory is the electronic capacity to hold and process information. This is measured in terms of Kilobytes or K (thousands of bits), Megabytes or Mb (millions of bits) and Gigabytes or Gb (billions of bits). In principle, the larger the memory the more information can be processed.

2) *Byte Rating of the System* -- Systems were classified as being 8-byte, 16-byte, 32-byte or higher. [Readers Note: Bits and Bytes are explained in the Cumulative Glossary.] In principle, the higher the byte rating the more information can be processed at the same time.

3) *Megahertz Rating of the System* -- Microprocessors run at different speeds which are expressed in megahertz (Mhz). The higher the Mhz the faster the processor, meaning that it can process information and run programs at faster rates.

4) *Single User/Single Function vs. Multiple User/Multiple Function Systems* -- Some microcomputers will allow multiple users to access the system and to perform different functions at the same time. Various computer systems were evaluated in terms of this capability.

5) *Potential for Expansion* -- Finally, computer systems were rated on their potential for expansion. Some computer systems are designed to be expanded, others are not. Memory, byte rating and the number and type of peripheral devices which can be added to the system are examples of system expansion.

The result of this rating process is the following classification schema.

The *Game or Home Use Computer* classification refers to computers which have a standard RAM memory of from 4 to 64K. Most of these use an 8-byte processor system. Examples of this type are the 1980 Atari 400, 800, 800XL, 1200XL, 5200 and 7800 game systems; Nintendo Systems; VIC 20; Commodore 64; TRS 80 Color Computer; and the Coleco Adam. These machines are capable of performing basic processing functions, and offer a learning opportunity for the novice computer user. They can perform simple word processing, record keeping, and can be used to develop basic computer literacy. Many have a good selection of entertainment and educational software which can be used at home or in a classroom. However, agency use, other than for classroom purposes (e.g. computer literacy, GED preparation, foreign language learning), is restricted by the limited capability of these computers.

The *Individual Use Microcomputer* classification refers to computers which are more sophisticated in technology than the previous class. Some of these computers have 8-byte processors with 48 to 64K RAM memory; some have 16-byte processors and 128K to 512K ; a few even advertise 1-4Mb and most operate at speeds between 4 and 8 Mhz. Most, however, have limited system expansion potential and the range of available software is narrow. Regardless of the amount of memory though, the systems listed in this class are suitable for many individual or small business uses. However, their standard capabilities are too limited to meet the needs of most agencies; if the system can be expanded, the cost is generally prohibitive. Additionally, all computers in this category are single user and single function systems. Examples of systems in this classification from the early 1980s include Apple I, II, II+ and IIe; TRS 80 Home Computer Models 1, 2, 3; Franklin Ace 1000, 1200 and, from the late 1980s, the Atari 520ST and 1040; and Commodore C64, Plus4 and C128 models.

The *Professional Application Microcomputer* classification refers to a broad range of flexible, expandable systems. Those marketed in the early 1980s had from 64K to 256K of RAM, operated at speeds between 4 and 6 Mhz, and were generally 8 or 16-bit systems. These routinely offered two floppy disk drives, or one floppy and a hard disk drive of up to 20 Mb storage, and were primarily single user, single tasking systems.

In contrast, systems marketed in the late 1980s offered from 640K to 1Mb RAM memory as standard, operated at between 8 to 25 Mhz, and were 16 or 32-bit systems. These routinely had one floppy or mini disk drive, and at least one hard drive with 20 to 80Mb of storage capacity. These were capable of single user, single tasking, or multi-user, multi-tasking (multiprogramming). Some of the newer products are being marketed as expandable to 10-20 Mb and some capable of running at over 25 Mhz. While the microcomputers themselves are capable of having their memories expanded to these levels and running at these speeds, many DOS (disk operating systems) and application programs can only make use of 640-750K and run at much slower speeds. Until DOS and application programs were redesigned to the new OS/2 operating system, expansion of some computers will not produce meaningful results. While some systems marketed before 1983 have 8-byte processors, most subsequent systems employ 16 or 32-byte processors. These systems can operate a wide range of currently available software. Many are also capable of networking, and all have the potential of multi-user access to the degree that information can be transferred from one system to another via a phone modem telecommunications link. When expanded to their maximum, some Professional Application Microcomputers satisfy the minimum standards for classification as minicomputers. Professional Application systems are ideal for both agency and individual use when word processing, records management, budgeting, inventory control and research capabilities are needed. All microcomputers in this grouping can operate multiple floppy disk drives or combinations of floppy and hard disk drives.

Professional Application Computers and the differences between them may be classified into one of two major subgroups:

1)   Single User/Single Tasking Systems, and
2)   Multi-User/Multi- Tasking Systems.

The category of *Professional Application Microcomputer: Single User/ Single Tasking System* includes systems essentially designed for one user to operate one program or task at the same time. Individual products offer RAM memories of from 64 to 1Mb, which can be further expanded, and generally operate at speeds between 4 and 8 Mhz. However, some systems can be expanded to use multi-tasking or concurrent tasking. In other words, the system can be capable of performing different tasks at the same time. These systems are not designed to be efficient multi-user, multi-tasking machines because processing efficiency slows down. The vast majority of professional use microcomputers are classified in this category. For example, included in this class would be:

All Z-80 based or CP/M80 machines (e.g. most machines marketed before 1982)

All "lap top" or "brief case" portable computers made by companies such as IBM, Kaypro, Tandy, COMPAQ, NEC

8086/8 chip based or PC/MS DOS machines (e.g. IBM PC, XT, PS/2 25 or clones, Zenith 100, Tandy 1000, Leading Edge, COMPAQ Deskpro 240)

M6800 and early M68000 chips (e.g. Apple II, Apple III, Apple Lisa, Apple Macintosh I, Macintosh Plus, and Macintosh SE, Atari 512 models)

The category of *Professional Application Microcomputer: Multi-User/ Multi-Tasking System* includes systems essentially designed for three possible user patterns: 1) a single user operating a complex program, such as a statistical analysis program using a large data set, 2) a single user operating multiple programs concurrently, or 3) a limited number of multiple users operating multiple programs at the same time. It should be noted that while the hardware of these systems are potentially capable of multi-user/multi-tasking, they require special operating systems and programs to perform these functions. Standard memory usually ranges from 640K up to 1 Mb with expansion up to 30Mb possible. Most of these systems operate at between 8 and 25Mhz. These computer systems offer the advantage of fast processing and the capability of linking several users to a single microcomputer. They are more powerful than other microcomputers, but considerably less powerful than minicomputers. Among IBMs and clones there are essentially two generations of true multi-user/tasking systems. The 80826 chip is a true 16-Byte processor and the 80836 chip is a true 32-Byte processor. The latter is the more efficient processor. Among Apple Computers, the 32-Byte Motorola chips, the Mc68020 and M68030 give the Apple MacIntosh II similar capabilities.

80826 chip based PC or DOS systems (e.g. IBM AT, PS/2 Model 50 or clones, Mitsubishi MP 286, PC Limited 286, Memorex 7000, Zenith 286)

80836 chip based PC or DOS systems (e.g. IBM RT, PS/2 Model 60,80 or clones, ACER 1100, COMPAQ Deskpro 386, PC Limited 386, Tandy 4000)

The Minicomputer category refers to microcomputers which have at least 1 Mb of memory and up to several hundred gigabytes. They operate at speeds from 10 to 30 Mhz. Actually, these are smaller versions of mainframe computers which are able to service several dozen users and functions at the same time. These minicomputers usually have hard disk drives with storage capacities in the millions or billions of bytes (e.g. 350Mb, 500Mb, 800Mb, 10Gb). Minicomputers have at least 32-byte processors, are capable of networking (meaning that many microcomputers or "dumb" terminals can use the memory and storage capabilities of the system) and can process several different tasks simultaneously. The minicomputer performs functions equal or superior to computers which might have been considered mainframe less than two decades ago. Among the specific models which fit this classification are: Data General MV/8000,10000; DEC VAX 11/750; Gould 32/6705; IBM 4361, Model L05; and PRIME 750. The upper range of minicomputers, sometimes called "super-minis," blurs the distinction between minicomputers and main frames even today. Costs of these systems (excluding additional terminals, networking hardware, systems software) range from $10,000 to $500,000. The linking of several Professional Application Microcomputers with a minicomputer can sometimes give an agency as much computer capacity and service as it would ever need from a mainframe at a fraction of the cost.

In summary, there are several points pertaining to the above typology which should be reinforced. First, as one moves from the category of Toy to Professional Application to Mainframe (shown in Figure 1-1) the sophistication of the computer system, the range of professional software available and the cost increases, while the entertainment and recreation value decreases. Second, emerging technology, together with market competition and mass production, have combined to expand the capabilities of microcomputers while reducing costs of technical features. One consequence is that the consumer is able to buy an increasingly more sophisticated small computer system for comparatively fewer dollars. Another consequence is that the distinction between computer categories is blurring. For example, in 1980, a microcomputer with a 16-byte operating system and a memory greater than 64K was a rarity and might have been classified as a minicomputer. By 1988, however, 16- and 32-byte microcomputers with memories in excess of 1Mb were common. The advanced microcomputer of today is capable of performing at levels which were only possible for mainframes in the 1970s.

UNDERSTANDING
MICROCOMPUTERS AND COMPUTERESE

Microcomputers are changing the organizational management of criminal justice agencies in ways which few people ever envisioned. Some of these changes are described in later chapters of this book. Before discussing these, however, it is important for the reader to have a basic understanding of microcomputer terminology and technology.

Microcomputers are tools which individuals and organizations can apply to a variety of different uses. After mastering the operation of the computer, individuals and organizations discover for themselves how these tools can best aid them. With experience, users develop their own user profile or pattern of usage. For example, one user may find that the best use of the microcomputer is to manage files, perform accounting procedures and statistical analysis; this user's profile is concerned with data base management applications. Another user applies the microcomputer to produce written documents; this user's profile is concerned with word processing or computer assisted writing (CAW). Still another user may apply microcomputers in training or education, this user has a computer assisted instruction (CAI) profile. The modern criminal justice organization normally has many user profiles; in contrast, an individual may have only one. Knowledge of a user's profile is essential in considering the purchase of computer equipment.

Until the microcomputer is understood and mastered, however, understanding the user profile serves no purpose. For many users, both individuals and organizations, the toughest problems in using a microcomputer are 1) overcoming the fear of "being humiliated" by a machine which is mistakenly assumed to be "intelligent"; 2) learning to speak "computerese" or the terminology associated with computers; and 3) spending enough time to learn how to use the computer. These three problems are interrelated. Fear is the most devastating barrier to effective human communication. (See, Archambeault and Archambeault, 1982: 283-315).

Understanding the microcomputer begins with a comprehension of two ideas, hardware and software. *Hardware* refers to the physical components or parts of computers (e.g. CPU, keyboard, disk drives, monitor). *Software* refers to programs which are either written by the user or purchased from commercial software manufacturers. There are two main classes of software required to operate most microcomputer systems: applications or source programs which allow the user to perform specific applications (e.g. word processing, accounting, graphics) and operating systems programs which co-ordinate all the parts of a computer system, allowing the user control over them. Hardware and software are discussed more fully below.

MICROCOMPUTER SYSTEMS: HARDWARE COMPONENTS

Every microcomputer system has certain common parts or components. These are input/output devices; data storage devices and the central processing unit or CPU.

Input/Output and Data Storage Devices

Input/output devices are also called peripherals. Technically, data storage devices are also input/output devices and peripherals; however, for clarity of discussion they will be discussed separately. Some of these devices are primarily input mechanisms through which the user communicates with the computer itself, gives the computer instructions, or feeds the computer information or raw data for analysis. Examples of input devices include typewriter and numeric keyboards, light pens, mouse, bar code readers, joy sticks, optical scanners and voice recognizers. What comes out of the computer is called output; printers are output devices. Other devices, such as video display terminals or monitors, phone modems, voice synthesizers and data storage devices, permit both input and output by allowing two-way communication between user and computer.

Data or information storage devices are input/output peripherals which hold information until needed and accessed. These devices must be used because most information is erased from memory once the computer is turned off. Even those equipped with bubble memories, which are really tiny batteries that continue to provide sufficient energy to hold the information in memory, do not provide permanent storage. A new microchip has been developed for computers which is capable of storing information even after the computer is turned off. If this technology becomes cost-effective it may change the entire relationship between computer memory and storage devices in the future.

The capacity of data storage devices is also measured in K, Mb or Gb. The amount of storage memory varies from device to device as discussed below.

In general, there are seven types of data storage devices in common use: 1) floppy disk drives, 2) hard cover mini disk drives, 3) hard disk drives, 4) bernoulli boxes, 5) tape drives, 6) tape recorders and 7)CD devices. *Floppy disk drives* allow the microcomputer user to access software, permit the storage of information, and allow interaction with the computer's memory through floppy disks or diskettes. A floppy disk is a thin, flexible, circular object whose surface is coated with a magnetic material that allows it to retain electronic impulses in a manner similar to cassette recording tape. The structure of a floppy disk resembles a phonograph record since information or data is stored on electronic grooves, called tracks. Floppy disks are enclosed in a plastic cover to protect the disk surface and allow the disk to rotate. These come in several sizes: 3 1/4, 3 1/2, 5 1/4 and 8 inch. Different computer systems require different sizes, but each performs similar functions. Floppy disk drives allow the computer to load or transfer data from the diskette to the computer, and to save the data to the diskette.

All floppy disks require formatting, and each computer system uses a specific formatting scheme. Formatting, sometimes called initializing, installs an operating system on the disk; this system is used by the computer to store and retrieve data or processing instructions. The amount of information which can be stored on a diskette varies based on several factors. Tracks or electronic grooves are divided into sectors; the exact location of a piece of stored information is called its address which is essentially the sector-track intersection. Some systems store data on only one side of a disk. For example, there are 36 tracks on the standard single sided 5 1/4 inch disk. Other systems store data on both sides of the disk. Some disks store twice the amount per sector-track address than standard; these are called double density disks. Finally, high density disks store about twice as much as the double sided, double density disk. Thus, for 5 1/4 inch disk drives, a double sided, double density disk can store approximately four times as much data as can a standard single sided, single density disk. A double sided, double density 8 inch disk may be able to store eight to ten times as much data as the single-sided, single-density standard 5 1/4 inch disk. As a rule of thumb a single sided 5 1/4 floppy will be able to store about 180K; a double sided, double density 5 1/4 disk will be able to store about 360K; a high density 5 1/4 disk will store about 1.2 Mb which is about the capacity of an 8 inch disk.

Hard cover mini disks perform the same functions and allow the same degree of portability as floppy disks. Most are 3 1/2 inches square, designed to fit into shirt pockets, and have a hard plastic shell protecting the disk with 1.2 - 1.5 Mb of storage. Apple first used these disks on the MacIntosh in the middle 1980s. IBM adopted them for their PS/2 line of computers introduced in 1987.

Hard disk drives function much like floppy disk drives except that they have ten to a hundred times more storage than a floppy disk, are faster in terms of data transfer, and are generally easy to use. They are also much more expensive. Another advantage of hard disks is that since they are not handled, they are not as subject to damage by carelessness as are floppy disks; therefore, the stored data is safer. Hard disk drives are ordinarily found only in larger organizations and used in combination with floppy disk drives. They are essential in any agency which intends to store a great amount of data.

Hard Card is a new technology miniaturized hard disk drive which is located on a printed circuit board which is fitted into a computer's expansion slot. These are available in capacities of 10-40 Mb. and cost slightly more than comparable standard hard disk drives, but can be carried in portable "lap top" computers without damage.

Bernoulli Box drives are data storage devices which can be used either for data backup or as another external hard disk drive. The box uses a cassette which is slightly larger than a VHS or BETA video cassette and has 10 - 40Mb storage capacity. The advantage of these devices is that the cassette can be removed and another inserted in its place, making it portable and giving a microcomputer system the capability of an unlimited number of hard drives. Units can be stacked, making switching back and forth as simple as switching from one hard drive to another. Newer units are now available which can be installed in a computer like a floppy disk drive. 20 Mb disks can be inserted or removed in the same way as floppy disks, giving the user an unlimited amount of storage.

Tape Drives are used with both mainframes and microcomputers. Tape drive systems range from the size of a large audio cassette to 16 inch spool. Tapes can store hundreds of millions of bytes of information. They can be used either to backup data or to input information. Tape drives are widely used in large agencies.

Compact Disk Drives or CDs use the same technology as CD players. Information is transferred to and from a CD disk via laser technology; no physical object ever touches the CD. The CD can hold thousands of times more information than a floppy disk and hundreds of times more than many hard disks. This technology, however, is still developing and costs are comparatively high. In 1988 Tandy, NEC and a few other developers introduced moderately price CD drive technology to the American market. Many of these products employ a *WORM* drive concept. That is, "Write-Once-Read-Many" technology which will not allow the user to re-use a sector of the disk. However, newer product lines which allow writing over previously used sections will be on the market by early 1989. However, CD laser technology may revolutionize current concepts of microcomputer data storage.

Illustration 1-1

THE GREAT BUS DESIGN CONTROVERSY

There is much controversy in the microcomputer market, particularly among IBM clones, about the relative advantage of different types of bus designs. A bus is a connection or junction of wires which feed signals into and out from the central microprocessor chip (e.g. 8088, 80286, 80386). Bus designs affect the speed of processing even for the same microprocessor chip. For example, IBM's original design for the AT bus when the model was first introduced was much slower than the new bus design employed in the new IBM PS/2 line of computers. Hence, an IBM AT, purchased in 1984, with an 80286 microprocessor, runs at a much slower speed than a PS/2 with the same microchip.

Bus designs are as important as the microprocessor chip itself. Application and systems programs have to be written in a special way to make use of the bus and microprocessor designs. Otherwise the program will not run as well.

When IBM introduced the new PS/2 line of computers it introduced a completely new bus design, called the micro channel. *Effectively, this design change made all pre-existing designs obsolete as well as programs and hardware components which had been designed according to earlier standards. IBM's apparent strategy was to regain control of the microcomputer market by controlling the production of software and hardware engineered to operate on the new design. Since IBM's micro channel design was protected by copyright laws, IBM could choose to grant a software or hardware company a license and charge the other companies a fee. The objectives were to force prices up, competitors out of the market and reestablish IBM as the controlling force in software development.*

However, IBM's strategy may have backfired. In late 1988 a group of IBM clone manufacturers, called the gang of nine, set out to present another industry bus standard, called EISA (Extended Industry Standard Architecture). The EISA is an extended AT bus design which allows a 32-bit processor to operate and is compatible with earlier software and hardware. It is as fast as IBM's micro channel bus and, if adopted, would provide a more competitive market, driving down the costs of new technologies.

The "gang of nine" include COMPAQ, AST, Epson, Hewlett-Packard, NEC, Olivetti, Tandy, Wyse and Zenith. Together, the "gang of nine" cut drastically into IBM's market share in 1987. For example, according to one industry research group, of all the personal computers shipped in 1987 the "gang of nine" accounted for 33.5% of shipments, IBM 26.8% and all other manufacturers 39.7% (Infoworld, Sept. 26, 1988, 10(39): 1).

Many organizations and businesses which have relied on IBM or IBM clone microcomputers have delayed purchasing new technology equipment until the bus controversy is settled. It is likely that the outcome of this controversy and whether or not IBM is ever able to dominate the market will shape the future of microcomputers for the next decade. The issue of competing bus designs goes far beyond debate about whether one junction of wires is better than another junction of wires. The central issue is one of power in an information dependent world.

Central Processing Unit (CPU)

The central processing unit, or CPU, is the heart and soul of any computer system. This term and its acronym have both common and technical meanings. In common use, the term CPU refers to the box or container which holds the central processing unit or CPU. If the box containing the CPU is opened (not advised), one would see a maze of printed circuits and other electronics. While the common meaning of CPU is sufficient for most situations, the technical meaning must also be understood. In a technical sense, the term CPU refers to the actual network of microcircuits, microprocessors, chips and circuit boards which make possible the "artificial or electro-mechanical intelligence" functions of the computer (see Sippl and Sippl, 1982:254). The CPU is the primary functioning unit of the microcomputer which contains all the circuits that control computer operations and receive instructions (Sippl and Sippl, 1982:63). Within the maze of circuits is the main CPU circuit board, sometimes called the motherboard, which functions much like the human central nervous system in terms of coordinating and relaying information to other parts of the system. Associated with the technical meaning of CPU are the concepts of computer memory and storage which are interchangeable terms (Sippl and Sippl, 1982:313). Memory applies to any device into which information is copied (saved), held for future use, and retrieved (loaded) as needed. However, for clarity, the term memory will be used only in association with the CPU and the term storage will apply to data storage devices (e.g. disk drives).

Computer Memory

Computer memory is also a commonly used term which has a highly technical meaning. In popular usage, memory may be thought of as the amount of electronic space which is available to process information. This electronic space is often expressed in terms of *K of memory* (e.g. 64, 128, 640 K), Mb of memory (e.g. 10, 15, 50 Mb) or Gb of memory (e.g. 10, 20, 50Gb). *1K or Kilobyte* of memory represents 1,024 bytes of information (2 to the 10th power); this translates roughly to 170 words or about two-thirds of a standard page (Naiman, 1982: 294). *1Mb or Megabyte* of memory represents 1,048,576 bytes or about 700 pages of text. *1Gb or Gigabyte* of memory represents 1,073,741,824 bytes or about 6700 pages of text. Most of the "current" state-of-the-art microcomputers offer between 640K to 15 Mb of memory. Gigabyte ratings are generally available in minicomputers and mainframes, but only rarely found in microcomputers.

Storage capacity and memory use the same measurements, but are very different in design and function. In general, information stored in memory disappears or is erased when the electricity is turned off, whereas stored information can be retrieved for later use. There are, however, types of memory in which information remains after the electricity is turned off, but these are usually associated with some sort of battery powered backup system. Memory and storage work together. Most current microcomputers have *DMA* or *direct memory access*. DMA allows the computer, through the program, to save information to a temporary file on a storage device (e.g. hard disk) even through the memory limits have been reached. In many microcomputers of the 1970s and early 1980s when memory limits were reached, the user was required to stop work and save the completed work to a disk, then clear the memory so than additional work could be performed. With DMA the amount of usable memory is limited only to the space remaining free on the storage device and the restrictions of the program being run. For example, running a word processing program with DMA the user is able to work with a document which is larger than that permitted by RAM only. During this process the user is generally not aware that the system is saving or retrieving a temporary file on the storage medium; this process occurs automatically. Game, home use and some individual use computers, particularly those marketed before 1983, seldom have DMA.

Memory measurements are often confusing. For example, until the mid-1980s it was not uncommon for some manufacturers to advertise their products in Kilobits, rather than Kilobytes. Since the latter category is approximately eight times larger than the former, it was possible to buy two 64K computers and one would have a smaller usable memory than the other. Fortunately, most manufacturers use "byte" ratings today as a standard measure of comparison.

Other sources of confusion arise because there are actually different kinds of memory. Computers using 8086/8, 80286, 80386, M68000 chip technology, reserve certain sections of a computer's memory for the processing of information and the storage of instructions from the program and user, this is called *addressable* memory. Other areas of memory which can not be addressed by the user or the program are reserved for instructions and information built into the computer which affect its operation. For simplicity, addressable memory may be classified as: 1) RAM or random access memory, 2) ROM or read only memory, 3) PROM or program read only memory, 4) EPROM or erasable read only memory and 5) virtual memory.

RAM or *Random Access Memory* is that memory which is free for the user to access for processing functions. This is the memory which allows the user to write and run programs, analyze data, compose text. However, RAM may not necessarily equal "usable memory." Consider the fact that whenever a program is run, electronic space or memory is needed to hold the program, the operating system, sub-routine programs which affect screen graphics, and space is needed for the computer to perform the processing required by the program (e.g. word processing, spread sheet calculations). Where is all this temporary information placed?

Within a computer's memory matrix certain areas are reserved for various commands and instructions which come from the operating system. These areas are called *ROM* or *Read Only Memory*. Simply stated, information stored in ROM gives instructions to the computer automatically without requiring the user to input that information. Instructions residing in ROM are permanently embedded into the ROM chip. These instructions are often called firmware. Binary code (ones and zeroes) is used to program the chip to indicate the presence or absence of electrical voltage. The transistor is either "on" or "off." The system works well with speeds ranging from 200 nanoseconds to 800 nanoseconds access time (Sippl, 1985:425).

Another sort of memory is *PROM* or *Programmable Only Memory*. PROM is similar in function to ROM. However, the stored instructions are not entered at the time of manufacture; they must be physically added through a PROM programmer system. Some PROMs can be erased and re-programmed. PROM chips may contain instructions for the operating system or for application programs.

Still another kind of memory comes from EPROM or Electrically Pro-grammable Read Only Memory chips or boards. Like PROMs, EPROMs contain programs encoded onto chips in the computer. Unlike PROMs, however, which are not generally erasable, EPROMS are intended to be erased through special techniques.

Illustration 1-2

THE EPROM CAPER

British customs authorities recently prosecuted a drug smuggler, allegedly guilty of smuggling $150,000,000 of heroin through Heathrow Airport. Conviction was due, in part, to an EPROM chip. The scenario of events involved the smuggler keeping an electronic ledger of his transactions on a small hand-held calculator/computer. Whenever the smuggler thought he was in danger of detection, he erased all his transactions from RAM memory. What he did not realize was that the particular computer he was using employed an EPROM chip to backup all data entry transactions as a safeguard against accidental erasure. To erase the EPROM, a separate set of procedures had to be followed. The smuggler never erased the EPROM. When the computer was seized, the EPROM contained all the smuggler's records which were reclaimed from the computer's memory and used by authorities in their prosecution. The smuggler received 28 years at hard labor.

Virtual Memory is the ability of a program to address or use more memory than physically exists. The operating system writes to the hard disk segments of memory not currently in use to make room for current memory demands. This type of memory is available with newer operating systems and 286 and 386 microprocessors.

Protected and Real Mode Memory refers to the ability of 286 and 386 microprocessors to section off segments of memory which can only be accessed by the operating system (Protected Mode) as opposed to other segments of memory which can be addressed by programs or user input (Real Mode).

In summary, computer memory is not simply a matter of advertised numbers, nor of descriptive CPU characteristics. The K rating of memory may have different meanings, given by manufacturers. The amount of addressable and usable memory is a complex interaction of many factors, including the physical design of the RAM, the amount of ROM, DMA and virtual memory capabilities, the sophistication of the program being run and the skills of the user.

Memory is also affected by the inherent limitations of the operating systems. On IBM compatible products a limitation of 640K RAM is imposed by restrictions of PC/MS-DOS. For several years MS-DOS machines have been marketed with RAM memories expandable to 10-15Mb, but PC/MS DOS 3.2 and earlier versions have simply been unable to address more than 640K of RAM. Auxiliary programs, such as TopView, and alternative operating systems, such as Unix and Xenix, have been able to address more than the 640 boundary with varying degrees of success. In contrast, the Apple MacIntosh M68000- and M680020-based machines and software overcame the 640K limit by the mid-1980s. The introduction of OS/2 operating systems in 1987 opened a new frontier for IBM compatible microcomputers. Within a few years microcomputer memories of between 1 to 15Mb will become standard. Application programs will be written to utilize potential of this expanded microcomputing power.

MICROCOMPUTER SYSTEMS:
SOFTWARE COMPONENTS

Computer hardware is a marvel in itself. However, hardware cannot serve a useful function until it receives instructions sent through a keyboard or other means of input or through a *program*.

Programs communicate instructions to the computer's CPU and establish a communications link between the user and the computer. Programs are written in computer languages, which are specifically discussed later in this chapter. Programs can be directly read by the computer, and yet they also make it possible for the user to interact with the computer. For example, at this moment, the author is writing this section using a word processing program. Through this program letters and words are entered on a keyboard and appear immediately on a monitor in front of the writer. The electronic impulse generated when a keyboard key is depressed is translated by the program into sets of instructions which are sent directly to the CPU, then translated into an English language character which is then saved temporarily in memory. At the same time, it is translated into a video image which is immediately sent to the monitor. Later, the text of this section is saved to disk, then printed out on a printer. Throughout this complex process the program translates and communicates instructions to various components of the computer system and interacts with the user.

Programs are commonly called by the generic term *software*. While there are many different kinds of software, there are two main classes which need to be understood: 10 application or source programs and 20 system programs.

Application Software

Application software refers to programs which perform specific functions for the user. For example, the word processing program used to write this section is an application program. Others would include spreadsheets, data base management programs, statistical analysis programs, communications programs, graphics programs, games and computer assisted instruction programs.

Application programs use interpreters to translate keyboard input into messages which can be read by the CPU and then translated back into language symbols understandable to the user.

In order for application software to run on any computer, another type of software is needed. This is system software. Different types of computers have different system software. Hence, application programs must be written to run on specific system software. This is why an application program which is written for one type of computer system cannot run on another system with different system software. On the other hand, if mutually compatible system software exists on different brands of computers, then the same application software can be run on them as well. For example, when the term "IBM compatible" is applied to application software it means that the program will run on any brand of computer which uses IBM compatible system software such as PC/MS-DOS. The following discussion of system software will further explain this relationship.

System Software

System software, in general, directs and controls all internal operations and management functions of the computer system. There are several types of system programs, each of which performs different functions. These are: 10 DOS, 20 utilities, 30 firmware and 40 program language.

Disk Operating System or *DOS* is the name most often used to refer to the system software of microcomputers. DOS provides the necessary coordinating instructions which link all parts of the computer system, allows application programs to run and permits the user to control all computer functions. DOS determines limits on usable RAM memory and on hard disk storage. DOS manages data storage on any medium, it assigns stored information to specific locations, called addresses and then "remembers" where the data is when it is needed. DOS establishes standards which any application program must satisfy in order for the application to run and to make use of the capabilities of the computer hardware.

The disk operating system (DOS) program is composed of two main sub-programs: the control program and the processing program. The control program manages input/output, communicates with the user through various input devices and coordinates all other parts of the operating system. The processing program contains the language translator or compiler, directs the procedures for storing data on the disk and includes utility programs for specialized functions, such as data transfer.

Another common type of system program is called *utilities*. These are programs which function as tools for the user. They enable the user to control, organize or manage the computer system and application program. The DOS contains several utility programs. For example, in PC/MS-DOS the command "chkdsk.com" allows the user to check the amount of memory or disk storage in use and how much remains. In addition, add-on utility programs can be purchased which give the user other tools. AMong the better known utility programs are Norton Utilities and MACE.

Still another type of system program is contained on a microchip and is in the computer's CPU, disk drive, printer, modem or other hardware components; this is called *firmware*. Firmware programs are installed by the manufacturer. Some firmware can be modified by the user, but most are very difficult, if not impossible to alter. Firmware programs send special instructions to various hardware components which allow it to be controlled by the DOS or by an application program.

The last type of system program which will be mentioned here is *program language translators* which perform the function of translating these programming languages easily understood by humans into the electronic signals understood by the computer. Some language translators are built into DOS and others require additional programs.

System programs play a critical and varied role in the operation of the computer. DEvelopments in computer hardware and developments in system programs are intricately linked because it is through the system programs that the hardware is controlled and its potential utilized. Correspondingly, when developments in system programs occur there is a rippling effect in application software development; that is, changes in system programs require that changes be made in application programs as well. For example, two recent developments in system programs have occurred in IBM compatible machines which have been prompted by advances in hardware technology. These are: 1) *multitasking* or *multiprogramming* and 2) *virtual memory*.

Multitasking allows the computer to run more than one program or more than one different type of program at the same time. In other words, a statistical analysis program could be run at the same time that the user is running a word processing program. This technique allows several programs in primary storage at the same time for processing, thus providing seemingly simultaneous execution of more than one program. This is possible because the internal processing speed is much faster than the speed of any peripheral device needed to receive output. The result is that the processor must continuously "wait" for the output device to "catch up." Multitasking or multiprogramming allows the operating system to work with more than one program in memory, on a rotating basis, while allowing the output device to continue to receive data from the previous program.

Virtual memory is a concept which allows the computer to apparently fill more memory than actually exists in the computer. Lengthy programs are segmented so that only the portion of the program actually being executed is resident in primary storage at any one time. The remainder of the program is stored on the disk until needed by the computer to complete processing. If the size of these programs exceeds "real" storage, then the technique of procedure gives the impression that primary memory is unlimited. The disadvantage of virtual memory is that extensive secondary storage must be available and overall processing time is less efficient.

If the concepts of multitasking and virtual memory are to be used, the system software, especially the DOS, must be written to utilize advances in hardware design. If the DOS used is not capable of accessing the hardware advances which enable multitasking and virtual memory, then neither are possible even if the machine and the application program offer the capability. Correspondingly, even if the hardware and system program make multitasking and virtual memory possible, but the applications program is not written in a way to make use of these developments, then neither can used. In other words, changes in hardware development must be matched with changes in system programs and application programs in order for new technological capabilities to be utilized.

The last statement is particularly important to users and agencies which may be attempting to cope with recent developments in IBM compatible hardware and system programs. Consider the following illustration.

Illustration 1-3

UNRAVELING THE MYSTERIES
OF THE IBM OS/2 AND DOS 4.0

IBM is attempting to prove the validity of Estridge's computer law, which states, "No matter how big and standardized the market place, IBM will re-define it." IBM is attempting to re-define not only microcomputer hardware standards with its PS/2 line, but software standards as well with its OS/2 and DOS 4.0 operating systems.

Early in the 1980s, IBM's PC-DOS and Microsoft's generic MS-DOS deposed C/PM as the "more or less" industry standard for microcomputer operating systems. IBM compatible machines which flooded the market in the 1980s, driving down the cost of microcomputers through cost intensive competition. By 1987 PC/MS-DOS was in its third edition. However, there were inherent limitations of DOS 3.3 and earlier versions which necessitated radical future changes.

For example, PC/MS-DOS 3.3 and earlier versions could only manage 32Mb. of hard disk storage, even though hardware technology made 40-120Mb. possible. Further, DOS could only manage a maximum of 640K of RAM, although many machines could be expanded to 15-20Mb. Additionally, the DOS was exclusively a single user, single tasking operating system. Hence, application programs could not take advantage of new hardware technology because of the operating system program.

Users who needed multitasking or multiuser capabilities often employed specially designed third party operating systems such as UNIX or ZENIX. UNIX, designed by AT & T, and ZENIX, designed by Microsoft, were originally written for mini and small mainframe computers. Later, they were adapted to linking micro and minicomputers. both programs provide telecommunications linkage or networking capabilities between computers, multitasking and multi-user processing. However, to make use of these capacities, software and hardware often had to be specially written or modified. In most cases, the costs involved prohibited most individual users from adding

these operating systems to personal computers. compatibility prob-
lems were often encountered as a user moved from an IBM based ap-
plication program to the UNIX or ZENIX operating system.

The need for an IBM compatible multi-user, multitasking oper-
ating system has been long recognized. Since 1985, rumors were wide
spread that a completely new version of PC/MS-DOS was under de-
velopment which would address these needs. However, IBM elected
to wait until after it had introduced its entire new PS/2 line of ad-
vanced technology microcomputers in 1987 before introducing the
new operating system. Finally, in December 1987, the Operating Sys-
tem/2, or OS/2, Standard Edition, version 1, was released, along with
an Extended Version. To confuse matters further, a new DOS 4.0 was
also introduced. The following discussions are intended to add some
clarity to this situation.

Operating System/2

The OS/2, Standard Edition, is a single user, multitasking oper-
ating system which was designed to run on 80286 and 80386 micro-
processors. While it is designed to take advantage of the new PS/2
model architecture, it will run on most IBM compatible 286 or 386
machines (e.g., AT 286 or 386 machines). It will not run on 8086/8
machines (e.g., PC or XT machines). In addition, OS/2 requires a
minimum of 2Mb. of RAM to operate.

The OS/2, Extended Version, adds multiuser and networking
capabilities to the standard version. When used with 386 based ma-
chines, this version effectively turns the microcomputer into a low
level minicomputer. With this version, a microcomputer becomes a
true multitasking and multiuser machine.

The OS/2 system is designed to take advantage of IBM's micro
channel bus architecture. This makes computers much faster. For
example, the OS/2 and the new bus design makes the 80286 chip,
used in original AT type computers, run from four to seven times
faster than the original AT. Given that the original AT was approxi-
mately four to five times faster than the PC/XT, with their 8086/8
chip, the newer 286 type machine with OS/2 runs 16 to 35 times faster
than the original basic PC/XT. Further, given the fact that the 386
chip is four to seven times faster than the 286, it is easy to understand
that the newer computer designs and operating systems are creating
much more powerful microcomputers.

There are both advantages and disadvantages to the new OS/2,
when compared to PC/MS-DOS 3.3. Among the advantages are

these. First, multitasking capabilities are available with both versions of OS/2 which allow a single user to run many different applications at the same time, meaning that time is not lost waiting on the computer to finish running one type of program before another can be run. Second, the Extended Edition of OS/2 provides true multitasking and multi-user capabilities. Third, the OS/2 system can manage RAM up to 1,024Mb., compared to the 640K limits of DOS 3.3, which means faster and more powerful application programs can be run. Fourth, much larger disk storage management is possible, but OS/2 still manages storage in 32Mb. segments. Fifth, a new drop-down menu-driven presentation manager will allow even the most inexperienced novice to perform sophisticated system management functions. In addition, other new features are available to programmers and application program designers which will allow more powerful and easier-to-use programs to be written.

There are, however, many serious disadvantages. First is cost. The Standard Edition costs about $325 and the Extended Edition costs $795 if purchased separately. Second, additional costs are also encountered because a minimum of 2Mb. of RAM is needed for the program to operate. This can add between $1000 to $1600. Total costs of between $1325 to $2395 are beyond the reach of most individual users and place heavy burdens on agency budgets which may have an many as 60 or 70 micro systems.

The third major drawback to the OS/2 is that not all Pc/MS-DOS software will run on OS/2. Even those programs that do run cannot make use of multitasking capabilities or extended memory capabilities. Only software which is specifically written for the OS/2 can make use of these new features. Additionally, there are comparatively few programs currently available which are written for OS/2. Those that are available are much more expensive than the PC/MS-DOS versions. In some cases, for example, software written for the OS/2 may cost from 50 to 200% more than the same software written for PC/MS-DOS.

The fourth major disadvantage to OS/2 is that many types of third party hardware, such as bernoulli boxes, print spoolers, modems and network coordination devices, do not operate under OS/2. This means that existing equipment must be replaced or other solutions found.

The fifth major disadvantage to OS/2 is that it simply has too many "bugs" in it to be reliable without extensive programming support. In time, the "bugs" will be worked out, but the current versions 1 and 2 are still flawed and a user is risking much frustration if current versions are purchased.

In summary, it is likely that OS/2 will become the standard for 80286, 80386 and later 80486 based microcomputers. IBM will likely prove the validity of Estridge's axiom. However, neither individual users nor agencies should be in any rush to upgrade existing systems until OS/2 Standard Edition, version 3 (or later) or Extended Edition, version 2 (or later) are released. By late 1989 or 1990, if history repeats itself, most of the "bugs" should be corrected, compatible software will be widely available and competition will bring prices down to more reasonable levels. Until then, IBM and Microsoft have introduced PC/MS-DOS 4.0, which will help bridge the technology-software gap.

DOS 4.0

IBM introduced DOS 4.0 in July 1988 after the introduction of OS/2. Like all other earlier PC/MS-DOS versions, 4.0 is a single use, single tasking operating system. It has some new features and advantages over earlier versions, but it also has some disadvantages as well.

Among the advantages of DOS 4.0 are that it can manage up to 1,024 Mb. of RAM, which means that DOS programs written to make use of this expanded memory can be run on PC, XT and AT type machines. Second, it has a DOS Shell menu driven management system, making it much easier to use than earlier versions of PC/MS-DOS. Third, it is much faster than other versions of PC/MS-DOS. This results in improved processing speed for all types of IBM compatible programs. Fourth, the new DOS contains new utilities programs, many of which used to be available only through third party vendors. Finally, a new purchase costs about $150 and an upgrade about $95, making the new DOS affordable by individual as well as agency users.

DOS 4.0, however, has several problems. First, memory-resident programs (e.g., Side Kick) and other types of software which were written for earlier versions of PC/MS-DOS will not run on 4.0. Second, there are "bugs" in the program which do not allow some parts of earlier DOS programs to operate correctly and some external devices do not operate properly either. Third, it is curious that Microsoft has a European edition of DOS 4.0 which is multitasking, but the version introduced in the United States is not. In time, later versions of 4.0 may include this function.

In summary, like OS/2, the new DOS 4.0 should not be pur-chased until later versions are released which correct some "bugs" and compatibility problems, unless the user has no other choice. New ver-sions or upgrades of 4.0 will be out in 1989. When these problems are corrected, DOS 4.0 should give renewed life and improved opera-tional capabilities to the IBM PC, XT and AT compatible computers. Newer programs with expanded capabilities and power will be able to run on these older machines, although not with the full potential available for the 286 and 386 based machines which run under OS/2.

[Note: In September 1988 IBM quietly introduced DOS 4.01, which was supposed to correct some of the problems associated with 4.0. However, no evaluation information was available at this writing.]

COMPUTER LANGUAGES:
AN INTRODUCTION AND OVERVIEW

Any language is a standardized set of symbols used by humans who understand the code to communicate information. To transmit information through the written word, both the writer and the reader must share a common set of symbols. In this text, the common set of symbols is the English language. As a consequence, the authors are able to communicate with the reader.

Computer languages serve a similar function between computer and human. Human communication with a computer is possible through the use of binary code. Binary code has only two symbols, 0 and 1. These two symbols represent the on or off nature of electrical circuits used by computers. Because all numbers can be expressed in binary code and all logic problems can be written to imitate binary code, all human language can be understood by the computer if it is first translated into binary. A typical binary code to represent "add" would be "01011010;" binary for "subtract" would be "01011011."

When used by the computer to represent information, each 0 and 1 is referred to as a *bit*. Units, or *strings*, of bits are called *bytes*. Different computers can process bits in units of eight, although the length of the string may vary. A 16 bit system, for example, reads strings 16 bits long; this is equal to one byte for that system. A 32 bit system reads strings 32 bits long; this is also one byte for that system.

Although early computers were programmed in binary code, the task was time consuming and mentally taxing. Today, computer programmers use a variety of computer languages to give instructions to the computer. Each of these languages is translated by the computer into binary code through a special program in the operating system called the translator, interpreter or compiler.

Computer languages are classified in several ways. One common distinction is between a *high level language* and a *low level language*. A high level language is similar to the user's own language; the higher the computer language, the easier it is for a human being to read and understand the logic and information of a program. High level programming languages must be translated by the computer into binary code before processing can begin. Thus, a low level language is one which is understandable to the computer, but far removed from human language. Another method of classifying computer languages is by purpose or procedures normally addressed by the programmer. For example, FORTRAN is primarily a scientific language, COBOL and RPG are primarily business oriented languages, and BASIC and PL/1 are multipurpose languages.

There are more than 400 different high level computer languages written in some form of English. Each of these requires a translator program, sometimes called an interpreter or a compiler, to convert the high level computer language into machine readable binary code. This translation occurs as soon as information is input into the computer. Processing is accomplished in machine code; the output requested by the user is translated back into the high level language and displayed on the screen or printer.

All application and system programs are written in some form of a computer language. Different types of computer languages are more efficient than others. That is, they consume less computer processing time and can be handled more easily by human programmers. As a general rule, the higher the level of a computer language, meaning that the human user can more easily understand it, the less efficient that language is in terms of processing time and memory requirements.

Examples of Computer Languages

Machine language is the most efficient for the computer, but the most difficult for human programmers to use. Programmers who work in machine language must possess a great deal of technical knowledge, mathematical facility and patience, and be able to consistently pay close attention to small details. Machine language is written in binary code.

The next step beyond machine language is *assembly language*. Assembly languages employ mnemonics, or easily recognized symbols, to represent instructions. For example, most assembly languages use "A" to represent "add" and "S" to represent "subtract." Both machine and assembly languages are difficult to use and require much attention to detail.

Prior to 1970, most programmers used machine or assembly languages because it was believed that these languages allowed the computer to function most efficiently. High level programming languages, on the other hand, are easier to use by the human, but require a great deal of computer time and memory. Different languages address different application problems with varying degrees of success because all high level languages are compromises between human language and machine language. One compromise more suitably resolves common problems in one field than in others. Consequently, some languages are more appropriately suited to problems associated with certain subject areas than others.

Among the languages which are in common use today are these: *FORTRAN, COBOL, ADA, LISP, BASIC, PL/I, APL, RPG, PASCAL, C*, and *FORTH*. Some of these languages are described below. *FORTRAN*, which stands for FORmula TRANslator, was developed by John Backus in the 1950s. It was the first high level programming language. It used symbolic formulas to avoid programming in the zeroes and ones of machine language. FORTRAN also provided a structure to organize programming loops. Many revisions of FORTRAN have been prepared since the language was first introduced. Initially designed to meet the needs of mathematicians, engineers, and other scientists, FORTRAN is ideally suited to complex mathematical calculations. By the early 1960s, it had been applied to business and the social sciences, and was accepted by many researchers as a standard tool. Statistical packages, such as SPSS (Standard Statistical Packages for the Social Sciences), were written in FORTRAN. SPSS uses English syntax, and is written in a rigid format or structure, reflecting the 80-column punched cards which were used to communicate with most computers until the 1970s. The strength of FORTRAN is in its ability to translate algebraic formulas into decision making statements (e.g. A > B, then C). Although FORTRAN is still widely used, it had some major weaknesses. A major weakness is that typographical errors do not stop the program from running, consequently, undetected calculating errors may occur. A second weakness of FORTRAN is that updating and changing stored files is difficult and time consuming. FORTRAN is available for microcomputers, although it requires a large memory.

BASIC is a multipurpose language developed during the mid-1960s. BASIC stands for Beginner's All-purpose Symbolic Instruction Code. Since it incorporates some elements of FORTRAN into a "user friendly" language,

BASIC has many applications, especially for casual or novice computer users. It was first introduced as a device to teach the fundamentals of programming, but it became so popular that the language has been continuously revised over the past two decades. One result of these revisions is that many versions of BASIC exist. With modification, programs written in one form of BASIC can be converted into another form. BASIC is used extensively as a teaching tool and as an introductory computer language. The strength of BASIC is that it is easy to learn; however, it is a relatively slow processing language. A frequent criticism of BASIC is that it encourages poor programming habits in beginners because it permits use of the GOTO statement. Without planning ahead, a novice programmer can begin with a relatively simple idea, add a GOTO statement, and create a confusing, unmanageable program.

COBOL, which stands for COmmon Business-Oriented Language, was developed in the 1960s by a team of U.S. Navy programmers, led by Grace Hopper. COBOL was designed primarily for business applications. Programs written in COBOL have four divisions or sections. The first is the identification section which contains general information about the programmer's identity, the date and program name. The second section is the environment; this contains information about the computer system on which the program is to be run. The third is the data section which describes the data elements and files used by the program. The fourth section is the procedure division which specifies the logic of the program and instructions to be executed. All instructions in COBOL are written in sentences and paragraphs combining standard English words and easily understandable symbols. Most professional programmers either love COBOL, or they hate it; few are neutral toward it. The strength of COBOL lies in its readability and in its ability to handle vast amounts of data. Its weaknesses lie in its wordiness and repetition. Although it can handle large amounts of data, it has limited computational capabilities.

PASCAL, named after Blaise Pascal, the 17th Century philosopher, mathematician and inventor, was developed by Niklaus Wirth in 1968. Originally designed to teach programming concepts to students, PASCAL is a highly structured language which requires that programs be prepared in sections and sub-sections. This language discourages the use of the GOTO statement, and is capable of handling complex problems involving many steps. However, PASCAL does not allow for dynamic arrays that can change size, and it consumes a large amount of memory. Although the language is available for microcomputers, it is not well suited for the small micro because of memory requirements. It is rapidly gaining popularity because of its flexibility and self-documenting features.

C is a powerful language which has been used by major manufacturers of computers and operating systems. It is used in many operating systems, particularly those associated with Local Area Networking. For example, UNIX, which was created by Bell Laboratories, and MicroSoft's MS-DOS, among others, recently developed networking programs applying C. Even the Hollywood movie industry has found a use for this highly versatile language; it is used to create many of the special effects and graphics for science fiction films. Major software manufacturers that historically used assembly language now use C in the preparation of application software. Agencies which plan to use LANS may need C.

FORTH was developed during the 1960s. Today groups of users, sometimes identified by their "FORTH DIMENSION" t-shirts, apply the language to a wide range of business, entertainment and professional applications. It is a non-conventional language which has unofficially been adopted by astronomers and a few major manufacturers of computers, including IBM and Hewlett-Packard. FORTH is most significant for the trend in computer languages which it represents. Computer languages are in a constant state of evolution. Recent developments in microcomputers and minicomputers are encouraging the development of new languages which are more compact, consume less memory, process information at faster speeds, are more adaptable to different applications and are still relatively easy to learn.

APL, which stands for A Programming Language, is an interactive language that functions best when used with a special interactive terminal and screen. APL first became available in 1968. Its primary advantage is that complex operations are possible with a minimum amount of programming. APL has two distinct modes which the programmer can specify: execution and definition. In the execution mode the terminal keyboard is used as a calculator. In the definition mode instructions are entered into the computer and the program is executed. A primary disadvantage of this language is that it requires a special keyboard. APL is primarily used in business.

PL/1 was introduced in 1964. It is a multipurpose language that has been revised many times. Its most common application is in the development of software for computer-aided design (CAD) used in three-dimensional graphic displays.

Generations of Computer Languages

Similar to the development of computer hardware, computer languages have developed through five generations. The first generation of computer languages was machine code. Instructions entered into the computer using these languages ranged from manually throwing electrical on or off switches to writing programs in binary code.

The second generation of computer languages was assembly language which used mnemonics to represent frequently used instructions. The use of such complicated assembly languages was believed necessary to ensure the efficient operation of the computer as it processed data. Programmers still use assembly language today when speed of execution is an essential part of the program.

The third generation of computer languages began with the development of FORTRAN, the first of the high level programming languages. These languages met the needs of the scientists and mathematicians who were the primary computer users of the time. The development of language compilers or translators encouraged the emergence of fourth generation computer languages.

Fourth generation languages are characterized by the use of more easily recognizable English words and syntax. Their development paralleled the development of fourth generation compute hardware. COBOL and PL/1 are examples of fourth generation languages. They overcome some of the error handling problems of FORTRAN. These languages rely on a structure which allows computer instructions to be specified in a language that more closely resembles human language than previous computer languages. Recent additions to the fourth generation of computer languages include BASIC and PASCAL which are more accessible to the novice programmer.

Application programs became common during the same time period that fourth generation languages were developing. The sophisticated application programs dealing with word processing, spread sheets, and data base management functions allow the user to access the power of the computer after learning a limited array of essential commands. The commands used in application programs were sometimes purposely constructed to parallel commands used in programming. For example, the primary commands used by the Wordstar word processing program were selected because they are very similar to the commands used in PASCAL to move the cursor on the screen.

The fifth generation of languages is only now emerging. With the advent of artificial intelligence, native language programming will be possible. Commands will be entered on the keyboard or through voice recognizer systems in standard English. These commands will be interpreted by the computer, and any programming necessary for execution of these commands will be performed internally by the computer itself.

NATIONAL CRIMINAL JUSTICE COMPUTER CENTER

It is difficult for any individual or agency to keep current on newer software and hardware developments. It is even more difficult to keep current on newer developments with specific criminal justice applications. Recognizing this, two new national evaluation and information centers have been established for use by the criminal justice computer user.

The Criminal Justice Statistics Association (CJSA) and SEARCH Group, Inc. have established a National Criminal Justice Computer Laboratory and Training Center in Washington, D.C. A second center has been established on the west coast in Sacramento, California.

In general, the new centers are clearing houses for criminal justice computer-related information. They provide training in software applications and in the use of various hardware technologies. They provide a network of information so that an individual or agency which is considering the purchase of specific types of equipment or software can be put in touch with others who are already using the technology or software.

For information on the centers and their activities, contact Jim Zepp, Computer Center Manager, Criminal Justice Statistics Association, 444 North Capitol Street, N.W., Washington, D.C. 20001 or call (201) 624-8560.

SUMMARY AND CONCLUSIONS

The information society and its economic reality will define the parameters of the operational environment within which today's criminal justice organizations must function. This environment is now being shaped by quantum increases in demands for information by today's police, corrections, courts and juvenile justice agencies and institutions. Technology for computerized information processing and dissemination is advancing annually, particularly in the area of microcomputers. So-called "state-of-the-art" hardware becomes obsolete within a few years after purchase. The marketing strategy of many manufacturers is designed to "change the state of the art" within eight to eighteen months after release for hardware and four to six months for software.

The net effect of the information society in the operational environment of criminal justice mandates that changes in organizational management occur. One of these necessary changes is the application of microcomputer and minicomputer technology to the routine management practices of contemporary criminal justice agencies and institutions. The remaining four chapters of this text make specific suggestions for applying the technology introduced in Chapter 1. Throughout the remainder of this text, the reader may want to refer to this chapter since the later chapters presume that the reader has some familiarity with the material and topics presented.

REVIEW QUESTIONS AND ACTIVITIES

1. Define the term "criminal justice organizational management" and relate it to the concepts of informational society and economy. What impact might these concepts have on the operations of American police, courts, corrections, and juvenile justice agencies and institutions?

2. Briefly trace the history of computers.

3. Explain the components of a microcomputer system. Differentiate among hardware and software, and between application or system programs.

4. Define RAM, ROM, PROM, EPROM, DMA and DOS.

5. Explain each of the following: input/output devices, storage devices, floppy disk drives, and hard disk drives. Explain how each can be used in a criminal justice organization. What kind of backup procedures would be appropriate?

6. Explain the difference between the functions and capabilities of game or home use computers, individual use microcomputers, professional use microcomputers, minicomputers and mainframe computers. Explain the advantages and disadvantages of each.

7. Visit three to six different computer dealers. Ask to see a demonstration of their computers. Integrate information concerning specific products in your answers to number six above.

8. What do the terms 8-bit and 16-bit mean? How do these terms relate to the memory and speed of a computer?

9. Identify the computer languages which are most often used in micro and minicomputer programs. Explain what is meant by the term high level language.

10. In evaluating the memory capabilities of any computer system, what four questions should the informed buyer ask? Explain the importance of each question.

Chapter 2

DATA BASE AND MANAGEMENT INFORMATION SYSTEMS: MICROCOMPUTER APPLICATIONS

CHAPTER PREVIEW

Contemporary criminal justice organizations are dependent on the rapid and accurate collection, analysis and dissemination of information. When a police officer investigates a crime, a probation officer prepares a pre-sentence investigation report, a court schedules a case for trial or a parole board tracks an inmate's parole eligibility date, information is collected, analyzed and stored for future use. Information stored for future use is called *data*. Data must be stored in a way which will allow it to be retrieved and organized in a systematic manner so that it will not be lost. Data or information is usually stored in some type of a *record*, and *clusters of records* are grouped in larger units called *files*. Centralized and systematic storage of case files, records or other kinds of information is called a *data base*. The physical form of stored data and the logic framework which allows data to be systematically retrieved is a *data structure*. Criminal justice agencies must store massive volumes of information because of the thousands of people with which they must deal and the nature of their work. Recent developments in computer technology have and continue to aid the management of information in criminal justice.

Two interrelated concepts are introduced in this chapter: *data base management* and *management information systems*. *Data base management systems (DBMS)* refers to a "systematic approach to storing, updating, and retrieval of information stored as data items, usually, in the form of records in a file, where many users, or even many remote installations, will use common data banks." (Sippl and Sippl, 1982: 127). In criminal justice, there are many different types of data or information bases (e.g. criminal information files, case investigation files, budgetary information files and personnel files). Some *data bases* are used by agencies in management decision making and are called *management information systems (MIS)*. By definition these refer to a "specific data-processing system that is designed to furnish management and supervisory personnel with information" required for decision making (Sippl and Sippl, 1982: 304). Microcomputer technology applications are examined in relation to the administrative functions of planning, budgeting, fiscal and resource management. All of these management processes are intricately related, utilize data bases and information management systems, and are found in most organizational settings. Also discussed are applications in field investigation, communications, and networking with mainframe computers.

STUDY QUESTIONS

The following study questions may be used as a guide to reading Chapter 2. Key terms and concepts related to these questions are printed in italics throughout the chapter.

1.   What is meant by the management functions of planning, budgeting, fiscal and resource management?

2.   What is the relationship of data base and information management to planning and budget management?

3.   What is meant by normative, strategic, planning and operational planning?

4.   Why are mainframe data bases frequently used in criminal justice? What are some examples?

5.   How are microcomputers used in networking with mainframe data bases?

6.   What are the potentials and limitations of microcomputer technology in other areas of data base and information management?

PLANNING, BUDGETING, FISCAL
AND RESOURCE MANAGEMENT:
A BRIEF OVERVIEW

Progress in mainframe computer technology set the stage during the 1960s for a major shift from manual to electronic record keeping. During the 1970s advances in minicomputer and microcomputer technology introduced computerized information processing and allowed more agencies to become automated. During the 1980s rapid improvements in microcomputer and minicomputer technology brought automation within the budgets of most justice agencies. With the advent of the 808286, 808386 and M68020 chips during the late 1980s, microcomputers became capable of processing very large files in a manner which had only been possible with mainframes a few years earlier. Recent and emerging enhancements are having three observable consequences in regard to data base and management information systems.

First, the accessibility of mainframe data bases allows a much broader range of criminal justice practitioners and academicians to retrieve information than ever before. With the advent of fifth generation-native language programming and artificial intelligence, millions more people will be able to access even more more information.

Second, more powerful minicomputers and microcomputers mean that data bases which previously required mainframes for processing now can be maintained on smaller computer systems, giving agencies more direct control over the input and retrieval of information than was possible previously.

Third, telecommunications networking opens up techniques of investigation and information acquisition which have heretofore never been imagined.

These changes are especially evident in agency planning, budgeting, fiscal, inventory and resource management.

Planning

Planning at the organizational, community, system or national level, is the process of reviewing information about the past, applying it to present goals and objectives, projecting toward the future and making decisions based on this process. Planning is foresight in the development and implementation of policy which involves the systematic analyzing of probable future events, evaluating alternative actions, within the limitations of present knowledge and decision making within political and economic realities. (Archambeault and Archambeault, 1982:10, 81-89, 137-175; Tansik and Elliott 32-75; Hernandez 1-16). In this context *planning* may be defined as the:

> orderly, systematic and continuous process of bringing anticipations of the future to bear on current decision making in order to achieve desired results. (*Criminal Justice Planning and Management Series: Criminal Justice Planning Course*, U.S. Department of Justice, 1981:IG2-5)

Consider the following example of planning. Imagine that a community, called Model Community U.S.A., is rapidly growing because of economic development and the migration of workers from all parts of the country seeking employment. As a consequence, the community government recognizes that it must expand its criminal justice services, chiefly in the numbers of police officers, available jail capacity and scope of services for juvenile offenders. However, the community political leaders want to know how many officers, how much more jail capacity, how many more services are needed. They need this information to cope with the problem of finding tax revenues necessary to provide these projected additions, since they also have to deal with increased demands for other types of public services, such as fire protection, roads, sewage and water. To address these problems, the community leaders rely on information provided by the local planning agency and on federal census tract data. This data is stored in planning agency and census bureau computers and includes data about past growth patterns and future projections. Based on summary information, the leaders of Model Community must develop consistent plans and timetables for satisfying projected demands for increased services. In turn, local criminal justice agencies (e.g. the police, sheriff, courts, and juvenile authorities) must develop specific organizational plans for their own agencies. This is an ideal planning process which combines community systems level planning and agency-specific organizational level planning. This model of integrated planning rarely occurs in real life. If it does occur, it is never finished, since planning is an on-going, continuous process.

Planning is a continuous process which involves a systematic review of information and continual analysis of possible implications. Planning is not a one time activity. The plans which result from the planning process must be updated and modified as more current information becomes available. In this process, there are three general types of planning which must be done: (1) normative; (2) strategic; (3) operational. In addition, there are several different classes of plans which will be discussed below.

Normative Planning

Normative planning involves two questions such as what should an organization do and why. The plans which result from this process are part of the policy of an organization and are reflected in the theoretical, philosophical, and ideological statements of organizational written policy. (Archambeault and Archambeault, 1982:144). Fluctuations in social, legal, moral, economic and political values and attitudes of the community and society as a whole impact on and alter the policy of any organization. For example, in Model Community U.S.A., as in other parts of the United States, changes in social and legal values of the 1960s shifted the emphasis of law enforcement toward a strict protection of individual rights. Changes in the emphasis on treatment and rehabilitation of offenders toward the emphasis on flat-time sentences and punishment substantially altered the ideological justification for dealing with adult offenders. Similarly, changes in definitions of juvenile rights altered the ways juveniles must be treated in courts, on probation and in institutions. All these changes required criminal justice agencies to modify the way they answered the questions of "what should be done" and "why" in the planning process. Normative planning, as far as Model Community U.S.A. is concerned, is influenced by the idea that problems should be anticipated and solutions developed "before" they become threats to the community. This basic value is reflected in the normative planning considerations for all criminal justice agencies within the community's influence.

Strategic Planning

Strategic planning is concerned with the questions of what can be done and how it can be accomplished. Strategic planning develops alternative plans, called *contingency plans*, to cover different possible future situations. Routine contingency plans are part of written policy. For example, the local jails and correctional institutions of Model Community U.S.A. have riot, fire, escape and other kinds of emergency plans. [See Archambeault and Archambeault, 1982: Chapter 13.] Police departments have plans covering VIP escorts. Juvenile authorities have public health plans for protecting juveniles in confinement, as well as plans for runaways, retarded and potentially vulnerable children in custody. Model Community also had contingency plans covering economic emergencies.

Criminal justice agencies of the 1980s in Model Community U.S.A. faced problems of reduced budgets, personnel layoffs, civil rights and union actions, as did other American communities in the 1980s. Planning for Model Community U.S.A. was based on certain revenue projections and anticipated growth. However, within a year after new personnel were added to the local police department, an economic crisis developed which required that all budgets be cut by ten percent. On the normative assumption that future cuts might be twenty to thirty percent, various contingency plans were developed, potential problems were analyzed, and alternative courses of action were considered. From these normative plans, various contingency plans were developed. Included were contingencies which anticipated different levels of budget cuts and how these cuts would impact on personnel. Operations were assigned priorities for possible reductions. The important point is that for each possible event which might affect a criminal justice organization, a contingency plan answering the "what" and "how" questions had to be developed. As a result, when the anticipated event actually occurred, Model Community's criminal justice organizations, were able to act in a consistent and orderly fashion.

Operational Planning

Operational planning involves answering questions concerning what an organization will do and when. When a strategic plan is activated, it becomes an *operational plan*. For example, when Model Community's jails became overcrowded and a disturbance broke out, the institution's riot control plan (a strategic plan) became an active operational plan. Once the disturbance had broken out and specific facts about it were established, specific elements of the strategic plan were implemented or operationalized. General and anticipated facts were replaced with specific and actual information. In this regard, answers to questions of "what will be done" and "when" become clearly defined in the form of orders and instructions from management personnel. In turn, when the specific details of the Governor's visit were made known to Model Community's police department (e.g. dates, time, routes and itinerary), then the department's strategic VIP escort plan became operational.

Budgets, Fiscal
and Resource Management

The administrative processes of budgeting, fiscal and resource management, and inventory control are intricately related to planning. A *budget* is a financial plan which is developed in several stages. First, most criminal justice organizations are required to submit annual budgets to funding agencies, such as the city council, county board of supervisors, state or federal legislature or other elected funding body. A particular plan might request a certain amount of money for the agency for the next year. Agency budgets must be justified in a variety of ways, including accounting for previous year's expenditures and the description of services to be performed. Next, the funding body allocates the agency a certain amount of money. Third, the agency must operate within the limits of the allocated budget. Hence the budgetary process, from an organization's perspective, starts first as a "normative plan" which states what the agency would like to do. It develops into a "strategic plan," and eventually becomes an "operational plan." The term budget ordinarily refers to the planned and/or requested amount of money to run an agency as well as to the actual amount of money provided by a funding agency. Once money is allocated to an agency, two other related concepts come into play: (a)fiscal management and (b)resource management or inventory control. *Fiscal management* within an agency is concerned with three areas: 1) planning for the efficient utilization of available resources; 2) accounting for the expenditure of budgeted funds; and 3) developing contingency plans to cover a variety of potential financial situations. *Resource management* or *inventory control* is concerned with three areas: 1) planning for the exigencies, both human and material, which will be needed for the organization to carry out its functions; 2) allocating resources as required; and 3) controlling and accounting for resources. Fiscal and resource management are components of any agency's total budgetary system. Both can be examples of an agency's management information system (MIS).

DATA BASE AND
INFORMATION MANAGEMENT SYSTEMS

In order for planning, budgeting, fiscal and resource management and inventory control functions to be carried out, information is required. In addition, information is also needed in association with functional operations such as case investigations, criminal background intelligence, offender profile information, court scheduling, juvenile health and medical records. Within any modern criminal justice organization, many different types of information are needed.

Stored information is called *data*. As noted earlier in this chapter, stored and systematically organized data are referred to by the general term *data base management system* or *DBMS*. However, data bases, also called data banks, which contain information specifically used by management in decision-making (e.g. planning, budgeting, fiscal, personnel management or inventory control information) are called *management information systems (MIS)*. Data bases which are used in agency operations (e.g. investigations, crime trend analysis, social history information, and arrest information) are called *operations data bases (ODB)*. Some ODB information is also used by management in decision-making (e.g. man-hours and costs connected with conduct of a particular investigation; also, see discussion of POSSE presented later in this chapter). Because of the overlap among different types of data bases, most discussions in this and later chapters will apply the general term data base management system.

Computerized data base management systems organize information into *records* which contain observations or other information composed of identifiable fields. These are assigned names or numbers and given particular locations or addresses on the data storage device (e.g. on a floppy disk, on a hard disk, or within the core of a mainframe). Records are organized into larger groupings called files; files may contain many different records. As noted in Chapter 1, it is through these names and addresses that files and the information contained in them can be recalled (loaded) or stored (saved). These data base systems require software programs, hardware, and communications links through which data can be input, stored, analyzed, retrieved or disseminated.

The types of data supported by data base software is important, generally these are either character type (e.g. letters, symbols) or numeric (e.g. 1,2,3). Numbers pose particular problems for data base management because they can be split into whole numbers (integers without fractions) or floating point numbers (real numbers which may have fractions or decimal values). The latter category is stored in a binary number format resulting in a fixed byte width, while the former is restricted to the *word* size of the microprocessor, meaning a character string of 8, 16 or 32 bytes. The same applies to character type data. That is, text material such as what you are now reading is composed of characters or letters which are stored in strings 8 bytes long if it is an 8-byte processor, 16 if a 16-byte processor.

A primary concern in selecting appropriate data base software is its ability to store and manage information and data. Some software and hardware limit the sizes of records, the number of files, the number of fields, and the types of functions or manipulations which can be performed. Early Z-80, CP/M microcomputers placed severe limitations on stored data, making them inefficient except for the smallest and simplest form of data management. In contrast, the new OS/2 operating systems and 80386 microcomputers allow high speed manipulation of extremely large data sets and files. Practical limits on this newer hardware and operating systems lie with the programming of the software itself. Hence, the software must be versatile, user friendly, provide on line help to the user, be menu driven and allow windowing of sections of stored data. In addition, good data base software programs should have easy to use, powerful report generators which allow transfer of stored information from the computer to some printed format. Further, with the newer types of equipment, the software should have multiuser capabilities. It should also have capabilities for recovery of information due to power failure or some other form of system crash. Finally, the software must provide some measure of security both in terms of permitting access to stored confidential information and protecting against purposeful sabotage or illegal manipulation of the data.

If interface with a larger minicomputer or mainframe computer system is desired, then issues of compatibility and file transfer become important. That is, in many agencies information is initially entered through microcomputers then transferred to larger systems to be integrated into still larger data base information systems. This means that the software used to create the microcomputer data base has to be compatible with the structure of stored data on the larger systems. It also means that communications link between the micro and the larger system must permit easy and accurate transfer of information.

One way to accomplish both compatibility and file transfer is to convert information files to ASCII or DIF formats. Most computers, whether micro or mainframe, have the ability to read standardized ASCII and DIF files. ASCII stands for American Standard Code for Information Interchange. An ASCII file consists of information stored into a form which is readable to most humans, such files are stripped of special characters and codes used by specific types of software programs. What results is a neutral or vanilla file which, within limitations, can be universally read by most computer systems. The DIF (Data Interchange Format) is similar but is designed to allow files written by one program to be read by another. ASCII and DIF capabilities are most important for the frequent uploading and downloading from one computer to another.

Another aid to compatibility and file transfer is the emerging technologies of artificial intelligence and native language input and retrieval. Artificial intelligence capabilities have been associated with certain mainframes for many years, but only recently have microcomputers become powerful and fast enough to make use of this potential. Artificial intelligence allows the user of newer data base management software to enter commands through native language statements, thereby avoiding the rigid syntax requirements for commands which have characterized data base software of the past. The artificial intelligence and native language proficiencies will provide links between systems which have never existed previously. The AI can build data bridges between non-compatible data bases, allowing transfer even without the intermediate step of transfer to an ASCII or DIF format. This will increase the speed and ease of information transfer between data bases because the AI will automatically generate the codes, commands, syntax, or data structures required by different systems. When additional instructions are required for clarification, the AI bridge will request additional input from the human user who can supply it in common, standard native language. Such augmentations mean that agencies will rely less on specially trained programmers and be able to use personnel trained in data management techniques. It will also mean less down time due to training, fewer mistakes because something is entered incorrectly, and less training. On the other hand, it poses new problems for data security and integrity.

Stored data and information is useless unless it can be cataloged, systematically retrieved and related to other data items. The ability of a DBMS to achieve these functions depends on its *data structure*. There are two essential components to data structure: 1) the *physical arrangement* in which data is stored, and 2) the *logic* which governs how data is stored within the DBMS. Physical arrangement is a direct result of both the hardware design of the computer and the logic of the program which is responsible for storing the data. There are many different models of data structure used, but three are most common: 1) network, 2) hierarchical, and 3) relational. To understand the differences in these, assume that an agency's DBMS consists of two different data bases: arrest information on adults and court disposition of cases. The agency wants to be able to track the characteristics of arrested persons, their crimes and the outcomes of their cases. In a *network data structure* data would be stored according to a logic which would allow characteristics of one data set to be related to those of another without any assumption of priority or hierarchy. For example, characteristics of arrested persons could be directly related to characteristics of the crime and then to disposition. In contrast, if the same information were stored using a *hierarchical* logic model, data would be stored in files according to some pre-determined priority of greater to lesser (or general to specific) relationships. Suppose the priority were categorical, such as type of offense, sex characteristics of offender, race characteristics of offender, disposition of case. Attributes of individual cases could not be related directly, rather, the logic would first seek out the largest category which contained the desired information (e.g. sex of offender) before it could access attributes (e.g. male, female). Hierarchical data bases are common in criminal justice because of the types of information recorded. The NCIC DBMS, for example, uses a hierarchical structure which means an electronic search for information must go through hundreds of layers of hierarchical categories in order to retrieve specific information. The third type of data structure, *relational*, establishes some other logical type of priority. The DBMS is constructed as a collection of already existing relationships or tables, making retrieval of information more efficient than either the network or hierarchical approach. Data is stored in the order in which output is desired. This of course requires that the questions or form of output desired be known before programming and input.

These are but three of the more common DBMS data structures for storage and retrieval of information. Individual agencies may elect to impose other systems of logic on their stored data. Further developments in computer hardware and software technologies will continually evolve newer and more efficient ways of storing and retrieving data. The increasing power of micro and minicomputers allow agencies greater flexibility in designing DBMS which meet the specific information demands of the agency. Artificial intelligence, native language programming, and voice recognizer technologies are on the verge of totally redefining the meaning of DBMS.

Within criminal justice, DBMS may also be differentiated as being: 1) self-contained mainframe systems; 2) self-contained microcomputer or minicomputer systems; and 3) interactive micro/minicomputer-mainframe data bases. Self-contained mainframe DBMS are those which can be accessed and used only within a mainframe computer network, usually through "dumb" terminals. Self-contained micro/minicomputer DBMS are those which can be accessed only by a particular microcomputer system, usually a single microcomputer or minicomputer. In contrast, an interactive micro/minicomputer to mainframe DBMS is a system through which either a microcomputer can communicate and exchange information with a mainframe computer or with other microcomputers, usually through some means of telecommunications. Because of the massive volume of information and millions of files which many criminal justice agencies maintain, mainframe computer data bases are essential. However, interactive microcomputer-mainframe systems allow smaller agencies to access huge state and federal data bases as well as other microcomputer systems. These also improve communication between individuals (e.g. police officers, probation officers, or court counselors) and their agencies, thus permitting direct input of field data into larger agency information systems.

Data base management systems are organized into *information networks* which are introduced later in this chapter and discussed extensively in Chapter 3. For the present, consider a network as being a means of communication among different computers. In this context, *data base management networks* may be regarded as communication links among different computer data bases which permit the exchange of information. Examples of different types of data base management networks follow.

MAINFRAME DATA BASED MANAGEMENT SYSTEMS

Mainframe computer systems are designed to store, retrieve, manipulate and analyze massive amounts of information. There are three mainframe data base systems in criminal justice. 1) The National Criminal Justice Information Center (NCIC) system contains detailed arrest and intelligence information on known criminals and may be accessed by any bona fide police agency. 2) The *Uniform Crime Report (UCR)* compiles, summarizes and reports national NCIC data on a quarterly and annual basis.   3) The *SOURCEBOOK OF CRIMINAL JUSTICE STATISTICS*, (Bureau of Justice Statistics, United States Department of Justice) which is published annually, presents a comprehensive summary of most published, governmentally funded criminal justice research and agency statistical reports for a given year.

Of these three, NCIC is the most frequently accessed by police departments. Begun in 1967, NCIC now houses more than fifteen million records and is maintained with an annual budget of more than six million dollars. It is estimated that NCIC contains entries on one out of every thirty Americans and maintains complete dossiers on more than eight million persons. These data files are managed by an IBM 3033 mainframe computer which is operated twenty-four hours per day, seven days per week, and which contains a fail-safe configuration complete with backup power. Annually, in excess of 64,000 federal, state, and local police agencies, prosecutor's offices and courts are authorized to access the system. Access is possible from any one of more than 17,000 remote terminals presently linked to the system. NCIC is supported by the National Law Enforcement Telecommunications System (NLETS) so that its control is not directly under the Federal Bureau of Investigation, although it administratively falls under the FBI.

Each of the above examples represents nation-wide data management reports and involves input from thousands of different sources. To directly access these data base systems, a user must have a terminal, access information, authorization codes and be a part of a national informational network. These data base management systems are used by federal, state and local authorities in planning and resource management. Planning at the organizational level, especially for police and corrections, is directly affected by reports generated from information stored in these files. For example, changes in UCR data may indicate that a particular community has a seriously increasing crime rate, compared to other communities of similar size. Such information may be used to justify expansion of justice services or the formation of special investigative units.

Mainframe data based management systems are also extensively used at the federal, state and local criminal justice levels in functions which range from preparing psychological profiles of terrorists, to plotting land use, to automobile registration. For example, the FBI uses mainframe computers to profile potential terrorists and criminals, and to construct descriptions and graphic sketches of potential criminal subjects from witness information; such programs also yield statistical information concerning the degree of correlation and consistency among reported characteristics. Similarly, psychological profiles of highjackers, kidnappers and other types of criminals are constructed using mainframe data bases. In conjunction with the Office of Juvenile Justice and Delinquency Prevention (OJJDP) and the National Institute of Justice (NIJ), the FBI established a National Center for the Analysis of Violent Crime which is the focal point for research and analysis of violent crime offenses. Its resources are available to assist state and local police in collecting, correlating and sharing information on unsolved murders, rapes and child molestations.

Most states and many large units of local government use mainframes extensively as well. Michigan, for example, uses a field report system which allows for optical input of investigative activities into data bases which interface with Michigan Crime Information and NCIC. Most state departments of correction maintain inmate data files and offender files on all persons committed to state corrections; such information is used not only for managing offenders (e.g. tracking of release and parole date information), but also for planning additional institutions, personnel and services. Computers are being used as investigative tools by the United States Department of Justice which operates a computerized Organized Crime Information System. This system is also used to identify hostile intelligence officers operating in the United States. FBI crime laboratories and other facilities around the country use computers to "read" and match fingerprints. The Forensic Science Research and Training Center at the FBI Academy also has a system that may allow positive identification of individuals through bloodstains.

Picture 2-1 above shows a SPERRY-UNIVAC mainframe terminal in the Investigative Support Center of the Louisiana State Police, Baton Rouge, Louisiana. Through this terminal, the operator can interface with NCIC, local police, and other public safety data bases (e.g. vehicle registration, prosecutors offices, warrants). This is an example of an interactive mainframe data system.

Some local cities, such as the St. Petersburg Police Department, use mainframe computers to dispatch emergency services (police, fire, medical) through a 911 emergency number. In San Diego, California, police use computers as collective, institutional memory banks for storing nicknames, scars, and marks. They are also used for field interrogations. Some courts, such as those in Orange County, Florida, use computers to schedule cases, monitor jail populations and ensure that prisoners scheduled for court appearances are brought to court on time. The Dallas, Texas, court system uses a mainframe computer to issue subpoenas and summons.

Picture 2-2 above displays an ADS mainframe terminal used by the East Baton Rouge Parish District Attorney's Office. Through this terminal, investigators can interface NCIC and state criminal files. This is also an example of an interactive mainframe data base system.

Table 2-1 illustrates the diversity in "systems functions" or types of mainframe data management systems employed in criminal justice (Table 3, *1986 Directory of Automated Criminal Justice Information Systems*, page 996, Bureau of Criminal Justice Statistics, United States Department of Justice, Government Printing Office). Mainframe information data base systems are used extensively in the United States by federal, state, and large municipalities. Use has been limited in smaller agencies because of high cost and levels of sophistication required to operate mainframe computers. Microcomputers, however, are changing this situation.

TABLE 2-1

Types of Data Based Management Systems
in Use in Criminal Justice Agencies
in the United States: 1986

Activity Reporting
Administration/Personnel
Alimony Control
Alphabetic Index
Arrests/UCR
Assignment-Attorneys
Assignment-Courtroom
Assignment-Judges
Automated Vehicle Location
Auto Registration
Calendaring/Scheduling
Case Analysis
Case Control
Case Disposition Reports
Child/Family Support
Citation Control
Command and Control
Communications:
--Message Switching
--Mobile Digital
--Other
Computer Instruction
Computer Assisted Dispatch
Corrections Personnel
Courts Personnel
Crime Lab
Crime Trend Analysis
Criminal Associates
Defendant Control
Docketing
Driver Registration
Evidence Control
Field Contact Reporting
Fines, Collateral, Bail
Fingerprint Processing
Geoprocessing (Geocoding)
Grant Tracking
Firearms Registration
Inmate Accounting/Records
Juror Payroll Processing
Jury Management

Jury-Random Selection of Panel
Juvenile Index/Records
Legal Information Retrieval
Licensing/Registration
Menu Planning
Micrographics
Missing Persons
Modus Operandi
Narcotics Control
Offender Based Transaction
Organized Crime
Parole Control
Pawned Articles
Performance Evaluation
Physical Goods Inventory
Planning
Police Personnel
Prison Industries
Prisoner Behavior Models
Probation Control
Process Service Control
Prosecution Management
Rehabilitation
Research/Statistics
Resource Allocation
Simulation/Modeling
Statute Retrieval
Stolen Property: Guns,
  Vehicles, Other
Subjects-In-Process
Summons Control
Traffic Accident Investigation
Training
Transportation of Prisoners
Trust Fund Accounting
Vehicle Inspection/Maintenance
Warrant Control
Warrants/Wanted Persons
Witness Control
White Collar Crime
Workload Analysis

MICROCOMPUTER APPLICATIONS
IN DATA BASE MANAGEMENT

All segments of American criminal justice, police, courts and corrections are part of the information dependent society. (See Naisbitt, 1982). Information, including its accuracy and speed of movement, is vital to every aspect of criminal justice. In police work, information can have life or death meanings. Consequently, it is not surprising that microcomputer technology has already begun to dramatically change American police management practices. As newer technologies reduce the size of microcomputers to portable and even "pocket-size" units, the impact on American law enforcement will probably continue. Police officers of the 1990s may be issued small pocket computers, similar in size to belt-carried two-way radios, which are now standard items of issue, together with pistol, handcuffs and badge (Shaw, 1969). Patrol cars in many jurisdictions now come equipped with computers. Similarly, microcomputers will change corrections as they are used increasingly to manage inmate records, conduct pre-sentence investigations, supervise offenders in the community, provide instruction to inmates, and train correction personnel.

Microcomputers are used in criminal justice data base management in four primary areas:

1. Data Base Management Networking with Mainframes
2. Small Business Management Applications
3. Field-Report Writing and Investigation
4. Information Systems Networking

These topics form the basis of the remaining portions of this chapter.

DATA BASE NETWORKING WITH MAINFRAMES

Data base networking with mainframe computers is possible in two ways. First, terminals can be linked through a communications chain to a mainframe CPU, usually through telephone lines, or other hard wire connection or sometimes through radio links. As noted in Chapter 1, such terminals are normally dependent on interaction with the mainframe CPU and cannot function if the communication link is broken. As a result, they are compromised by problems with telephone lines or other means of communications, a shut-down of the mainframe system for repair, and time sharing conflicts in priorities and protocols. Second, another form of networking can be based on interconnected microcomputers or minicomputers, which have functionally independent CPUs, memory and processing ability.

With the advent of affordable microcomputers, the potential of networking with large mainframe data bases became a possibility for many criminal justice agencies. Microcomputer systems, electronically linked to mainframe computers (e.g. by phone modem, wire, radio or microwave transmitters) were able to interact with the mainframe computer data bases. However, several problems remained. For American police, three critical problems were: 1) the development of compatible software which was capable of achieving functional linkage between microcomputers and mainframes and between different microcomputer systems; 2) the cost involved in writing software programs which were compatible with so many different types of systems; and 3) the development of interactive and multi-tasking management information systems (MIS) and operations data bases (ODB). Fundamentally, these problems were the result of each agency's choice of software, data base and operating systems. Hence inter-agency and even intra-agency software programs often could not easily exchange information with mainframe computers. For instance, within the same agency, accounting or payroll might use different computer hardware or software than equipment used by personnel or research-planning, thereby making it impossible to exchange information either within the same agency or between different agencies. Without compatible software, computers cannot interface or interact.

Recognizing these limitations as they applied to local police agencies, the Bureau of Justice Statistics (BJS), United States Department of Justice entered into a cooperative arrangement with the International Association of Chiefs of Police (IACP) to develop a compatible software system for data based management which would allow any police department using this particular software system to share information with another department using the same software. This compatible software system would be provided free upon request to participating police departments. The central program, called POSSE, was a field reporting, search and record keeping system which allowed various types of information bases to be combined into a single report and allowed information from one program to be combined with information from another. Interfacing with this were three other limited use data management systems: 1) CASS; 2) IMIS; and 3) FMIS. These are explained below.

1. *POSSE*, which stands for Police Operating Systems Support-Elementary, is the central operating system which provides the capability of field information input and report preparation, as well as file search and record keeping. This program coordinates other data base management programs and serves as a central clearing house for all information stored in other program components of the software system.

2. *CASS*, Crime Analysis System Support, represents an attempt to provide some standardization to the future development of computerized crime analysis. CASS provides information for detection of crime patterns, identification of potential suspects by matching characteristics, identification of potential crime targets, forecasting crime trends, and evaluating efficiency resource allocations. It also provides for statistical analysis and graphic display of results. (See Robertson and Chang, 1980).

3. *IMIS*, Investigative Management Information System, is a sophisticated program which interfaces with POSSE and CASS and allows field investigators and managers to more efficiently utilize personnel and material resources involved in case investigation.

4. *FMIS*, Fleet Management Information System, is a program which allows a police agency, or potentially any agency which uses many vehicles, to deploy and maintain those vehicles efficiently, to determine cost-effectiveness measures, and other information related to the management of motorized vehicles.

Thus, it was possible for an agency to conduct a management study and learn how many personnel, vehicles and man-hours it took to solve a particular case or to track the development of a specific case. (See *Law and Order*, February, 1982:14-18; Ioimo, 1981:56-57; Damos and Stepanek, 1982:32-34; Robertson and Chang, 1980:41-43). To assist police agencies in overcoming the cost barrier and to encourage standardization, the Bureau of Justice Statistics (BJS) made the POSSE data base system and its interfacing programs available upon request to local police agencies. POSSE has also been integrated into previously developed regional data base management systems such as REJIS (REgional Justice Information Service) in the greater St. Louis area (see Damos and Stepanek, 1982). However, despite federal efforts, many police agencies either lacked compatible computer equipment or operating systems. Other agencies have preferred to develop and maintain their own systems or were locked into "time-sharing" arrangements with other divisions of government. Hence, the POSSE model is not standard in all agencies or settings.

Besides POSSE, the federal government has made available to criminal justice agencies other free data base management software. These include ATHOS and MAPPS which are used in drug investigation information collection (*Law and Order*, February, 1982: 14-18). Similar free software is available to jails and institutions as well. *JAMS-II*, or the Jail Administrators Management System, was developed by the Department of Justice and made available to participating agencies. JAMS-II provides jail administrators with daily reports on court schedules, inmate rosters, time served, statistical reports, maintenance costs and other data. Under a cooperative arrangement with the Bureau of Statistics, The SEARCH Group, Inc. of Sacramento, California, maintains a National Clearinghouse for Criminal Justice Information Systems and currently has an index of over 860 different criminal justice software systems from all over the country. Some of these are free upon request, while others are copyrighted and must be purchased.

POSSE and JAMS-II are attempts to develop compatible software for police and corrections. These, however, are not the only examples of mainframe-microcomputer networking software. *ORDAIN*, or the Online Rape Data Analysis Information Network, represents an example of an intra-agency network (Hughes and Pedroncelli, 1982). This system was designed to interface with *MEDUS/A*, a general purpose public health data base system originally written by the Harvard School of Public Health for use in public health agencies and also used by the Albuquerque, New Mexico, medical investigator's office (Oson and Chang, 1980). Still another recent example of interfacing and compatible criminal justice software, is *IMPACT* (Interactive Model For Projecting Arrests and Corrections Trends), developed by the Criminal Justice Statistical Association (CJSA) of Washington, D.C., for prison population forecasting. IMPACT is also part of current efforts to design software which can run independently or interactively on microcomputers or mainframes.

Microcomputers are also used in police information networking to link officers in the field with centralized data files, such as NCIC. For example, the Chicago Police Department uses a mobile terminal system consisting of a vehicle-mounted computer terminal, a logic unit (CPU) and a radio transmitter with receiver sites on top of high buildings to communicate with the communications center. As a result, the police officer in the field is linked with NCIC and other crime data bases. Unit commanders and precinct captains can also use this system to allocate and manage the personnel and equipment resources of the department (Rodriguez, 1982). When "pocket-size" computers become standard pieces of police and correctional officer equipment, even smaller departments may be able to provide this type of direct field link.

Similar direct field links may increase the effective use of probation and parole officers who supervise offenders in the community. Pre-sentence investigations and social history updates may be produced from the field, a vehicle or an agent's home, thereby reducing time lost in transit. Supervisors could more effectively control and account for an officer's activities, since filed transmissions would document time, location and activities of probation and parole personnel. Dr. Joe Waldron has developed an automated social history for criminal justice related agencies, *ASH Plus* (Cincinnati, OH.: Anderson Publishing Co., Software, Criminal Justice Division), which is designed to produce a structured social history report from subject responses to field-interview questions. Similar types of software will become more common within a few years.

Correctional officers, whether human or robotic, could be in direct contact with an institution's control center as they patrol various areas of the prison. Corrective actions, disciplinary matters and conditions of security systems could be reported and data encoded instantly. Potentially dangerous situations could be identified and handled before they become major problems. Inmate behavior (both positive and negative) and conduct files could be accurately and comprehensively recorded for later analysis, thereby improving the quality of decision making for parole and institutional classification. Diagnostic and assessment functions could also be improved through computerization. [See Waldron, et.al., 1983: 41-49]. Medical records and treatment in correctional institutions could be improved at reasonable cost by accessing medical diagnostic and prescriptive mainframe data bases located at major hospitals around the country. Future applications are limited only by human creativity, energy and financial support for research and development.

Pictures 2-3 and 2-4 above show the microcomputers used in the patrol cars of the Hillsborough County Sheriff's Office, Tampa, Florida. Picture 2-4 shows the type of information which an officer receives. Pictures provided by the Hillsborough County Sheriff's Office, Tampa, Florida.

Agency Profile 2-1

THE COMPUTERIZED POLICE AGENCY

The Sheriff's Office, Hillsborough County, Tampa, Florida, has made extensive use of computers for more than eleven years. It is one of the first law enforcement agencies with a fully computerized dispatch system which includes computer terminals in patrol cars. The mobile terminals are linked to an integrated state and national crime information system, in addition to fully computerized dispatch operations. (See pictures 2-3, 2-4.)

The dispatch system is networked with approximately 384 mobile digital terminals in patrol cars. The system allows patrol officers to interact with communications dispatchers and other mobile units and office terminals in addition to being able to access state and national data banks. The original system once supported by two PDP- 1145 computers was replaced with a Unisys (formerly Sperry Corp) System 1100/72 with dual CPUs for redundancy and 6.4 gigabytes of disk storage capacity. In addition, four tape drives serve to transfer and store data. One of the CPUs is dedicated for the exclusive use of the dispatch system. The second CPU is available for backup and for future development of records and management information systems. The present dispatch system utilizes personal computers as terminals, and the entire system is designed for communications between personal computers, the mainframe and mobile digital terminals.

A network of more than eighteen personal computers links remote district offices, detective division squads, crime analysis and other special units and commands. Each of the personal computers can operate independently to do word processing and specialized office tasks or to access the larger shared data banks of the mainframe computer. (See picture 2-5.) Other personal computers are distributed throughout the Sheriff's Office for specialized uses, but are not currently linked to the mainframe computer. All of the personal computers use color monitors, including those in the dispatch center. Within this center, the computer positions each have the capability of making personalized adjustments to the screen background color, angle of display and keyboards, as well as many other personalized ergonomic considerations. These color personal computers facilitate the implementation of an enhanced 911 telephone system that directly interfaces with dispatch positions. Color is important because they aid in computerized mapping of areas served by the Sheriff's Office. Nearly all activities are electronically recorded. Vehicle fueling is automatically recorded, in addition to dispatches, vehicle maintenance schedules, parts inventory, radio maintenance and gasoline consumption, and other operating facets of the department. Calls for service, response time, crime reports and patterns are all automated and subject to electronic review and analysis. Within the agency computers maintain warrant files, known offender files, modus-operandi files, field interrogations files, stolen property files, pawn shop files and vehicle accident files, among others. When a communications dispatcher receives a telephone call reporting a crime or need for police assistance, the location and basic information is entered into a personal computer and then routed to a dispatch console. During this routing, the computer searches a gobase file, verifies the address, lists intersecting streets near the complaint's location, and identifies any known hazards reported at that location. The computer then searches for available zone cars, conducts an analysis of priority and availability, then displays a list of available cars within or near the zone. This whole process takes less than two seconds. (See pictures 2-6 and 2-7.) The human dispatcher can then forward the dispatch information onto a receiving patrol car, or override the recommendations and designate another unit. The system also includes a special consideration file for officers with specialties or bilingual abilities. The system is programmed using a fourth generation language which allows flexibility without the necessity of hiring professional programmers. As a total system it is a prototype, not without its own bugs and problems. However, this agency is committed to improving and expanding its computer capabilities because it is the only way to keep pace with the demands placed on it.

For more information on this agency write to Major Stephen W. Appel, Hillsborough County Sheriff's Office, PO Box 3371, Tampa, Florida, 33601.

Picture 2-5 above shows the central computer facilities of the Hillsborough County Sheriff's Office. Notice that mainframe and microcomputers are networked so that the capabilities of each can be utilized. Microcomputers can be used independently for word processing, filing or other administrative functions. When there is a need to interface with the mainframe, the microcomputer becomes a terminal.

Notice also that the central computer facility is a specially designed room. Its floors, ceilings and walls are insulated to reduce static electricity and interference from other parts of the building. Its electrical system is independent from the rest of the building. Not shown in the picture is a backup electrical system. If power is lost, batteries temporarily maintain operations while an emergency generator is activated. When power returns the emergency system shuts off. Picture provided by the Hillsborough County Sheriff's Office, Tampa, Florida.

Pictures 2-6 and 2-7 above show the process of taking a complaint by phone and then relaying it to dispatch. Notice that these microcomputers are used both independently and as mainframe terminals. Picture provided by the Hillsborough County Sheriff's Office, Tampa, Florida.

SMALL BUSINESS MANAGEMENT APPLICATIONS

Every criminal justice organization is a business in the sense that it has revenues, resources and personnel. In this context, departments and smaller agencies can make extensive use of business applications software developed for microcomputers. Business software which may be of particular use in criminal justice management includes: 1) electronic spreadsheets, 2) electronic accounting, inventory and resource control, 3) personnel management, 4) statistical packages and 5)data base management systems. Examples of these are discussed below.

BUDGET MANAGEMENT:
Electronic Spreadsheets,
Accounting and Inventory Control

Budgets are a reality of any organization, as are the maze of reports which explain and justify them. Small agencies and individual departments or divisions within larger organizations can tap into a large variety of microcomputer software which has been developed for business applications. Adequate planning in this regard can allow the microcomputer user to access and interface with data bases of other departments or higher organizational divisions, which can help with the development of agency-wide budget control and accounting. Some examples of the types of programs which are available are discussed below. It must be stressed that any time an agency initiates a new software system, three to ten weeks will be needed to thoroughly train and orient personnel. So much time is required in the initial stages because even the best software packages require the user to apply the program to the particular needs of the agency. [For more information see Antonellis,1983: 78-82; Bonner,1983: 73-78; Hersch and Cushing,1983: 14-18,20,23.]

Electronic Spreadsheets

One common type of small business applications software which is available to the microcomputer user is the *electronic spreadsheet*. This is a program which presents the user with an electronic ledger sheet and then provides a range of commands which enable the user to input headings, numbers, and to perform mathematical and statistical analyses of data. Spreadsheets also allow the generation of integrated reports from the same basic ledger sheet. For example, from one electronic sheet or template of budget information (e.g. accounts payable for a given week), several other reports may be prepared at the same time (e.g. total expenditures to date for the year, month or by line item). These programs also allow for "forecasting," or using present budgetary information to project the future status of a budget or related item.

Among the more popular spreadsheet programs are: Lotus 1-2-3, Symphony, UP-Planner, Multiplan and SuperCalc4. Each of these provides slightly different user features, costs between $200-$400 and is available for most major brands of microcomputers. Each provides program functions that allow a user to personalize accounting functions and report preparation. Such programs are suitable for personal use, small business applications, small department budgeting, special project or program budgeting, but are not adequate for general accounting and control of a large department or agency.

ACCOUNTING, INVENTORY
AND RESOURCE CONTROL PROGRAMS

While electronic spreadsheets meet some management-information needs, they do not meet all of them. Thus, a wide range of professional business applications software packages have been developed. Among the more common programs are Symphony, SMART, Framework, Peachtree, Lotus, IBM, Wang, Applied Business and Ashton-Tate brands of accounting, inventory control and project management software. These packages are designed for extensive level use, require a considerable sophistication to operate and are more expensive. Individually purchased, such software may cost $400-$500. However, once installed and in operation, the quality and complexity of functions which can be performed are far superior to those of electronic spreadsheets.

Personnel Management

Personnel or human resource management involves another type of data base which contains personal information on employees, their productivity and career development. Performance evaluation is a major problem for many criminal justice agencies. Evaluations are conducted for many purposes, including promotions, retention, re-assignment. Personnel evaluations are often criticized on the basis of their objectivity and the innate difficulty involved in comparing human beings because of individual differences. One example of the kind of assistance which a microcomputer can give an agency in the area of personnel management software is Computer Assisted Personnel Evaluation (CAPE) which is a performance evaluation system. *CAPE* was developed for Utah's Department of Public Safety and was originally a mainframe computer program (Lehtinen, 1984: 20). Recently, however, it was redesigned to run on the IBM making it adaptable to other microcomputers and, with modifications, usable in other criminal justice organizations. CAPE has two main components: 1) a performance evaluation manual and 2) the program itself. Performance evaluation items include job performance, physical fitness, personal appearance, knowledge of policies and procedures. These are assigned weights or degree of importance by a particular agency. These scales can also be modified for different jobs or grades, such as patrolman, technician, sergeant, lieutenant, then applied to individual employees in a department or agency. Once completed, each evaluation is loaded onto the CAPE program. The result is a fair and defensible comparative performance profile of any employee, in relationship to other personnel by rank and job description. [See Cannon, Debenham, and Smith, 1983; Morgan and Lehtinen, 1983.]

Programs are also available for microcomputers which allow small police departments to optimize scheduling of manpower [see Davis, 1981: 84-87] and which could be modified to fit the needs of most small criminal justice agencies. Software is available for payrolls, records, income tax preparation and addresses. The cost of such software ranges from a low of $400-$600 per software program to $1200, depending on the type of software needed.

Statistical Analysis

Statistical analysis of data is an essential element of organizational planning and budget control. The use of the microcomputer for this purpose is limited only by two factors: (1) the memory limitations of the hardware used and (2) the cost limitations imposed on such decisions. Memory problems can be overcome through proper planning of equipment and through networking with mainframe computers to store data sets. Cost limitations of pre-written statistical software programs become less significant when compared to the investment of time required to enter the program through the keyboard into the computer. Electronic spreadsheets, as previously described, also provide the user with a range of basic statistical tools for use in budget analysis and forecasting. These tools can be modified to serve a broad range of statistical functions. However, if an agency wants highly sophisticated research capability, software is available for microcomputers which comes close to the technology of mainframe computer systems.

At this point, a definitive limitation of microcomputers must be mentioned. Microcomputers will never replace mainframe computers for the storage of data files that contain thousands of cases and variables. Neither is the microcomputer's memory capable of applying high powered statistical tests, such as multiple regression, to thousands of cases; mainframe core memory and processing are required. However, some high quality statistical packages are currently available for microcomputer applications which are well suited to data sets of up to several thousand cases. Such software is expensive; some programs cost over $2000.

Carpenter, Deloria and Morganstein (*BYTE*, April, 1984:234-264) published an in-depth analysis of twenty-four statistical packages for microcomputers which are currently on the market. They concluded that "there was no clear favorite" among the products now available. However, other evaluations indicate that individual preferences, different types of hardware and software systems, and specific applications make some packages more useful than others in certain situations, although no particular package was superior in all situations. Similar conclusions were reached by later program evaluators. (See Fridlund, "Statistics Software," *Infoworld*, Sept. 19, 1988, pp. 55-76.) Several statistical packages available for microcomputers are discussed below.

MICRO-CRUNCH is an inexpensive SPSSX compatible micro based statistical package. The program allows for export to LOTUS 1-2-3 and SPSS. The program can be used to put together data sets using a format that does not allow the keypunching of numbers that are not within the set range of numbers which are expected. The program also allows for the labeling of variables and values for easy referencing.

The statistical functions in the package allow the user to analyze data using most of the current statistical methods. This program runs considerably faster than either SAS/PC or SPSS/PC because the program and the data are loaded into RAM all at the opening of the program. This does create some limitations to the program in the number of variables, values and cases which can be analyzed in a single data set.

The program is a good instructional aid for students in entry level research methods and statistical classes. The cost per student at a site-licensed institution is low enough that each student can afford an individual copy.

The program is IBM PC, XT, AT or compatible with two disk drives. The program and the data are loaded into RAM at the start up of the program, therefore it will use 640K if that is the size of the data plus the program. For example, if you have 6,000 observations, you will be limited to 20 variables; if you have 1,000 observations, the limit is 125 variables.

Micro-Crunch sells for between $89 and $300 and is available from Softex Micro Systems, 7915 Glenbrae, Houston, Texas 77061.

PC SAS is published by SAS Institute, Inc., and is a microcomputer version of mainframe program which is in wide use throughout the country. It is a very sophisticated statistical program which lends itself to use by serious statisticians and researchers who want control over statistical formula used in calculation. It minimally requires an IBM XT or AT clone, with 512K and 20 Mb hard disk. It operates less efficiently, however, in a microcomputer environment than the SPSS/PC+, discussed below. It is also expensive, with licensing fees in excess of $1000. The written documentation which accompanies the program assumes a high level of user knowledge concerning statistics and mainframe SAS. This program requires a very sophisticated user.

SPSS/PC+, v 3.0, published by SPSS/PC, Inc., offers exciting statistical power for the microcomputer. It contains about 95% of the commands and functions of its mainframe and minicomputer versions, SPSS/X. It has a good editor, excellent "pull down" menus, clearly written manual and interfaces with a number of data base, word processing, spread sheet and graphics programs. The basic statistics package costs about $700. It requires an XT or AT clone, 640K RAM, and at least a 20 Mb hard disk drive. The authors have tested the program with satisfactory results using data sets of up to 75,000 cases on an AT clone with an 80286 processor. The program is designed to fully utilize the 80386 and OS/2 technology. Statistical packages are also available for the Apple and other major brands of computers. The numbers of microcomputer-minicomputer statistical programs are likely to increase as the cost of mainframe statistical packages increases. Economic factors are forcing agencies and departments to find less costly way of processing needed statistical data. For example, the annual leasing costs for the SPSS/X mainframe package, used in many criminal justice agencies and academic institutions, is around $8500. This represents a major recurring expense. Such costs, along with others, are passed on to "time-share" customers, those agencies or individuals who access mainframe computers and are charged on a pro-rated basis for the amount of computer time used. Some runs on a mainframe may cost as much as $1000 in computer time. Many agency and university research departments charge organizational subdivisions for the use of these services. Consequently, the demand for utilizing the less expensive micro-minicomputer systems in statistical analysis is increasing.

In response to these economic pressures, at least three different trends in agency handling of statistical data can be projected. First, where possible, an increased use of microcomputers and self-contained statistical packages, such as SPSS/PC+, PC SAS Statistical Package, can be expected. If data can be entered and analyzed with a microcomputer as opposed to a mainframe, tremendous savings in time and expense will be realized.

Second, spinning off this first trend is likely to be an increase in competition among software manufacturers. If past patterns are any indication, then this competition may result in more sophisticated statistical packages, lower costs and wider product availability for a broader range of computer brands.

Third, the increased use of interactive microcomputer-mainframe networking can be anticipated. Networks between microcomputer and mainframe reduce time and processing costs. For example, interfacing and interactive micro-mainframe software allow the user to enter all the instructions or data on the micro. Then, when the micro interacts with the mainframe, both computers exchange information at rates hundreds of times faster than a human being could enter instructions or data directly to a mainframe terminal.

Agency Profile 2-2

THE VIRGINIA DEPARTMENT
OF CRIMINAL JUSTICE SERVICES

The Virginia Department of Criminal Justice Services is divided into several sections; each section has specific goals and objectives. Below is a brief description of the use of computers to accomplish the goals of each section.

SPECIAL SERVICES SECTION. This section uses a variety of computer equipment. One of the section's most important functions is the monitoring of legislation as it affects criminal justice. Each year when the State General Assembly meets, a terminal and modem are used to link with the state's mainframe computer. This link provides a printed copy of the lawmaker's activities which is updated continuously. A Diablo 630 terminal and acoustic data coupler/modem are used for this purpose.

STATE AND LOCAL SERVICES SECTION. This section uses information compiled on the state's IBM mainframe. The information needed for research analyses is downloaded onto a 1600 BPI tape for use with the 9-track tape unit. The complete data file, each 880-byte record containing more than 200 elements, is transferred onto a 130 megabyte fixed disk located in a COMPAQ Deskpro 386. The file is divided into subsets for transfer to microcomputers through 10-megabyte Irwin tape units. The data is analyzed using the SPSS/PC+ statistical software package. Various procedures are implemented to provide information to state and local government officials on a wide variety of criminal justice issues. The analyses range from producing basic descriptive statistics to carrying out complex multivariate statistical techniques. The results are interpreted in charts, graphs and written reports which aid executive, legislative and judicial branch officials in various policy-making decisions. All statistical analyses are performed on microcomputers (286 and 386 machines) because it is less expensive than mainframe time. Data sets as large as 4 Gb have been handled in this manner. The information is also graphically represented through the use of packages such as MS-Chart and AtlasAMP. The information is plotted on an HP-7550-A, a plotter that includes automated sheet feeding and high speed graphics production. The system is frequently used to produce state maps, highlighting various data by city and county. This section is also involved in desktop publishing. An Apple Macintosh II system with a laserjet printer and an optical scanner produce reports and newsletters without the added expense of typesetting and the time consuming technique of "cut and paste" for document layouts.

TRAINING SECTION. This section is responsible for maintaining training and certification records for all Virginia law enforcement officials and police academy instructors. Over 120,000 records are maintained on an IBM AT microcomputer with a 30megabyte fixed disk using the Dbase III application program. The system provides various reports, letters and certificates. The computer is used to send local law enforcement agencies reminder letters indicating the need for recertification and training. The system accommodates inquiries from any local police department desiring a complete record of an applicant in order to verify certification for use of firearms and other special training. Another valuable function offered by this system is a complete training calendar of courses offered by various police academies; this calendar is continuously updated by training personnel.

FINANCE SECTION. This section currently uses five microcomputers to perform a variety of functions, including: automated interface into the state's mainframe, electronic spreadsheet analysis, graphics and word processing. Through a Sperry-Link system, Finance is able to access either a Sperry-Univac mainframe or an IBM 4381 for financial systems processing. Three of the microcomputers are linked to the system through a multiple-access interface unit or "MAIU" device, a high speed modem and dedicated telephone line.

The application includes on-line access to the personnel management information (PMIS), electronic bulletin boards and the electronic mail system. The Finance Section uses Lotus 1-2-3 electronic spreadsheets to perform budget analysis and to monitor daily operations. The program also allows Finance to produce graphics illustrating any spreadsheet. The Finance Section uses a variety of hardware including IBM ATs, IBM PCs, Compaq Portables, a Hewlett-Packard 7475 Plotter and C.Itoh 4000 printers.

For more information on this agency write to Richard P. Kern, Ph.D., SAC Director, Department of Criminal Justice Services, 805 East Broad Street, Richmond, Virginia, 23219.

Data Base Management Systems

With the advent of more powerful microcomputers a number of updated data base management programs are available for the microcomputer which offer great potential for smaller to medium size criminal justice agencies. Products such as Dbase IV, Rbase, Foxbase, Clipper, Cornerstone, Knowledgeman and VP Expert allow the user to develop relational data base systems tailored to the need of individual agencies. Through the use of fourth generation languages, the user can program the system by using commands from the program to create financial, inventory or personnel records of all types.

In addition to expanded power, many of these new programs have moved toward integrated software designs, allowing the user to move easily from data base to spreadsheet to word processor to data charting programs. These trends are likely to continue, making data base management and file processing much easier.

Finally, a few examples of artificial intelligence are also becoming evident in data base management systems. Lotus introduced a product called "HAL" which functions with Lotus 1-2-3, giving it a rudimentary artificial intelligence capability. More products of this nature will become available in the near future.

Other data based needs exist within an agency such as storage and retrieval of information files on offenders, or cases under investigation. To address these more general needs, software programs such as INFOSTAR, Verso-File, PMAIL, PEARL, MAG, EDBS, Cardfile, Milestone may provide possible solutions to a variety of "file-cabinet type" information storage problems. [For product description and evaluation see *INFOWORLD: Re-*

port Card, Vol.5, No.48A, December 1, 1983:59-86. Also see, Brin, 1983: 74-80,154.] This type of software is highly flexible, since it can be adapted to a broad range of data storage and retrieval uses.

Integrated Multitasking Software

Throughout this text, reference to single-tasking and multi-tasking software programs are found. An understanding of these terms is essential in understanding the term integrated software. Single-tasking software refers to the ability of the software to perform one function at a time (e.g. word processing, budget management, or inventory control). Multi-tasking software, in contrast, permits several separate but related tasks to be accomplished with one software package (e.g. word processing and budget computations). Multi-tasking program routines store data and disk files common to multiple tasks. As a result, budget information can be more easily integrated with inventory control information and can be displayed within a report prepared by the word processor. *Integrated software* is a term which refers to the commercial packaging of multi-tasking software. That is, within the software package are different programs (e.g. word processing, speller, index and table of contents generator, thesaurus, accounts receivable or spreadsheet) which are *interactive*. In this context interactive means that all the programs interface, use the same operating system and are compatible with the same computer, and that information from files in one program can be transferred to another. For example, suppose that an agency manager must prepare a report which should include budget information, inventory information and personnel report information. The needed information was stored on three separate programs. If the manager was using an integrated software package, then the needed files could be loaded and printed through the word processing program. On the other hand, if the separate programs were not designed to be integrated, then it would not be possible to merge the needed information. Instead, each file would have to be printed separately, making the final report less refined than it could be.

Integrated software packages, such as Peachtree, Lotus 1-2-3, Symphony and Framework, have several advantages over single-function packages from a criminal justice organizational perspective. First, it is easier for employees to learn these materials in the sense that once personnel have mastered one set of operating instructions in order to use the software, they can use all the programs in the series. Second, once data is entered into a system it can be re-used for multiple purposes. Third, such packages allow the user to jump from one task to another. For example, a user may have previously input current budget information and now needs to prepare a written report with tables and graphs to support it. An integrated software program reduces the time required to accomplish this task. Fourth, although the initial purchase of such packages is expensive, when compared to buying the least expensive individual single-function programs (e.g. word processing, electronic spread sheet or graphics package), the difference in cost to an organization may be recovered rapidly through reduced employee labor costs and the quality of the final product produced (e.g. a current budget report with narrative explanation, tables and graphics). Finally, the integrated packages apply the state of the art technology which makes use of the package easier. These developments include *windowing* capabilities which allow the user to see several different miniature electronic screens at one time, use of a mouse, light pens and other input devices make it easier to operate and use the system.

FIELD-REPORT WRITING AND INVESTIGATIONS

Microcomputers, because of their size and flexibility, can be adapted to many different field reporting functions which would not be possible with mainframe computers. The development of lap size microcomputers has encouraged the portability of the micro. These allow agents or investigators to collect information in the field and then transfer this information to larger computers for processing. The following examples are ways in which data may be collected, assimilated and then entered into larger mainframe systems.

The IRS field officers use lap size computers to conduct field audits, then transfer this information to mainframe computers thereby reducing the time associated with entering field data into the main system. Information is collected in a format which allows instant mainframe input, allowing immediate integration with other stored information about a case.

Microcomputers may be directly used as investigative tools in other ways. For example, the *ETHNOGRAPH*, developed by Qualis Research Associates of Glagow, Colorado, was developed for collecting field notes of participatory researchers, coding observations and then quantifying them for statistical analysis. The same type of software could allow police investigators to collect field note information and report on specific subjects from a variety of different sources, then assemble them into a simple data set for investigation and evidence assimilation. Likewise, investigators who input field observations into a microcomputer using a good word processing program could use program functions such as "SEARCH" to identify and mark the locations of names, addresses, phone numbers or other data strings. These data could then be transferred into a single file for investigation and analysis. [See Waldron, et.al., 1983, for other examples.]

Mainframe data base information systems are not always desirable in criminal investigations. For instance, interfacing criminal information systems may give an impression of truth and accuracy which may not yet be justified in a given case. The use of a parallel, yet separate, microcomputer data base system provides the advantage of collecting and verifying a wide range of information before entering it into a mainframe data bank. Microsystems may also be used to track informants whose identities must be kept secret, yet whose activities may need to be monitored by several investigators working on a given case. In Ocala, Florida, microcomputers are used for a variety of field investigation, report writing and personnel management functions which would not otherwise be possible because of cost and access factors with mainframe systems (See McGehee and Whiteacre, 1983: 24-26). In Westminster, Colorado, P.D., St. Petersburg, Florida, P.D. and many other departments across the nation, lap top microcomputers are used to produce field reports and are carried in squad cars with the officers. Officers prepare reports, then "dump" shift reports to a minicomputer system at the end of a shift.

PLANNING MICROCOMPUTER DATA BASE SYSTEMS

Introduction of microcomputer technology into any criminal justice agency must be a carefully planned process. Failure to plan adequately may prove disastrous and waste limited resources. Regardless of the nature of the mission of a criminal justice agency, planning for the introduction of computerized data bases should follow a sequence of steps similar to those described below.

First, computerization of an agency's work functions must be planned. Decisions must be made concerning which areas are to be computerized first and which are to follow according to a defined order. This is especially true when phasing in microcomputers, because everyone is inclined to think that his or her job can be better done with these new tools. Planners must consider networking designs to allow the most efficient use of small computers. Planners need to define total system capacities and consider both the potentials and limitations. If adequate planning is not done, more may be expected from equipment and software than such systems are realistically capable of delivering.

Second, planners should determine the requirements for each computer application. These requirements can be regarded as: a) fixed, b) flexible and

c) optional. *Fixed systems* must perform computerized operations in a specific way each time. Processing accounting and budgetary matters are examples of such requirements, since procedures must be followed exactly if these efforts are to be successful. *Flexible systems* are computerized operations which may be handled in a variety of different ways. For example, the general form of field investigative reports may be flexible in the order of information entered. *Optional systems* are those which are desirable, but not necessary for daily operations. Optional systems features may also concern certain periodic functions such as quarterly reports, which may be generated from daily or monthly budgetary, resource or personnel reports.

Third, future requirements must be considered. There is a temptation when new equipment becomes available to view the purchase as a final act. In reality, equipment and software purchases are first-step propositions at best. If equipment is not bought with the potential for expansion already present, it may soon have to be replaced. Software should be purchased with plans for multiple users and multi-tasking. Microcomputer systems purchased today need to have the potential of 16 and 32-byte processing to make use of the state of the art software.

Software, in turn, must be capable of meeting the demands of future expansion. Features must match the intended planned use, both present and future.

Fourth, the cost-benefit comparisons of different systems should be considered before purchase. Different products and vendors need to be contacted. Too often, what appears to be a good conservative choice in the short run becomes a nightmare. The purchaser may have assumed that the dealer would reveal all information needed about the particular system at the time of purchase; this may or may not occur. Agencies would be wise to consider obtaining professional help in determining needs and in assessing equipment potential and limitations. Microcomputer technology changes so rapidly that no one individual or company can remain current unless it is their specific business to do so.

Fifth, a competent support system needs to be established. User groups, seminars and product evaluations such as those referred to later in this chapter, are all components of a support system. Many brands of equipment such as IBM, Apple, NEC and DEC have their own product magazines which offer insight into problems and future trends in technological advancements. Support systems place users in contact with other users. The problems solved by one user may be the problems currently faced by another.

Sixth, in purchasing equipment, consider the availability of software and be aware of "hidden cost" factors. For example, IBM computer systems are in many respects the standards of the industry. Consequently, IBM systems probably have the greatest volume and range of compatible software of any brand, followed closely by Apple. Unfortunately, IBM is one of the most expensive computer systems. Makers of IBM clones actually produce equipment which is superior to IBM, but often do not have service centers readily available to support their equipment. Consequently, there is a continuous trade-off which must be considered between the initial cost of equipment, its quality and longevity of use, and the availability of service centers. For agencies which depend daily on equipment the availability of service is critical.

The key point made here is simply that any individual or agency considering the purchase of a microcomputer system should carefully research the product, the reputation of the manufacturer, the support given by dealers, and attempt to discover all hidden costs before purchase. Careful comparisons prior to purchase can save a great deal of grief and expense. As an agency begins to plan the purchase of equipment or the establishment of a data base, the following five steps are suggested:

1. Identify personnel in the agency who have microcomputers and who are familiar with their use as well as individuals familiar with mainframe data processing.

2. Identify the persons in charge of those portions of the organization which are dependent on information (e.g. records, communications, accounting, maintenance, security).

3. From these two lists of people form Quality Control (Q-C) circles in each major department or sub-division. Q-C membership should represent all levels and information needs of the organization.

4. Divide these Q-C's into areas of anticipated computer use (e.g. word processing, fiscal accounting, records, investigation). Establish time-lines for reports. These groups will be asked to read the popular magazines, journals and trade publications for descriptions and reviews of microcomputer hardware and software for that specific area. Members will visit local dealers and inquire about specific brands of hardware and software. This information will be compiled into a report.

5. Use the information prepared by the Q-C groups to assess different brands of equipment and software. While management will make the final decisions on equipment and software purchase, the information obtained will be the basis for that decision.

Although this process may appear to be time consuming and initially cumbersome, it will pay long-term dividends, provide up-to-date information on new products and prepare agency managers to ask probing questions of potential competing vendors. Most important, it will involve the people who will use the equipment in the decision-making process.

The purchase of micro or minicomputers constitutes a major investment for any agency, both in cost and human effort. Unlike the purchase of a typewriter, automobile or another piece of equipment, a microcomputer or minicomputer system is not yet a common household item. Consequently, few organizational managers possess information necessary to make competent, informed decisions on state of the art microcomputer equipment. Involving others in the decision process is essential.

Computer salespersons, like the infamous used car salespersons, tend to play on both manager ego and ignorance. A basic understanding of facts can be quickly obscured through the application of computerese and technical jargon. Assurances concerning equipment capability and product "after sale services" made by dealers and vendors may exceed their own expertise and authority. Ideally, limitations should be discovered before, not after the purchase. Because of the complexities of computer purchase and the agency-wide potential impact, managers are strongly advised not to make solo decisions, although they may have the authority, and in some cases, the knowledge, to do so. The five step process described above is the best insurance against buying a "computerized pig-in-the-poke."

INFORMATION SYSTEMS NETWORKING

The concept of informational networking is more comprehensively discussed in Chapter 3. However, its relationship to data base management is introduced here. The microcomputer literally opens up a world of data systems to the user. Various information retrieval services allow one to use phone modems, and to access thousands of data base information systems. For example, DIALOG (an information services company in Palo Alto, California) is a subscription service which is available at many libraries and through which computerized literature searches can be conducted. The same searches, however, can be conducted and printed out by anyone having the necessary equipment and software (costing between $500-$2200).

Among the 175 different data bases which can be accessed through DIALOG; several have direct applications to criminal justice management. These include medical and bio-science literature, energy and environment literature, science and technology literature, materials science literature, directories for all phone systems in the United States, National Criminal Justice Reference Service, GPO Publications Files, Social Sciences and Humanities literature, ERIC and education research, and foundations and grants directories. DIALOG, moreover, is just one of several similar types of information networking systems.

WESTLAW and LEXIS are two other important data bases for criminal justice. These are computer assisted legal searches of federal and state laws, case precedents and legal opinions. They operate in a similar manner to DIALOG in that an individual or agency can enter into a contract to access these legal data bases. Many professional microcomputer systems can be used and configured to interface with these services via a phone modem.

In addition, newer technology is allowing microcomputers to directly access telecommunication satellites. With the use of microwave disk antennas, weather information seen on the evening news as "radar scans" can be received through the monitor and graphed on a printer. This technology is of use for marine patrols which are concerned with drug smuggling or rescue type operations in which weather may play an important factor. Such hardware is portable and could be made mobile, allowing it to be taken to the scene of an operation or emergency.

Other telecommunications monitoring may allow for "phone taps" without requiring physical "bugging" of phones. Still other types of communications links with satellites can allow access to business and banking transactions, electronic publishing, electronic mail and mailgrams and telex communications.

SUMMARY AND CONCLUSIONS

American criminal justice is dependent on the rapid and accurate collection, analysis and distribution of information. It is part of what Naisbitt terms an "information society and economy." Information and those who control it are the most powerful forces in our society. Newer technology increases this power and its potential abuse. It is the mission of criminal justice to keep this power in check and to apply technology to its justice efforts. This chapter has introduced some of the potential data base applications of microcomputers in criminal justice. Networking with mainframe computers, business applications and field investigation reporting are only a few potential areas of application. The true potential range of microcomputer and minicomputer technological applications are limited only by the creativeness of the human mind. The examples provided in this chapter are intended only to stimulate thought and experimentation. It is the reader's task to expand this knowledge beyond its present limits.

REVIEW QUESTIONS AND ACTIVITIES

1. Describe the functions of planning, budgeting, fiscal and resource management. Explain how microcomputers can be applied in each. Give specific examples relating to police, courts and corrections.

2. What is data base management? What are management information systems? What is the role of each in planning, budgeting and resource management?

3. Define and differentiate between these terms: normative planning, strategic planning and operational planning. Include examples in your definition.

4. What is a mainframe data base? Give five examples of mainframe data bases in criminal justice. Where would you find additional information on this topic?

5. Discuss these concepts in relation to criminal justice management and give examples of each:

    a) networking with mainframe computer data bases;
    b) business applications;
    c) field reporting and investigation; and
    d) interactive multi-tasking software.

6. Imagine that you are an agency head and that you want to develop a microcomputer data base technology in your agency. Describe the steps you would take in planning and implementing an agency-wide microcomputer system. Where would you find product information? Use specific examples to explain your procedure.

7. What is information systems networking? Describe how it could be used in a police department, in a correctional institution, in an individual's home.

8. Visit three criminal justice agencies (e.g. police, court, corrections, pros-ecutor's office) which utilize a mainframe and/or microcomputer data base system. Prepare a written report on the types of computer systems used, the types of hardware and software used, and describe in detail all the uses to which computers are applied (e.g. investigations, records, statistical analysis). Ask the agency to demonstrate it for you (e.g., NCIC). Ask the agency what uses it plans for computers in the future.

Chapter 3

COMPUTER ASSISTED ORGANIZATIONAL COMMUNICATION:
Information Networking,
Computer Assisted Writing,
Desk Top Publishing,
Telecommunications Applications

CHAPTER PREVIEW

Organizational Management Communication is a general term used to refer to a diverse range of vital and complex functions, including the collection, assimilation, generation, transmission and dissemination of information. Accurate information is essential for sound administrative and management decision making and for the direction and control of subordinates. Accurate information is necessary for the police officer on the street to investigate a crime, for the judge to hand down a fair sentence, for the probation officer to supervise offenders in the community, for an institution to identify the security risk of prisoners and for a counselor to determine the psychological and emotional needs of a child in trouble. Every criminal justice agency is information dependent and no agency can function without it.

In its broadest sense, management communication includes the usual methods of communicating information, normally classified as written, verbal and non-verbal. It also refers to a wide range of electronic media, including radio, telephone, teletype and computerized data bases.

Criminal justice organizations are experiencing an information revolution in which information is not only vital to organizational survival but is also a source of economic and political power. As the extent of information dependency increases, radical changes are being forced upon traditional bureaucratic management structures. This chapter identifies key problems in bureaucratic management communications in criminal justice agencies and institutions, then focuses on Computer Assisted Writing (CAW) applications in management communications. Finally, this chapter examines selected theoretical and applied aspects of information networking and its potential ramifications in criminal justice management.

STUDY QUESTIONS

The following study questions may be used as a guide to reading Chapter 2. Key terms and concepts related to these questions are printed in italics throughout the chapter.

1. What do the following terms mean as related to criminal justice agencies: *organizational management communications, filtered communications, scalared communications* and *bureaucratic communications*?

2. What are computer assisted writing (CAW) and desk top publishing? How are they related to organizational communication? What are the principles of professional CAW writing?

3. What is information networking?

4. What is readability? How does readability influence organizational communication?

5. What is telecommunication? What is its potential in criminal justice management?

COMMUNICATIONS IN THE
CRIMINAL JUSTICE BUREAUCRACY

The typical American criminal justice organization is a modified Weberian-Fayolian bureaucracy (Archambeault and Weirman, 1983; Archambeault and Fenwick, 1980; Archambeault and Archambeault, 1982: 68-80; Archambeault, 1983). "Weberian-Fayolian bureaucracy" is a more specific name given to the organizational model which other authors have described as "para-military" or "bureaucratic." It is a management model that is typical of American-style organizations in general. This model is characterized as impersonal, authoritarian and creating hierarchical work environments where management demonstrates only segmental concern about worker welfare. Management control is implemented through formalized written policy and procedure. These characteristics often combine to create a wasteful, inefficient and ineffective organizational structure that is incapable of rapidly and consistently adapting to change (See Ouchi, 1982; Pascale and Athos, 1982; Naisbitt, 1982).

In criminal justice organizations, the para-military aspects of bureaucracy are more obvious among police agencies and custody institutions. These are overtly seen in the use of military-like uniforms, rank (e.g., corporal, sergeant, lieutenant) and customs (e.g., saluting, standing in ranks for inspection). They are less obvious in other types of criminal justice agencies (e.g., juvenile, probation, courts). Nevertheless, Weberian-Fayolian principles of management are present in the use of authority, in the formalized and explicit mechanisms of employee discipline and control and in the patterns of organizational communications.

Bureaucratic organizational communications are formalized through *written communications*, which include policies, rules and regulations, forms, memoranda. Written communication, as used in this chapter, describes the generation and transmission of information through the printed word as hard copy (paper) or electronic (video) display. As used within the scope of this chapter, the term "written" may include an electronic display screen, a report typed on paper and may be generated by direct human input through a word processing program, or a printed report which is generated by computer with only indirect human intervention. Regardless of its origin, the intent of the written communication is to transmit information requiring action to a human. Unfortunately, the effectiveness of any form of written communication, whether human or computer generated, is limited by similar organizational management factors which influence all forms of communication (Also see, Archambeault and Archambeault, 1982; 1983).

Criminal justice bureaucracies are noted for their great volumes of written communication. In recent years, this volume has increased dramatically because of court imposed standards, EEOC Guidelines, and the ever-increasing caseloads processed by criminal justice agencies and institutions. In addition to volume, three other characteristics of Weberian-Fayolian bureaucratic communications negatively affect the capability of organizations to manage themselves and to react promptly and effectively to changing conditions. These are 1) scalared communications; 2) filtered communications (Tansik and Elliott, 1981; Swanson and Territo, 1983); and 3) problems of readability and reading comprehension.

Scalared and Filtered Communications

Scalared communication is the Weberian principle of organization which states that all management policies must be in writing; that written policy must be interpreted by someone in a higher position within an organization; and that all instructions and orders must be initiated at upper organizational levels and implemented at lower levels. This results in a "funnel effect." Orders from superiors become the responsibilities of those lower ranking persons who "stand under the funnel" by virtue of their position in the organization. Bureaucrats carefully guard this principle as a source of power useful for organizational fiefdom building and maintenance.

Scalared communication often inhibits the accurate flow of information within an organization. Official written policies of many agencies require that workers in one division or department who wish to share information with workers in another department or division must obtain permission from a supervisor to do so. For example, before a detective working in vice can share information with another detective working in burglary, permission must be obtained from a supervisor to transmit the information. The information must then flow "up" through channels, "over" to the other division and then "down" to the intended officer. In reality, even where such archaic policies exist, officers usually subvert the system and share information "unofficially." However, if something negative happens as a consequence, such as an "information leak," the officer who passed the unauthorized information may face disciplinary action. Furthermore, subversion of "official" channels of communication tends to strengthen the credibility of the "organizational grapevine" through which incorrect, as well as correct, information travels.

Filtered Communication is a term which describes the fate of information flowing "up" through an organization's bureaucratic channels. All organizations require information from the field be sent up the chain of command so that persons in higher positions can monitor policies and control the actions of subordinates. When a correctional employee submits a report on the safety conditions of a prison, the report is often directed through several levels of the organization before it ever reaches the warden's desk. At each level of the organization, official policy may allow management personnel to either attach comments or rewrite the report itself. In a large organization such as a prison, the initial report may be altered several times before it reaches the warden's eyes, particularly if the report negatively reflects on superiors or managers within the chain. Filtered communication, whether written or verbal, reduces upper management control, because it biases or distorts information needed by upper management to make sound decisions. It delays critical information from reaching persons in authority who must act on it.

Contemporary organizations are in a dilemma. On one hand, they cannot ignore recent developments in computer technology. On the other, the availability of information through computer technology threatens to erode established canons of bureaucratic management. What often results is an unstable and inconsistent set of procedures. For example, in some settings the covert informal sharing of information between employees from different divisions or departments is expediently "overlooked," although the need for information sharing may be recognized. If negative consequences result, then violation of procedures or "information leak" is alleged, and the organization seeks an individual to scapegoat, prosecute or discipline. Through this double standard, the typical bureaucracy seeks to survive in a world of rapid change, while at the same time attempting to avoid acknowledging the ineffectiveness of scalared and filtered communication in meeting the needs of the organization in an information dependent world. This is especially true for criminal justice organizations since few realistic alternative models of organizational management have been developed.

Readability and Reading Comprehension Problems

The dependency of bureaucratic management on written communications makes it essential that employees, who must act on the information contained in the communications, must be able to understand the message communicated through the written word. Unfortunately, this is not always the case. Communication through written policies, procedures, memoranda and other forms of written communication is complicated by problems of *readability* and *reading comprehension*.

Readability refers to the level at which written communication has been prepared. This level is generally expressed in grade level equivalents or some other measure of difficulty. [See Archambeault and Archambeault, 1982, Chapter 11; Archambeault and Archambeault, 1983.] Written materials intended for employee use in the performance of their duties must be prepared at grade levels appropriate to employee education and reading levels. Otherwise, employees will neither read nor follow the written instructions. For example, if an agency's policies and procedures are written on a 13th grade level (college freshman), but intended for an employee audience which reads on an average sixth (middle school) to tenth grade (high school sophomore) reading level, management will lose its ability to communicate effectively with employees through written communications. The employees will not be able to read or understand what has been written.

Even if the readability level is appropriate for the audience, employees may still not be able to understand the communications sufficiently to act on them. This is primarily a problem of reading comprehension. Technical and specialized terms, bureaucratic styles of writing, unfamiliar concepts and other aspects may block comprehension and application, even if individual words are understood. In agencies, "mastery level" comprehension, the ability to correctly carry out the actions stated in the written communication, is required. [See Archambeault and Archambeault, 1983.]

Problems related to readability and reading comprehension among employees have become targets of recent court actions concerning the rights of criminal justice employees. In the broader context of concern about the job relatedness of entry level employment and promotional testing and evaluation measures, courts have focused on issues of readability and reading comprehension. Tests of these measures have been accepted by the courts as screening techniques for use with potential employees, provided the tests meet the criteria of job relatedness as established by readability levels, and content and predictive validity. [See Elliott, 1981; Swanson and Territo, 1983; Baehr, 1979; Chaiken and Cohen, 1973; Rothenberg, 1977; Schacter, 1979; Territo, Swanson and Chamelin, 1977.]

Microcomputer technology, particularly *Computer Assisted Writing (CAW)*, offers possible solutions for addressing problems associated with criminal justice organizational communication. *Computer Assisted Writing* and specific applications to criminal justice agencies and organizations are discussed below.

COMPUTER ASSISTED WRITING (CAW)

Computer Assisted Writing (CAW) may be defined as the application of computer technology to the preparation, editing, printing, distribution and electronic storage of written material. In criminal justice organizations, written material may include policies and procedures, correspondence, budget reports, statistical summaries, client records, memos, case investigation materials, training manuals and other agency-specific forms. CAW addresses numerous problems associated with organizational management communication.

Individuals working with criminal justice agencies are expected to communicate professionally through written documents and correspondence with the public, Congress, the legislature, the funding body, other agencies, community leaders, educators and other professionals. The competency of an agency's management, as well as individual members of the agency, is often judged by the quality of the written documents. Grammatically incorrect writing, gross misspellings, or incomplete thoughts, reflect negatively on the agency itself (Archambeault and Archambeault, 1982). Quality writing is also hampered by the great volume of reports, letters, memoranda and forms which must be completed on a daily basis. Further adding to this problem is the redundancy of many items which must be sent to a variety of individuals.

Advances in computer technology offer potential solutions for dealing with the information demands placed upon the contemporary criminal justice agency. Some of these demands relating to data based management were discussed in Chapter 2; those relating to word processing and desk top publishing are discussed below.

CAW: Word Processing

The most common form of CAW is *word processing*. By definition, word processing is the application of computer technology to the preparation and printing of text material, through a printer or typesetting device. Printers, discussed later, are typewriter-like devices which print hard copy or paper output, and are most commonly found in offices. Typesetters, often called phototypesetters, are commercial printing devices used to set type-face, and are normally used with printing presses to produce newspapers, magazines, books and other commercial publications. Word processing is the computer's answer to the best typewriter available, although the comparison between word processing and typing is similar to comparing the ball point pen to the caveman's chisel. Word processing simplifies routine tasks because the writer is permitted to edit the text on the monitor before preparing a printed copy. As a result, the writer can correct misspellings, add words, delete lines or rearrange paragraphs until the final product is satisfactory. Then, when editing is complete, the revised document is stored in the computer or on disk for future use and a paper copy is made. Word processing is one of the most versatile and adaptable computer applications, particularly for the professional who must write to fulfill job-related responsibilities. For example, word processing can be used to produce manuals of standard operating procedures, training manuals, correspondence and memoranda. When these documents require revisions, only the new sections need to be typed into the computer and the old sections deleted before a printed copy is made, thus eliminating the need to re-type major sections or the entire document. Word processing networks are able to monitor and log the individual performance of operators, thus adding to efficiency. The advantages of word processing over conventional typing are many. They are summarized below.

First, the word processor permits fast typing. Word processing programs employ a technique called "word wrap," which automatically begins a new line of print when the previous line is full, thus eliminating the need for a carriage return. Another technique used by word processing programs is the type-ahead buffer; this permits a typist to enter text as fast as the keys can be pressed. If the text cannot appear on the monitor as fast as they are entered, the computer stores the letters until the monitor can "catch up" with the typist. These features result in marked improvement in typing speed, even for average (or below average) typists. Once a system is mastered, production of final typed copy may be increased by a factor of three to four times the rate achieved through conventional typing.

Second, word processing allows flexible and immediate editing before hard copy printing. Screen format allows the typist to preview text saved in the processor's memory or disk. Any corrections, additions or deletions can be made on the screen before printing. Changes can be made by anyone with a compatible input terminal or micro system, reducing the problem of "waiting on the typist." As a result, an administrator can make last minute changes to a report or letter from his or her own office, then direct the system or an operator to print a hard copy.

Third, individually produced documents can be integrated by the computer, rearranged in any order requested and reprinted in the new format. This is especially useful and important for budgets and reports which must integrate data from a spreadsheet or a narrative to be organized into chapters or in integrating parts of a large document.

Fourth, word processors can automatically center, make boldface headings, italicize words and other specific printing enhancements in the text before a printout is requested.   These capabilities vary according to specific word processing programs, hardware and software configurations.

Fifth, and perhaps most important, are the auxiliary programs which can be used with basic word processing programs to edit and refine the text (e.g., reports, letters, news releases) before printing. These programs allow computer analysis of readability and reading comprehension levels of the text, spelling correction, word use, verb tense consistency, capitalization, punctuation and frequency of repeated words. Other auxiliary programs can automatically prepare a table of contents or an index of the written document.

Sixth, Computer Assisted Writing offers several methods for addressing the problems of readability and reading comprehension in criminal justice agencies and institutions. Auxiliary software programs, which interface with word processing programs, are available to determine the readability level of printed materials, based on one or more standard methods for calculating readability. Most programs are simple to use. Material, already stored in the word processing program, can be analyzed, the readability level determined, and results printed for later use.   Other auxiliary editing programs (e.g., Random House Proofreader, Grammatik II) will routinely provide information (e.g., number of words, number of sentences, sentence length) which can be applied to standard readability tables used to classify the readability level, expressed in grade level equivalents (e.g., fifth, tenth, twelfth, fifteenth). Among the readability tables which can be used in this manner are the Fry Readability Graph (Fry, 1977), the Fog Index (Gunning, 1968), the Raygor Readability Estimate (Raygor, 1977), or the SMOG Readability Formula (McLaughlin, 1969). Once the readability level, or the reading level necessary to easily understand the written material is determined, this level can be compared to the average reading level of employees who are expected to read the material. If, for example, material was found to have a readability level of fifteenth grade (college junior), while the average reading ability of employees was eleventh grade (high school junior), then the written communication would be considered too high and adjustments should be made. (See Archambeault and Archambeault, 1983, for additional information.)

The auxiliary word processing software listed above also provides information needed to address the problem of reading comprehension (e.g., sentence length, number of prepositions, number of unique words and number of imperatives and questions). This information, together with the calculated readability level of the written document, can be invaluable in examining text for sexist or racially biased terms or phrases, and for vocabulary and concept levels which are too advanced for the intended reader. The final product can be written communication which is more effective and defensible in court when allegations of bias or discrimination are concerned (Archambeault and Archambeault, 1983).

Dedicated Versus Microcomputer Word Processing

Increasing volumes of written communication motivated many large agencies during the 1970s to purchase one of the dedicated word processing systems offered by Lanier, IBM, Xerox and other companies at costs of from $10,000 to $25,000. "Typing pools" were renamed "word processing pools" and many agencies became dependent on these systems for the production of paperwork. However, as the volume of work increased, these systems were stretched to their production limits. Backlogs of work, sometimes several weeks old, were not uncommon. Individuals with small jobs were often the most frustrated, usually because these carried a lower priority for production than larger jobs. Such delays exaggerated employee frustration, reduced efficiency and increased wasted time and effort. The cost of the expansion required to make dedicated word processing systems and pools more efficient was often greater than many agencies and departments could afford.

At this point it is necessary to distinguish between a dedicated word processor and a microcomputer with word processing capabilities. While a dedicated word processor and a computer contain similar components, such as a Z-80 microprocessor, the hardware and software design of a dedicated system restricts use to word processing. Furthermore, brands such as Lanier, are designed so that a user must continue purchasing blank storage disks from specific suppliers since only Lanier disks are suitable for Lanier equipment. The same criticism also applies to IBM, Xerox and other major brands of dedicated word processors.

In contrast, a microcomputer or a minicomputer is a multi-functional system. It is capable of virtually all the functions of a dedicated system in addition to the full scope of other microcomputer functions. Because these systems are multi-function, however, they are more complicated and operators must be carefully trained. The advantages of such a system are worth the investment. Interestingly, as the expanded use of microcomputer based word processing has occurred over the past few years, many dedicated word processing brands have not only moved into the microcomputer market (e.g., Lanier, Xerox, IBM), but have "discovered" that their word processors are capable of performing functions other than word processing. Lanier, for example, now offers the equivalent of a complete budget data base management system and communications protocol package. In addition, third-party manufacturers, or companies which are not connected with either the original hardware or software, are marketing a variety of software and hardware products to convert "dedicated" word processing systems to microcomputers.

CAW: Software Programs

Software manufacturers have responded to the increased demand for word processing software by providing the consumer with numerous programs from which to chose. These range in price from $65 to $500. Any agency planning to purchase software will quickly learn that even "expert opinion" does not agree on the worth of all word processing programs. The value of a particular program will vary among users; what may be an adequate word processing program for one individual or agency may be wholly inadequate for another. Information on CAW software is readily available from many sources. These include other agencies or institutions currently using word processing programs, numerous periodicals and trade journals and manufacturers, distributors and retail dealers.

Word Processing Programs

There are many good word processing programs currently on the market which are IBM compatible. Many are examples of integrated software, designed to interface with a spelling correction program, thesaurus, spread sheet or data base manager. A 1986 sampling of Fortune 1000 companies showed that approximately 37% used Multimate, 37% used Display Write, 20% Wordstar, 11% used Wang, 9% used Microsoft Word, 6% used Word Perfect and 9% used other types of word processing software (See *Info World*, Oct. 20, 1986, page 1). These are described below.

One popular and versatile word processing program is *Word-Star* by MicroPro International Corp. Wordstar was first introduced in June, 1979, and has reportedly sold more than a million copies. Since the program is not copyright protected it is difficult to estimate exactly how many copies are actually in use. WordStar is available for almost all operating systems including CP/M, CP/M86, MP/M, MS/DOS, PC-DOS or OS/2. Wordstar has become the standard of comparison for all other word processing programs (Miller, 1984). WordStar is available in several versions; this text was written using WordStar Professional 4.0. Originally written to compete with dedicated word processors, little if anything, was left out of the program. As a result, the program can be adapted to a wide range of equipment and specific work tasks. Because of its complexity and versatility, WordStar is not an easy program to learn; even skilled users report that they are still learning the intricacies of seldom used commands. WordStar is an excellent word processing program and is suitable for office or home use. Version 4.0 Professional costs around $500 retail and requires 256K of RAM, two disk drives and DOS 2.0 or later.

WordPerfect, by Wordperfect Corporation, is fast becoming a popular word processing program. It is somewhat easier for beginners to learn than Wordstar. It contains many features similar to Wordstar, as well as some variations in standard word processing features. In addition, an integrated data base manager system and spreadsheet are available to interface with the word processing program, allowing data from one to be easily transferred to the other. The current version is 4.2 and costs about $500, requiring 256K of RAM and two disk drives.

Multimate Advantage II is widely used in business corporations and is made by Ashton-Tate. It contains a spelling correction program with a dubious reputation for accuracy. Multimate is also an integrated software program, designed to interface with the company's data base and spread sheet programs. The current version is 1.0 and it costs about $600, requires 384K of RAM and two disk drives.

Display Write 4 is IBM's entry into the word processing market. It contains a spelling checker which also has a dubious reputation as to accuracy and speed of operation. Like other word processors in this class, it interfaces with other IBM products (e.g., spreadsheets, data base management) making integrated operations possible. Version 1.0 is currently being marketed for around $500 and requires 310K of RAM and two disk drives.

Microsoft Word, marketed by Microsoft Corp., is available in version 4.0. It is another integrated program which contains a speller and interfaces with a thesaurus. It functions on a level competitive with Wordstar and Wordperfect. Microsoft Word costs about $450 and requires 256K of RAM and two disk drives.

XyWrite III Plus, marketed by XyQuest, Inc., is a powerful word processing program that combines traditional editing functions with some unique features. It includes a spelling checker that can review each word as it is typed or scan an entire file for errors. The unusual redline editing feature keeps an on-screen record of deletions and additions by displaying these in reverse mode. Cost is approximately $500 and 384K of RAM is required.

Auxiliary Word Processing Programs

One distinct advantage of selecting IBM compatible word processing programs is the availability of separate auxiliary programs to check spelling, determine readability levels, check grammar and punctuation and suggest alternatives for often used words. Many word processing programs contain one or more features of auxiliary programs. However, not all spelling checkers are of equal quality and the user may wish to try another brand. In addition, some separate auxiliary programs offer features not available with a particular word processor. Some of the available auxiliary programs are described below. This is not a comprehensive list; it is intended to serve only as a guide to the various types of auxiliary software currently available.

Editor's Toolkit, marketed by BestInfo, Inc., is a professional editing package which consists of a spelling checker, thesaurus, grammar checker, note pad and other functions. It is designed to operate with XyWrite, WordPerfect and MultiMate word processing programs. It requires 512K of RAM, DOS 2.1 or later to operate and costs about $350.

Electric Webster, marketed by Cornucopia Software, Inc., is another editing package that works with most IBM compatible word processors and consists of a spelling checker and a grammar checker. It requires 64K of RAM and DOS 1.0 or later. It is a bit dated but still useful package which sells for about $129.

MicroSpell, version 7.4, is marketed by Trigram Systems, and is primarily a fast spelling checker. It requires 128 to 320K of RAM and DOS 2.0 or later. It is a stand alone speller which sells for $69.95.

The Random House Proofreader, marketed by Digital Marketing, is considered the grandfather of serious professional spelling checkers. It is a stand alone program which requires 192K of RAM and DOS 2.0 or later and sells for under $50. This program is used in combination with other word processing products and sold under other names.

Reference Set, version 3.0, marketed by Reference Software, combines the Random House Dictionary with a thesaurus and other editing tools. It requires 128K of RAM and DOS 2.0 to operate and costs $89. Specialized dictionaries containing medical or legal terms can be purchased and added to the set for $49 each.

Webster's New World Spelling Checker, version 1.4 is published by Simon and Schuster Software. It is a fast, efficient stand alone spelling checker which requires 128K of RAM and DOS 1.1 or later and sells for under $60.

Webster's Electronic Thesaurus, version 1.0 is marketed by Proximity and is a stand alone thesaurus. It requires 256K of RAM and DOS 2.0 or later. It sells for under $90.

Word Finder, version 2.0 is marketed by Writing Consultants and is a stand alone computerized thesaurus with between 90,000 to 22,000 synonyms; it is the same thesaurus integrated into Wordstar 4.0. It requires only 35K of RAM because most of its dictionary remains on a disk until activated. The size of the dictionary used depends on the amount of storage space on a disk; it is best used from a hard disk drive. It sells for under $80.

Grammatik II, marketed by Reference Software, is a sophisticated grammar checker originally developed by Wang laboratories for CP/M machines. It analyzes style, syntax, identifies spelling errors and makes suggestions for corrections. It is not interactive, meaning that the user does not correct the edited file at the same time the program is running. Rather, it marks the file where errors have been detected and gives the user a print out of errors with suggestions. This way the user can choose to accept or reject the suggestions made. It uses norms of writing found in business and general usage. It also has a function which alerts the user to frequency of word usage. It requires 128K of RAM and DOS 2.0 or later to operate and costs under $90.

Only a few of the available programs which may be used with IBM compatible word processing programs listed above. In addition, there are other auxiliary programs available for many specialized purposes including preparation of mailing lists, compilation of indexes, numbering and editing footnotes and automatic paragraph and section numbering. As with all auxiliary programs, it is essential to remember that not all programs will run on all computers or interface with all word processing programs.

It is also important to recognize that none of the software mentioned has been written for the OS/2 operating systems. Software specifically written for this system will undoubtedly have more capabilities and be easier to use than CAW software available at this time.

Desk Top Publishing

Desk top publishing is the term given advanced word processing capabilities which allow organizations or individuals to produce publications similar in quality to that produced by professional printers using offset printing techniques. However, desk top publishing is actually a totally different system of communicating with the computer than the system used in word processing. Word processing software uses the American Standard Code for Information Interchange (ASCII) to interpret keyboard strokes to the internal circuitry of the computer. In word processing individual characters are moved about in a manner similar to movable type. Word processing was a considerable improvement over traditional typewriters which can only produce static, unmovable characters.

Desk top publishing software displays individual characters as though they were part of a graphics display. The tiny dots which are used to compose each letter are actually individual pixels, or the smallest unit of the video screen addressable by the graphics application. These pixels can be used to form circles, squares, cones or even photographs, thus producing a true "what you see is what you get" image. Not everyone needs desk top publishing, but often an agency produces its own reports, advertisements, public relations materials, manuals, newsletters or pamphlets. Historically, these were prepared by professional printers using offset printing techniques. However, as the cost of printing has increased and the capabilities of desk top publishing software have expanded, many agencies find that they can prepare their own materials at considerable cost savings.

High quality desk top publishing is accomplished through the combination of microcomputers, special publishing software and laser printers. Printing of slightly less quality can be achieved less expensively with twenty-four pin dot matrix printers. In terms of hardware, the Apple Macintosh systems are currently recognized as industry standards for desk top publishing. The newer IBM PS/2 line of computers and compatibles were designed to compete in this market, but the software currently available is not as easy to manipulate as the software available for the Macintosh. With the older IBM line and compatibles desk top publishing can still be performed, but with more difficulty.

Among the current IBM compatible desk top publishing software are *GEM Desktop Publisher*, *The Office Publisher*, *PageMaker*, and *Ventura Publisher*. These cost about $400. To maximize their potentials, laser quality printers are required which may add another $2000 to $5000 to printing costs. Minimally, serious desk top publishing requires 80286 or 80386 computer systems (e.g., ATs) or the newer PS/2 Models 50, 60 or 80, although less satisfactory operations are possible with 8086/8 XT class systems.

However, despite IBM's attempt to capture this currently developing market, Apple Computer's Macintosh SE and Macintosh II machines are still judged to be superior. Many agencies continue to rely on IBM based machines for "number crunching" (e.g., spreadsheets, statistical analysis) but have turned to Apple Macintosh for word processing and desk top publishing because of the ease with which employees can be trained. In fact, some major newspapers (e.g., *U.S.A. TODAY*) use Macintosh machines to write copy and to create the graphics for which the paper is famous.

It is not possible at this juncture to predict how successful IBM's new PS/2 line will be in competing with Apple. However, the area of microcomputer technology is volatile and subject to quick changes. These realities must be taken into account whenever the purchase of new equipment is concerned.

PRINTERS

Printers enable a computer system to produce "hard copy" or printouts. The selection of printers for word processing is important for several reasons. First, not all printers work with all computer systems unless modifications of the system are made or special boards or interfaces are added. Second, not all printers work equally well with all types of word processing programs. Third, printers and print quality vary directly with the price of the printer. Although the pricing structure of printers may change as technology develops, for the present it must be recognized that less expensive printers, those under $300, may not be able to perform adequately under heavy use. High quality printers capable of performing for long periods without problems may cost as much as the other components of a microcomputer system combined. Fourth, most printers, regardless of the brand name on the front of the machine, are made by one of about half a dozen manufacturers. In buying a printer, it is often less expensive to purchase it under the "generic name," than under a better known brand name such as Apple or IBM. Fifth, some printers are capable of graphics, such as printing charts, tables, histograms and other images, while others are not. Sixth, printers vary in speed, which is measured in characters per second or cps. The speed of most printers is between 25 cps and 550 cps. Generally, the faster the printer, the more expensive. Seventh, printers in general use today are one of four types: 1) *dot matrix*, 2) *ink jet*, 3) *thimble* or *daisy wheel* and 4) *laser*.

Dot Matrix Printers

Dot matrix printers form characters in a manner similar to the formation of characters on a video display. Letters on a video display or CRT are formed electronically by the grouping of dots into patterns or symbols. Dot matrix printers operate at a speed of from 60 to 550 cps and create dots through three different principles: 1) impact transfer, through which small needles strike against a ribbon which roughly corresponds to the electrical impulse that produces symbols on video screens; 2) thermal transfer, which "burns" dots into paper; and 3) electrosensitive transfer which requires special types of paper and operates much like the transfer process in photocopying. Of the three principles, the dot matrix impact printers are the most common and practical for word processing purposes. They are also the most noisy.

One measurement of the quality of a dot matrix printer is the number of pins which make up its head or striking surface. The higher the number of pins, the better the quality of character created. The more pins which are used to produce individual characters, the more the finished printout will resemble output produced by a traditional typewriter. Today, better quality dot matrix printers are twenty-four pin. These printers are described as letter quality. Under normal conditions it is difficult to distinguish such printing, often called "near letter quality" from true letter quality print. Dot matrix printers which use fewer pins form characters with clearly distinguishable dots. Low quality dot matrix printers form characters using widely spaced dots. These printers are suitable for draft copies, memos and other routine paperwork circulated within the agency office. However, for materials which will be sent outside the agency's office, a higher quality printer is desirable.

Ink Jet Printers

Ink jet printers produce dots through another principle. Literally, characters are formed by spraying ink through micro-jets onto paper; the shape of the spray is electronically configured to form letters and symbols. The end product is usually equal to the quality produced by letter quality printers. These printers are also excellent for graphics; some print in several different colors. However, the technology for this type of printer has not been fully developed; maintenance is high because ink jet ports (openings) become blocked by paper dust. Additionally, dirt, temperature and climactic changes affect the viscosity of the ink. Hence, because these printers are more sophisticated and sensitive, their reliability for high volumes of work does not equal the reliability of impact printers. On the other hand, they are excellent for preparing graphs and charts, especially those involving multi-color presentations.

Thimble or Daisy Wheel Printers

Letter quality printers is a general term referring to a group of high volume printers which produce a print type comparable to electric typewriter print, usually without a keyboard. Symbols and letters are formed in a manner similar to a conventional typewriter. Daisy wheels or thimbles contain preformed characters which strike a typing ribbon. The daisy wheel and thimble differ only in their physical shape: one looks like a daisy flower with print elements on the ends of the petals, and the other looks like a sewing thimble which has been cut into spokes each containing a character. As a group, these printers are slower than dot matrix printers and average from 25 to 180 cps.

Good quality, reliable, letter quality printers in this category cost between $500-$1000. However, high quality, reliable, letter quality printers which are designed for sustained high volume agency use cost from two to ten times more. Some of the high cost is due to the addition of special features needed for specific office functions. These special features may include alternative print heads, form print track feeds, individual sheet feeds multiple sheet feeds, and various other paper feeding or print options. Printer costs, however, continue to decline because of increasing competition among manufacturers.

Laser Printers

Laser Printers employ a technology which borrows from photocopying technology pioneered by Xerox. Instead of printing each letter or symbol, as is the case for other kinds of printers, laser printers print an entire page at one time. The image sent from the computer is printed on paper using laser light beams. No mechanical parts ever touch the paper, except those parts required to move the paper in and out of the printer. The end result is a very high quality end-product that rivals professional typesetting or offset printing.

A significant advantage of laser printers is the variety of print fonts which can be selected. The user can choose to change print fonts each time a page is printed, or the user may combine several print fonts on one page. Even less expensive laser printers have five to ten fonts from which to choose. Some printers have as many as 35 resident fonts.

Laser printers are generally slower than higher quality dot matrix printers but faster than many letter quality printers. They are very expensive ranging from around $2000-$5,000. However, competition is becoming stiff and prices are falling. Within a few years good products will be within the financial reach of many individuals and most agencies.

Printer Memory and Buffers

Another factor to consider in word processing is the size of the printer buffer. A buffer is nothing more than the memory storage of a given printer. Except for certain brands, such as the IBM and Xerox Memory Typewriters, most typewriters do not have any memory. Those with memory employ a microchip arrangement which is similar to that found in printers. All printers have some memory, ranging from 1K to 95K. This memory allows the printer to receive information from the computer's CPU and to store it until the printer can print it. In most instances, internal print buffers cannot store more than several pages at a time. This means that the microcomputer system cannot be used for other functions, such as editing or typing new text, until the printing has been completed.

More sophisticated systems add a piece of equipment called a "print buffer" which allows the microcomputer to "dump" up to several hundred pages into memory, which is then fed to the printer at a rate it can process. Dedicated word processing systems usually include a print buffer. Recent advances, such as the 16 or 32-bit UNIX and OS/2 operating systems, contain a sub-program called a "spooler" which also allows printing storage. The latter has many disadvantages primarily because the software technology has not standardized "spooling" for all computer/printer systems. Print buffers cost from $50 to $500 and are a reliable mechanism for storing pages awaiting printing.

It should also be noted that some memory typewriters, such as the IBM 85, can be converted into a computer printer. An investment of less than twenty dollars in a parallel or RS-232 plug is all that is needed. As a result, an agency which is making a transition from typewriters to microcomputers may be able to make use of equipment which has already been purchased. However, such conversions would be temporary solutions since memory typewriters were not designed to be used at the sustained speed and workload of a computer printer, and they will therefore require more frequent maintenance.

PROFESSIONAL WRITING: CAW CONSIDERATIONS AND TECHNIQUES

Academics, researchers, managers and others who have the responsibility for writing professionally can increase their own productivity by mastering a computer system and a word processing program. Computer assisted writing (CAW), however, is different from typing. While the advantages over the typewriter are many, computer assisted writing has some unique features which must be discussed. These are summarized in the following points.

First, software must be selected before hardware. Evaluate various computer systems for potential use as word processors. Consider the arrangement of the keyboard and the touch of the keystrokes. Many individuals have personal preferences in these two areas. Some prefer a traditional clicking sound and a "metallic" touch; others prefer a "soft" keystroke which produces no sound. Other important considerations are the operating system and the availability of software.

Second, consider the cost of the total system. This includes the initial purchase price, additional cost for microchips and boards to operate a word processing system, the cost of cards needed to operate printers and the cost of additional peripheral devices, such as interconnecting devices and additional disk drives. Additional costs of peripherals and "system add-ons" make many *Game-Home Use Microcomputers* expensive. Furthermore, some *Individual Use Microcomputers* (e.g., Apple II, IIe) require the addition of several expensive boards (to total around a $1000) for reasonable word processing capabilities. Even after additions, some of these otherwise excellent general-purpose computers are adequate for limited individual usage as basic word processing systems, but not for high volume agency use. Physical arrangement of keyboards and keystroke, and the wider variety of word processing software make the following *Professional Applications Microcomputers* good word processing systems: IBM PC, XT, PS/2 systems, DEC, NEC APCIV, Apple Macintosh SE, Macintosh II.

Third, if an expensive letter quality printer is available for typing, it may be advisable to get an inexpensive dot matrix printer for drafting. It is often cheaper to buy ribbons for the dot matrix than for the letter quality printers. However, with the advent of twenty-four pin dot matrix printers, the speed and quality may make the purchase of a letter quality printer unnecessary for many professional applications.

Fourth, the minimum software needed for professional computer writing is a good word processing program, spelling checker and grammar checker. A thesaurus is also desirable, as is a table of contents generator. Most of the major brands of word processing programs today have spelling correcting and thesaurus programs integrated into their main programs and it is not necessary to purchase these separately.

Finally, special attention must be taken both in the care of hardware and software. The best use of these CAW aids can be made if the following sequence of steps is followed:

1. Clean the heads of floppy disk drives regularly and keep computers in environmentally clean conditions. Extended use causes static electricity and dust build-up which can result in disk failure. This problem can be eliminated by routine cleaning with a specially designed disk drive head cleaning kit. Hard disk drives cannot be cleaned directly, but proper procedures for caring for hard disks such as keeping air circulating and fan openings clean and free of obstacles are essential. It is also important to retract hard disks before turning off the system to prevent accidental erasure or damage.

2. If the system depends on floppy disks, use only high quality floppy disks. Less expensive disks tend to be less reliable and the probability of a disk "crashing" is greater. In addition, the less expensive disks are not finished as smoothly as the more expensive brands and may damage disk drive heads.

3. Write material with the word processing program and make screen corrections as needed. Then make a backup copy of the document onto another disk. This extra copy is insurance against the possible loss or "scrambling" of the text during editing. This procedure is essential for important files. For important, difficult to replace files, a third copy on a third disk, stored separately, is recommended.

4. If the system depends on floppy disks, keep the word processing and operating system programs on one disk (usually drive A or 1) and the writing on another data disk (usually drive B or 2), particularly if 5 1/4 inch disk storage is used. When a disk is more than 60% filled, there is greater danger of data loss. This danger is diminished if the word processing program is stored on one drive and the data disk on another. Many word processing programs make a "working file" on the disk during editing; this also requires additional space. If a disk becomes full during the editing of text it may be difficult, if not impossible, to save the edited copy. Problems of this nature are minimized if hard disk drives are used.

5. During writing, the first editing program to use is a spelling checker and the second is a thesaurus. A good checker will identify spelling errors, provide lists of incorrectly spelled words and allow corrections to be made automatically on the

file. A thesaurus helps keep the writer from using the same word again and again. Both editing programs are RAM resident in many of the newer integrated word processing programs, meaning that both the thesaurus and spelling checker can be activated while the user is editing a file with the word processor.

6.   The next editing step is to use a grammar checker to identify punctuation, syntax and other errors. Grammar checkers should not be used until after all spelling is corrected, or misspelled words may be read as grammatical or style errors. A good program, such as Random House Grammatik II, will provide a printout of grammatical errors and style inconsistencies, and make suggestions for revisions which the writer may or may not choose to make. It will also provide a "redundancy" analysis which will tell you how often you are using certain words. Finally, it will give you a readability level analysis which is important in organizational communication.

7.   Other auxiliary programs, such as index generators, Table of Contents generators and footnoting programs can be used to polish and refine the writing.

8.   The use of a program to determine the appropriate readability of the written document may prove invaluable to some agencies, especially those departments directly concerned with training aspects.

9.   If floppy disks are used for primary or backup storage, use dust free storage containers.

CAW IN PERSPECTIVE

Criticisms of bureaucratic forms of communication have led to the conceptualization of alternative organizational models and ideas. One of these is *Computer Assisted Writing*. *CAW* offers tremendous potential to criminal justice agencies and institutions as an aid to effectively handling the massive volume of written communications that they encounter daily. *CAW* also offers alternative methods for achieving more effective methods of written communication between management and employees. CAW also provides management with a more defensible foundation for satisfying EEOC Guidelines. However, CAW is only one tangible result of rapidly evolving computer technology.

Another general consequence is the emergence of *information networking*. Information networking is a term which has at least three distinct meanings. First, it refers to a theory of organizational management which orients the structure and processes of management to the flow of information, in sharp contrast to traditional principles of bureaucratic management which structures organizations on the distribution of power and authority. Second, the term pertains to the electronic linking of multiple computers through a physical *limited area network system (LANS)*. Finally, it refers to the linking of computers through *telecommunications*. Each of these meanings is discussed below. The following is intended only to be a brief overview of the subject matter and to guide the reader to other sources of detailed information.

THE INFORMATION ECONOMY:
AN INTRODUCTION

The increasing importance of information as a commodity and the rising level of education in the United States since 1900 has had a significant impact on traditional bureaucracies. The criminal justice bureaucracy is no exception. The U. S. Department of Commerce calculated in 1967 that 46% of the GNP was directly due to information generation or information facilitating jobs. These jobs included persons working in education; printing; communications; computer manufacturer, sale and use; mass media; accounting and banking; advertising; publishing; and those individuals who spend the majority of work time preparing written reports.

Occupational data can be used to illustrate the beginning of the information economy. The chart in Figure 3-1 indicates that the number of individuals in agricultural related occupations declined steadily from 1800, while the number of people in occupations related to industry, service and information increased. The early years of this century marked the beginnings of the free public library system and the publication and distribution of newspapers on a large scale. In addition, telegraph messages, telephones and phonographs soon became commonplace. All these events contributed to growth in the occupational category of information related jobs.

Figure 3-1

EVOLUTION OF INFORMATION SOCIETY

Occupational Category	1850	1900	1950	1980
Agriculture	85%	35%	10%	2%
Industry	2%	35%	45%	22%
Service	10%	20%	20%	29%
Information*	2%	10%	25%	47%

*Information is defined as those workers involved primarily in production, creation, processing, or distribution of information, e.g., lawyers, accountants, data clerks, educators, etc.
(Source: U. S. Census Bureau Report, 1982.)

The development of modern computers during World War II was soon followed in 1950 by a surge in the information occupational category. This trend has continued today. Census information such as this clearly indicates that the information society was in existence by 1950.

The shift in occupational categories is only one measure of the information society. A more dramatic measure of this phenomenon is the degree of change which the emphasis on information has caused and will continue to cause in organizations. The information society will have four specific influences on the organizational structure and the people within all bureaucracies. First, slowly but surely, administrators and managers will acknowledge that the information society is an economic reality not an abstraction. Second, technological innovations in communications and computers will accelerate the rate of change in all fields. Third, new information will be applied to old tasks and existing institutions. Fourth, employee reading and writing skills will become more important than ever before.

One of the influences of the information society has been the application of information networking to organizations. One of the earliest networks established to share information was a computer link between computer specialists in the U. S. Defense Department and computer specialists employed by the Computer Corporation of America which had been hired as a consultant by the Defense Department. These computer links were established to transfer data easily and quickly. *Unintentionally*, human networks sprang up among the various contractors and consultants hired to work on the project. The result was a spontaneous exchange of information on computers, computerized weapon systems and strategies for computer controlled systems. Defense Department officials immediately recognized the security problems involved in such information networks. As a consequence, the military adopted the policy of using "closed" communication systems. Closed systems are dedicated to a single purpose and have limited access. From this informal beginning the concept of information networking has evolved into a principle of organizational management.

INFORMATION NETWORKING:
THE THEORY AND ITS IMPLICATIONS

Information networking, as a theory, refers to a set of management principles which maintain that organizations must be flexible and structured around the central flow of information, instead of structured by the distribution of power and authority that is typical of bureaucratic management. Organizations structured according to the flow of information are more capable of rapidly adapting to change than traditional bureaucracies. To structure an organization on the basis of the flow of information is a normative or ideal model which has never been fully operationalized or tested. However, its component ideas are directly related to computer networking and its application to criminal justice organizations reveals information-related problems that all managers of the 1980s face. The theory begins with the observation that technological developments in communications have exacerbated the great volume of information which must be collected, assembled and distributed by traditional bureaucracies through their characteristic "scalared" and "filtered" patterns of information flow. As a consequence, bureaucracies are increasingly less able to cope with the demands for information.

Information as a commodity has replaced industrial production as the controlling factor in economies of the U. S. and the entire world (Smith, 1983: 27-29). The National Commission on Libraries and Information Science report (1982) states that there is:

...an increasing awareness of information as something of economic value, as a commodity, as a tool for better management of tangible resources, as an economic resource in and of itself (1982: 26).

Power, which refers to the ability to persuade others by overt or covert means to one's will, is now shifting from those who control industrial production, to those who control information and its flow (Molitor, 1981: 24). Naisbitt writes:

> We need to create a knowledge of theory of value. In an information economy, then value is increased, not by labor, but by knowledge. Marx's "labor theory of value," born at the beginning of the industrial economy, must be replaced with a new *knowledge theory of value*. In an information society, value is increased by knowledge, a different kind of labor than Marx had in mind...the notion that knowledge can create economic value is generally absent from most economic analysis, though there is some evidence that it is now beginning to be taken into account (Naisbitt, 1982: 17).

Nations are evolving from an industrial-based economy and society into an information-based economy and society. Further, the full potentials of this shift will be felt in democracies which permit "open" inquiry and allow "challenges to authorized conventional wisdom" (Dizard, 1982: 99). As this occurs, significant social and organizational restructuring will result.

> The restructuring of America from an industrial to an information society will easily be as profound as the shift from an agricultural society to an industrial society (Naisbitt, 1982: 18).

The computer can enhance the power of organizations in a variety of ways. First, it enhances the ability of the organization to collect, store, organize and retrieve information about individuals and groups at a level of sophistication which has never before been experienced by mankind. Second, computers enable organizations to organize and store information in ways which make it accessible to thousands of people instantly. Those same computers can prevent everyone from obtaining access to information except only a few selected individuals or groups, depending on the decisions of those who control the information. Thirdly, organizations can assimilate and integrate information from a broad range of different sources. This permits an analysis of individual and group behavior leading to prediction about future actions, decisions, desires and fears. Organizations possessing such power can use this information to further enhance their own power or that of selected individuals in the infrastructure. The full potential and implications of computer power can only be the subject of conjecture. There is no comprehensive historical precedent to rely upon. It is a phenomenon which requires constant vigilance and monitoring; the computer as a source of power cannot be ignored.

The normative theory of information networking has several implications for American criminal justice management. These implications suggest extensive changes in justice organizations will be necessary for survival in an information-dependent society. Change begins with the twin goals of, first, adjusting management structures to be more flexible and capable of adapting to change, and, second, increasing the efficiency of organization communications. One way of achieving these goals is to restructure justice agencies into smaller units, each with increased independence of action and decision-making. Each agency would be directly connected with the central flow of information within the agency. Organizational unit structures of teams and departments would remain accountable to supervisors, managers, or team chiefs, and to the chain of organization. However, to accomplish their assigned functions, jobs and duties, the teams or departments would be semi-autonomous and free to directly obtain needed information from any other organizational unit, instead of being hampered by "scalared" and "filtered" limitations. These changes, however, would not be without problems.

One problem that can be expected is that both organizational units and individuals will have more information available to them at any specific time than they desire or can effectively utilize. Hence, information access, storage and retrieval systems must be carefully designed for ease of input and retrieval. Another problem to be faced is overcoming the "informational float" or the time delay encountered by an organization as information moves from the point of collection (input) to the point of delivery (output or final destination). Both of these problems will be addressed by technological advances in computer technology (Naisbitt, 1982; Dervin, 1983). However, other problems will not be as easily solved.

While microcomputer technology may solve electronic hardware and "float" problems associated with information networking, technology alone will not overcome the traditions of bureaucratic management, especially scalared communications, paths to success, guarding rather than sharing information and organizational values. New organizational management values regarding information and how it is to be handled must be developed. New multi-directional communications patterns including bilateral, diagonal and bottom-up, must be established to replace the efficiency plagued scalar pattern (Naisbitt, 1982: 198). Still another related problem is that in order to bring about these changes, criminal justice organizations will have to shift the emphasis of their reward systems from an emphasis on "climbing over" others success to an emphasis on "empowering others with knowledge" in order to accomplish organizational goals.

Success in any typical bureaucratic organization often means that individuals and groups prey on each other, instead of cooperating. Individuals are constantly in competition for limited resources or symbols of success, whether it be budgets, equipment, new positions, titles, power, wealth or influence. An overemphasis on individual attainments and competition discourages cooperation and defeats organizational loyalty. In this context, information is a source of power and the sharing of information is discouraged both overtly and covertly through bureaucratic management practices. In sharp contrast, the concept of information networking requires that an organization must reward the "sharing" and communication of information, rather than discouraging it. Paths to career success in criminal justice agencies of the future must recognize the benefits of "empowering others with knowledge."

Consistent with the ideas of information networking are newer organizational management models, such as Management Theory Z, Quality Control Circles and Search for Excellence approaches which provide for management information flow in all directions (up, laterally, and down). Management should emphasize rapid and accurate dissemination of information to all who have a vested interest, and to facilitate input. For example, the success of Japanese business and industrial organizations, particularly the use of Management Theory Z, may provide the processes and principles which organizations of the future will use to manage themselves (Ping, 1983; Ouchi, 1982; Pascale and Athos, 1981). Management Theory Z has also been applied to a comparison of American and Japanese criminal justice (Archambeault, 1982; Archambeault and Weirman, 1983; Archambeault and Fenwick, 1983). The essential features of this applied model stress holistic or total concern for the welfare of employees, clearly defined and life long employment paths, shared decision-making, and complete loyalty to the organization. Management Theory Z has been equally successful in both Japan and the United States. Management Theory Z may provide the applied management framework within which to achieve the ideals and goals of information management theory, and an effective alternative to traditional bureaucratic management.

In relation to police organizational management, Archambeault and Weirman (1983) provide insight into how an organization can be structured to accommodate concepts of Management Theory Z, with its emphasis on shared decision-making. By separating the "administrative and operational spheres" of management, policies and procedures are developed through shared decision-making in the former and implemented through a command structure in the latter. This conceptualization can be extended to account for information networking.

Within each of these respective spheres of decision-making, is an information dimension. The information dimension of the "administrative sphere" involves information gathering and sharing related to management responsibilities (e.g., budgets, staff studies, operational research, health care, personnel policies); computer assistance in this area is called management information systems (MIS). By comparison, the information dimension of the "operations sphere" is concerned with information and intelligence gathering relative to: (a) routine operations (e.g., patrolling, investigation, supervision of offenders) and (b) tactical operations (e.g., the para-military or armed force actions performed by a criminal justice agency arising from riot conditions, emergency and disaster management, and criminal arrests). While the information needed by each sphere is different, both information dimensions are interdependent. For example, the traffic division needs research information on traffic problems, manpower and equipment availability, all of which must be provided by management information data bases. Similarly, once a traffic control plan has been developed and operationalized by the traffic division, then information on equipment use, man-hours and accident report data are needed by management to schedule vehicle maintenance and replacement, pay personnel and continue analysis on traffic patterns.

The information dimension in both spheres requires that those persons engaged in information collection and transmission should have the freedom and flexibility to deal directly with sources of information and to share this information with others who have legitimate needs. Furthermore, organizations need to analyze information requirements and determine the most productive pattern of information flow in both the administrative and operational spheres. Based on this analysis, organizational structures must evolve which are flexible enough to adjust to changes and tailored to achieve an optimal flow of information.

INFORMATION NETWORKING:
LOCAL AREA NETWORK SYSTEMS (LANS)

Local Area Networking System (LANS) refers to a special hardware and software combination which allows individual microcomputers to share common data bases, operating systems, programs, memory and storage. In many ways, LANS use physical connections similar to main frame computers.

LANS are physically connected computer systems, sometimes through standard telephone lines, other times through a special area telephone connection, within an agency, within a building or between offices on the same floor. What distinguishes a LANS from a main frame computer's system of terminals, is that what is being connected is a series of microcomputers, all of which are capable of autonomous processing, and all of which possess independent memory.

In some LANS, one microcomputer or minicomputer may function as the central processing unit. Through this arrangement, single integrated word processing and data base management programs, as well as centralized hard disk storage, can be shared. LANS may be used in settings where several individuals, such as engineers, accountants, secretaries, police officers and field reporters are working independently on a joint project or where the day's work production from different departments is to be combined into a single day's-end report, whether it is the amount of typing done, the record of the day's receipts, updates on casefiles or inventory accounting. LANS has three basic configurations: the *bus*, *ring* and *star*.

The *LANS bus* consists of a single line shared by several computer work stations which may be independent microcomputer systems. All stations along the bus are able to transmit and receive information from others on the line. The bus is easily expandable. Such arrangements may be useful when several people are working on different parts of a project and want to share information with others. There is, however, no central controlling computer.

The *LANS ring* provides a point to point link between microcomputers arranged in a physical circle. Like the bus, the ring does not have a central controlling computer.

The LANS star links several different work stations with a central control unit, either a mini or super-minicomputer. The physical configuration may take different shapes, but all information is fed through the master computer. This system is most often found in educational or training situations where an instructor can monitor the activities of several students at different computer units. This type of network may also be used by a word processing pool in which a supervisor who operates the control unit can assign, monitor and track work done by individual operators along the network.

LANS are also distinguished by the terms proprietary and non-proprietary. Proprietary refers to networks which can use the hardware of only one manufacturer, such as Apple, Xerox or IBM. Non-proprietary refers to networks which can integrate components of different hardware or software manufacturers.

What differentiates LANS from telecommunications information networking is suggested in the word "LOCAL." A LANS is a limited area network, in contrast to telecommunications linking which can be worldwide.

Picture 3-1 shows part of a LANS network used by Patuxent Institution, Jessup, Maryland. Three Burroughs B-25 microcomputers are connected via LANS for office automation purposes in the Research, Personnel and Fiscal Offices of the Institution. Photo courtesy of James "Chip" Coldren, Jr., Director of Research, Patuxent. Photography by Tommy Foster.

INFORMATION NETWORKING: TELECOMMUNICATIONS LINKS

Telecommunications Information Networking refers to the linking of multiple microcomputers to each other or to main frame computer systems through the electronic linkage of any communications equipment, including telephones, closed-circuit cable television and microwave-satellite connections, among others. These information networks allow a microcomputer user to access a wide variety of information services, including library literature searches, and the Dow Jones stock market information; interface with short-wave operators around the world; receive weather and news information directly from satellites; complete banking transactions; and shop for and purchase products via the computer. In 1983, computer networking made it possible for ham radio operators to talk to Space Shuttle astronauts. Communication networks permit the microcomputer to send information or data from one computer to another through a telephone modem. Some "smart" modems are capable of receiving information without the user being present. Through telecommunications, a potential user can access any main frame data base anywhere in the world, provided that the user has the necessary software, hardware and password or security codes.

Glossbrenner (1983: 7-8) notes that there are more than 1350 different public access computer data bases and nearly 500 are free. These data bases evolved from the remote data processing (RDP) companies which started in the late 1950s as low-cost alternatives to buying or leasing main frame computers. The RDP companies grew and the demand for services expanded to the present point where electronic delivery systems, hardware and software are standardized and reliable. Glossbrenner (1983: 10- 16) offers a seven category typology of different computer networking services which are available to the microcomputer user, and gives detailed information on their use. These categories and their applications in criminal justice management communications are summarized below:

1. *Information Utilities* is a type of electronic networking service which provides both information and a variety of services to subscribers. Among the services available are electronic mail delivery and shared-time game playing. Also included in this category are services such as CompuServe Information Service (CIS), Dow Jones News/Retrieval Service, Telex, Forbes, airline schedules, hotel reservations and job finders. [See Glossbrenner, 1983: Chapters 3, 4, 5.] Information Utilities may be of value to criminal justice management in selected areas. Electronic mail service between physically separated offices, sub-stations and districts may be less expensive and faster than conventional mail or delivery services. Job finder services may be of use in corrections work where employment may be part of a probation, parole or pre-release program. Some agencies whose personnel must travel by air may find that they can make their own reservations and select the lowest fares themselves at a reasonable savings. Computer utility services, such as CompuServe, may provide a more cost-effective method of employee training and debugging new equipment and software than contracts with dealers who are not available twenty-four hours per day, seven days per week.

2. *Encyclopedia Data Bases* is a type of networking service such as DIALOG, described in Chapter 2. Other services falling into this category are the Congressional Record and Readers Guide to Periodic Literature Index. [See Glossbrenner, 1983: Chapter 6.] This service, as noted in Chapter 2, is of value to researchers and academicians. In addition, prison libraries may find that subscription to such services may actually reduce expenditures for new books and periodicals. Legal reference services may in some instances be less costly than maintaining a law library, yet meet court standards relative to ensuring access to courts. Medical services may be enhanced within institutions at considerably lower costs than hiring additional or consulting medical doctors.

3. *News and Business Information Databases* is a type of service which provides general news coverage (e.g., *New York Times Information Service*), industrial information and business information newsletters and reports (e.g., *Hazardous Waste News, Tax Notes Today*). [See Glossbrenner, 1983: Chapter 7.] This type of service has limited applications in criminal justice, except for libraries which can access many periodicals without paying individual subscriptions. Hard copy printouts can be made for the reader who needs a copy of a particular article.

4. *Computer Bulletin Boards* is a service ranging from special interest boards for ham radio operators to information for computer programmers and computer-specific user groups. [See Glossbrenner, 1983; Chapter 8.] These boards may be of value for agencies with various offices physically separated or housed in one huge complex. Individual offices can be immediately notified of meetings, changes in schedules, deadlines for reports, personal announcements or other pieces of office information. For example, the Federal Bureau of Prisons in Washington, D.C., maintains a bulletin board for members of FBP to keep them informed of information affecting the agency. The Arlington, Virginia, Parole Department maintains a bulletin board to coordinate its neighborhood watch programs and list recent break-ins. Other police departments provide boards to keep members informed of events or incidents which occurred on other shifts. The list of uses for bulletin boards are limited only to the imaginations of the users.

5. *Electronic Shopping, Banking, and Barter* is a category which allows the average user to shop and purchase catalog items by computer, do banking, and trade services and goods. [See Glossbrenner, 1983: Chapter 9.] This type of service may have limited value in criminal justice, except to those involved in purchasing.

6. *Computerized Conferencing* is a category of networking which is similar to teleconferencing by phone in which participants from different locations can enter interactive audio/video conversations. In computer conferencing, the medium of communication is the computer, either alone or in combination with teleconferencing. Computerized conferencing allows individuals who are working on different parts of a project to share data, narrative descriptions or reports at the same time. [See Glossbrenner, 1983: Chapter 10.] This technique can also be used by police officers, probation officers or other investigators to report field notes or findings from hotel rooms or homes back to a central office, thereby allowing closer supervision of cases and personnel.

7. *Telecommuting* is a category of networking which allows persons to be physically located in one place, usually a home office, and to transmit work to another computer at another location. Persons engaged in occupations ranging from computer programming, accounting, word processing and education can engage in telecommuting. This enables the employee to complete tasks on the microcomputer, save it if necessary, and send the completed work to another location without leaving home. Telecommuting is the "cottage industry" of the information society. [See Glossbrenner, 1983: Chapter 11.] Telecommuting could be used in criminal justice agencies in several ways. Undercover operatives could make their field reports without returning to a police station. Probation or parole officers who must work in large metropolitan districts or on a state-wide basis and travel long distances from their office could use this technique to update case records. Management records, reports, budget and personnel information could be transferred from a state police post or sheriff's sub-station to a central office, thus eliminating the need to physically deliver

the reports. Telecommuting also has educational and training applications as discussed in Chapter 4.

One criminal justice information network which provides the first six of these functions is ACAnet, sponsored by the American Correctional Association. This on-line service is available twenty-four hours per day, seven days per week. It is designed for the individual and agency user who is interested in applied corrections issues and information. It offers on-line teleconferencing, software oriented to corrections users, electronic mail services and data base mini-networks on such varied topics as prison construction and AIDS. For more information call 1-800-ACA-5646. There is a one-time connect charge. Access is through 300 or 1200 Baud modems.

Another type of information network which may be of value to criminal justice agencies and individuals is an electronic bulletin board system or BBS. A BBS can be set up by an individual or by an agency and allows access via a phone modem to either a select group of individuals or to a wide range of persons having interest in a particular subject. There are a number of BBS software programs such as FIDO which are available for little or no cost and can be adapted for criminal justice usage. While there were no criminal justice bulletin boards known to the authors at the time of writing that serve as good examples of what an information network should be, there are two examples which are accessible by anyone with a computer and phone modem. One example of a well-maintained, private bulletin board is the "Old Frog's Swamp," operated by BFM Computing of Rhinelander, Wisconsin, which operates a FIDO information network. This board can be accessed at 1200 or 2400 Baud by calling 1-715-362-3895 twenty-four hours per day. Electronic mail, messages, forums and public domain software services are provided. Another example is the bulletin board at the University of Wisconsin at Madison which can be accessed at 1-608-263-6057. There are thousands of such bulletin boards throughout the United States and Canada which can provide computerized information linking between computer users.

FAX Technology

One of the more recent forms of computer assisted organizational communications to gain popular acceptance is *facsimile transmission*, or FAX, which involves sending graphics images through the telephone lines as a series of scanning impulses. This technology is similar to that used by cable TV to send and receive pictures, but is different than sending impulses through a standard phone modem and communications program. In the latter, messages and graphics are created, transmitted, and received in ASCII code, which limits the range of possible graphics characters. In FAX technology, the image is sent line by line and then re-assembled by a FAX machine on that receiving end. The end result is that the copy received is an exact replica of the original, including signatures, logos or other special graphics. The faxing of documents may be important to agencies which frequently need to deliver large volumes of documents with unique character graphics (e.g., signatures, pictures, maps, sketches) or desk top publishing quality in shorter periods of time than normal mail services provide.

FAX technology is available through three different sources: 1) computer assisted FAX technology, 2) dedicated FAX machines and 3) commercial FAX services. These are briefly discussed below.

Computer assisted FAX technology essentially involves the addition of a FAX board to a computer and the purchase of FAX software. FAX boards can be added to most major brands of microcomputer hardware for from $400 to $1000. In addition, FAX processing software may add another $300-$400 in costs. However, these allow documents which are created by word processing, desk top publishing or other specialized computer graphics programs to be sent to hundreds of different locations in a matter of seconds or minutes. However, there are inherent limitations to existing FAX technology. For example, computer generated signatures can be sent, but original signatures could not be without having the document containing it read back into the computer. Additionally, documents which are received through FAX technology are not immediately readable by computers. Such documents must be translated back into ASCII format in order to be read by a word processor or other program. In doing so, some unique characters may be lost or altered. Further, the FAX format of one computer's software may not be readable by another system's, making the transfer of files between systems difficult.

Dedicated FAX machines look like miniature copying machines which are attached to phone lines. A document is fed into the FAX machine in a similar manner to feeding one into a copy machine, then it is read by the sending unit and instantly sent to one or more destinations. There are a number of different types of stand-alone FAX machines on the market which do not require a computer interface. These range in price from a few hundred to several thousands of dollars. To be useful, an agency has to have compatible machines, which stand idle except when involved in transmission or reception, at each of its locations. The advantage of the microcomputer based system is that the computer can be used for other functions as well. However, as stated previously, the dedicated FAX machine can send a copy of an original signature, while the computer cannot.

For individuals and agencies alike, there is another alternative, *commercial FAX services* which charge a per page fee. There are a number of different communications companies such as Western Union's Easy Link, Electronic Courier's Xpedite and Hotelcopy, which provide facsimile transmission services. The disadvantage of these services is that the user has to go to the nearest outlet for the service to receive the faxed document, or it has to be hand delivered as a telegram. The advantage of the microcomputer based system is that transmission is instantaneous, providing that the sender and receiver have compatible equipment. Further, the micro system ensures privacy and security in ways that no commercial service can. Finally, commercial services are expensive if high volumes of documents need to be sent daily, and commercial services may not be available twenty-four hours per day, seven days per week. Micro based systems can pay for themselves within a few weeks and can provide twenty-four hours per day operations. On the other hand, if the individual or agency infrequently needs to FAX only small numbers of documents, then commercial services would have the cost advantage.

There is, however, a growing trend among the business and manufacturing organizations to apply microcomputer FAX technology. Nonetheless, it must be stressed that the current state of computer assisted FAX technology is about where desk top publishing was a few years ago. Existing hardware and software technology has not yet been perfected and costs are higher than they will be when more products enter the market and competition increases. However, industry trends indicate that numerous advances can be expected in the next few years.

MICROCOMPUTER SYSTEM REQUIREMENTS

To engage in telecommunications, a microcomputer user must have the required equipment. First, the computer's CPU must be capable of telecommunications; some systems require the addition of "cards" or microchips, while other have this capability built in. Second, a microcomputer must have an RS-232 port or one has to be connected to the computer through some other means. Third, a micro system needs communications software to coordinate all the components of the system, and interact with the computer on the other end of the line. Finally, the system needs a telephone modem.

A modem is a device which allows the computer to "hear" or receive electronic impulses from other computers as well as to transmit messages. In doing so, the modem becomes both an input and an output device to the CPU. Modems can be classified as either acoustic or direct link. An acoustic modem typically uses a pair of rubber couplings to hold the mouth and earpiece of a standard telephone. Information is transmitted similarly to normal human usage. A direct link or direct connection modem permits the use of a standard plug-in wall jack, similar to that used to plug in a telephone. The advantage of the latter is that transmission between computers is a direct physical electronic link that results in improved accuracy of the data transmission over acoustic modems which are dependent on sound transfer and are more subject to outside interferences. Another way in which modems are differentiated is the rate or speed at which information between computers can be exchanged. This is called a Baud rate, named after the inventor of the Baudot telegraph code, J.M.E. Baudot (Glossbrenner, 1983: 29- 30). Baud rates generally correspond to another measure of modem speed, bits per second (bps). Although there are some technical differences, they are not significant for present discussions. Baud rate, as far as microcomputer modems are concerned, is typically 300 to 9600 Baud, although most mini and mainframe systems function at 9600 Baud. The user's decision to buy a 300, 2400 or 9600 Baud modem should be shaped by several considerations:

First, cost must be considered. A good quality 300 Baud acoustic modem can be purchased for under $300, while a high quality direct link 2400 Baud modem may cost up to $1,000 and a 9600 Baud modem at $1500-$3500. Furthermore, contracted services, such as DIALOG and WESTLAW, charge a higher rate per hour, in some instances, twice as much, to access the service at 1200 or 2400 Baud than at 300.

Second, a more sophisticated user can make 2400 or 9600 Baud rates less expensive than 300 or 1200. The key in this equation is the technological sophistication of both the user and the equipment. With adequate planning, it is possible for a user to minimize "on-line service time," or the amount of time that a user is charged for accessing the service. This can be accomplished with the correct configuration of hardware and software. The user must also have the intended information request saved to disk or computer memory, so that when the transmission communication sequence begins, the result is a computer to computer interaction. Any time a human enters this equation, the time usage variable increases by a factor of from eight to ten. As a result, if a user's system is configured in a way which allows the human to state all the information needs and save this within the system, the user's computer can directly interface with the computer of the main frame data base service, obtain the information, and save it to disk or CPU memory. Even if a service is charging double for a 2400 or 9600 Baud link, the elimination of the human time factor can reduce the charged time sufficiently to be five to seven times less costly per unit of measured time, than a human interacting with a 300 or 1200 Baud system.

Third, users have to make sure that their modem is compatible with the main frame system or other computer network with which they want to communicate. Some systems may not allow the use of 300 Baud modems. Hence, telecommunications systems must be carefully planned.

Fourth, one limitation of most modems is the requirement that both the transmitting and receiving systems must be "up" or operating. This means if an agency uses microcomputers to receive field reports, someone has to be at the receiving computer. For this reason, many law enforcement agencies which use microcomputers, house them in their communications sections which are manned twenty-four hours per day. An alternative to this procedure is a product such as a Hayes Smartmodem (costing around $700) which can be programmed both to dial and to answer automatically (see Markoff, 1983: 116-118). Such features permit communication during hours of least expensive telephone rates at nights or on weekends, and yet avoid the necessity of having someone awake and ready to operate the computer system.

Telecommunications Information Networking is a rapidly developing technology whose potential for criminal justice management has not yet been appreciated. It is also an area whose potential problems for criminal justice have only begun to be recognized as discussed in Chapter 6. Through telecommunications links via a personally owned microcomputer and an inexpensive telephone modem, an investigator in Chicago could transmit information to a personal microcomputer belonging to an investigator in New Orleans and possibly not be subject to provisions of the Freedom Of Information Act. An accountant for a large bank in New York could leave work on Friday, travel first to California, then to Florida, return to California, then back to New York on Monday. While in Florida, the accountant could use his lap-size microcomputer and the telephone of a rented motel room to transfer several hundred thousand dollars to an account in another state. Meanwhile, after visiting clients in the field or preparing a pre-sentence investigation, a probation officer in Indianapolis, could transmit the information to the office, ready for court the next day. A new generation of challenges for American criminal justice has emerged.

SUMMARY AND CONCLUSIONS

This chapter introduced microcomputer applications in organization management communications. It presented informational networking in both theoretical and applied contexts, and discussed implications for criminal justice administration and management. Issues of readability and reading comprehension and current legal and management-labor concerns facing criminal justice were discussed. Suggestions addressing these issues through computer technology were made. An overview of telecommunications microcomputer applications was presented.

The information society is a present reality facing American criminal justice organizations. It is creating pressures for radical changes in management strategy, organizational structure and technology. If criminal justice is to cope with the increasing demands of the future, it must continue to expand the creative applications of microcomputer technology. One way to address present needs is for agencies to establish information networks which can be accessed by agency personnel through microcomputers and phone modems. These networks provide an opportunity for valuable information exchange.

REVIEW QUESTIONS AND ACTIVITIES

1. Define the following terms: organizational management communications, filtered and scalared communications, and bureaucratic communication.

2. Explain the concept of information networking and how it relates to contemporary and future criminal justice management.

3. Relate each of the following terms to criminal justice organizations: written communication, word processing, dedicated word processors, and microcomputer word processors.

4. Visit a computer software store. Ask for a demonstration of two different word processing programs. Evaluate each according to the features listed in the chapter.

5. Discuss the advantages of CAW over preparation of written documents by traditional means.

6. Discuss the various applications of auxiliary word processing software packages.

7. List the different types of printers. Explain how characters are formed by each. Discuss specific applications for each.

8. Define readability and reading comprehension. How are these terms related to communication problems within criminal justice organizations? Explain how applications of CAW can be used to resolve these problems.

9. Define telecommunications and explain its potential impact on criminal justice.

Chapter 4

COMPUTER ASSISTED INSTRUCTION (CAI): THEORY, APPLICATIONS AND ISSUES

CHAPTER PREVIEW

Developments in microcomputer and information networking technology are evolving new methods of education and training which may be of value to criminal justice management. Agencies and institutions have legal, moral and professional obligations to adequately train personnel and to provide educational opportunities for offender populations under official control. They must also deal with the reality of computer literacy and take steps to develop the knowledge and skills employees need to cope with this technology.

Building on the discussions of telecommunications presented in Chapter 3, this chapter focuses on Computer Assisted Instruction (CAI), which by definition is a computer application in which a dialog is established between students and a computer program that informs them of their mistakes as they occur (Sippl, 1985:90). Topics discussed in this chapter include the theory of

137

CAI, its demonstrated and potential applications in criminal justice training and education. Evaluation criteria for educational courseware and the potential uses of diagnostic expert systems are also discussed.

STUDY QUESTIONS

The following study questions may be used as a guide to reading Chapter 4. Key terms and concepts related to these questions are printed in italics throughout the chapter.

1. Define and discuss the term Computer Assisted Instruction (CAI).

2. Explain the potential applications of CAI to criminal justice training and education.

3. Define and discuss computer literacy in terms of management's responsibility to train employees.

4. Discuss the applications of CAI to offender treatment and rehabilitation.

5. Discuss CAI effectiveness, advantages and disadvantages and courseware evaluation criteria.

CRIMINAL JUSTICE TRAINING AND EDUCATION OBLIGATIONS AND ISSUES: A BRIEF OVERVIEW

Microcomputer technology is changing the information processed in criminal justice, and is bringing increasing pressure on the criminal justice organization to adopt more efficient management methods. This same technology is also developing new, innovative methods of education and training which may be of value to criminal justice management. Agencies and institutions have legal, professional and moral obligations to train personnel and to provide educational opportunities to offender populations under their official control. They also must deal with the reality of computer literacy and take steps to develop employee skills and knowledge. Management must also evolve strategies for coping with computer-related employee stress (e.g., eye and emotional stress from working with a CRT, pressures to produce specified quantities of work, fear of being monitored by the computer, feelings of inadequacy and fear associated with learning about computers). As discussed later in Chapter 5, computer-related employee stress is becoming a major management-labor issue; it is also one which can be addressed through management and employee education and training.

Training the Employee

One principle of criminal justice organizational management, about which there exists general agreement, is that agencies and institutions have an implicit legal and professional obligation to train their personnel. Failure to adequately train personnel can make both individual agency administrators and their agencies criminally and civilly liable (Archambeault and Archambeault, 1983, Chapter 12: 317-320). General agreement also exists that what was once the satisfactory entry standard of a high school education is no longer an acceptable minimum educational level (Swanson and Territo, 1983). Beyond these points, however, deep philosophical, ideological, and pragmatic controversies exist about the nature, standards, content and methods of training criminal justice practitioners. Space limitations will allow only a cursory overview of selected issues which are directly related to the focus of this text.

With the introduction of computer technology to the criminal justice work environment, agencies have assumed additional training obligations toward their employees. Not only must management make provisions for training personnel to handle new equipment, but supervisors also need to be taught new skills for addressing the needs of employees experiencing CRT stress syndrome. This particular kind of stress is found among a wide range of employee work groups who spend many hours each day working at computer terminals.

Computer Literacy and Competency

Computer literacy has become a commonly used term, although its meaning is often vague and varied (Mace, 1983). Literacy, as used in this text, refers to the minimum level of computer competency that an agency or a department within an agency expects from its employees. Thus, the meaning of computer literacy may be different from scholar to scholar and agency to agency. For most criminal justice agencies, a four level classification of computer competency will be useful: 1) awareness; 2) operator; 3) programmer; and 4) systems analyst. These classifications are explained below.

The computer *awareness level* denotes a general knowledge of computers, their functions, and the general social, economic and legal issues associated with computers. All criminal justice agencies of the 1980-90s have an increasing responsibility to develop at least this minimum level of computer literacy among employees through in-service training. Awareness may be achieved through in-service training and demonstrations aimed at familiarizing all employees with the types of computer functions performed by the agency. It may be particularly important to develop an appreciation among employees whose work involves the production of information used in the agency's computer system in the form of field reports, incident reports and inventory reports. It may also be of value to help employees understand how they are directly affected by the computer through payroll and scheduling of vacation time. Beyond in-service training, the awareness level may also be achieved by encouraging employees to take basic computer courses at local schools or colleges.

The computer *operator level* is the second level of computer competency. This level of competency involves learning specific hardware and software skills by those personnel expected to operate the equipment for data management or word processing. If an agency widely employs computers, and if such knowledge is necessary for promotion, or other merit consideration, an agency should define minimum computer literacy in terms of level two computer competency.

The computer *programmer level* describes persons with knowledge of different computer languages, who can write or modify the computer programs to better meet the needs of the agency. Competent computer programmers will have advanced education or degrees in computer science.

The *systems analyst* or systems designer is knowledgeable of detailed computer microcircuits. They often determine equipment specifications and planning expansion of existing systems. Such persons must be highly trained and educated in computer technology. Many agencies may elect to hire a computer design firm or individual on a consulting basis, instead of employing persons with this competence level. Other larger agencies may find it is cost effective to have one or more system designers on staff.

As more of the new technologies are introduced and implemented in criminal justice agencies and institutions, all employees will need to become computer literate, although the level of computer competency required for individual employees will vary. Advocates of computer literacy believe that computer use will increase to such an extent that a secure job future will be dependent upon knowledge of computers.

In the 1960s many secondary schools with access to main frame computers began to teach computer programming. During the late 1970s and early 1980s, the spread of microcomputers created a demand for separate programming courses, especially for the microcomputers. The 1980s have witnessed a greater proliferation of computers in the schools. It is estimated that 20-35% of all secondary schools in the United States had at least one microcomputer in 1980; in 1983 99% of all secondary schools and 20-35% of all elementary schools had at least one microcomputer (Dennis, 1983). Most states now require a minimum level of computer literacy for high school graduation; many colleges and universities have similar requirements. Agencies can expect that within the next few years high school and college graduates will have at least an awareness of, and some will possess operator levels of, computer competencies. Supervisors and managers must be prepared to effectively utilize this potential talent.

Picture 4-1 shows the Computer Science Lab at Catholic High School, Baton Rouge, Louisiana. The lab contains 28 Apple IIe computer stations and seven computer printers. All secondary students in Louisiana are required to take a Computer Literacy course for graduation. This lab is used by students acquiring computer literacy skills. As similar facilities become more common throughout the country, agencies can expect entry level employees to possess an increasing degree of computer competency.

Picture 4-2 shows the Advanced Programming Lab at Catholic High School, Baton Rouge. This lab contains 20 Compaq computers, three regular computer printers and one printer capable of printing in multiple colors. This lab is used by students learning to program in BASIC and PASCAL. Photos of Catholic High School courtesy of Bro. Francis David, S.C, Principal.

Traditional Approaches to Training

Criminal justice agencies have traditionally discharged their obligations to train employees, with various degrees of success, in one or more or the following three ways.

First, the agency provides "on-the-job" training under the supervision of an experienced employee. This informal approach alone does not provide the quality, consistency, or documentation necessary to either adequately prepare the employee or protect the agency in the event of a law suit.

Second, the agency provides "in-service training" (e.g., legal, report writing, search techniques, rules and procedures, first aid training, firearms training) to its personnel. This approach allows an agency to document its training efforts, and in combination with "on-the-job" training can produce satisfactory results.   However, other problems and costs are generated. Training staff must be hired, programs planned and materials and equipment purchased.   Instructors and training support personnel, although trained to do other jobs, cannot perform agency tasks (e.g., patrol, investigate, work with offenders) while performing training functions.   Other problems are created when competent agency field personnel are more qualified or experienced than instructors, and professional instructors hired from educational institutions may not have appropriate field experiences.   The problem of instructor qualifications has often led to the practice of sending personnel outside their agencies for training.

Third, the approach taken in states with mandatory training requirements, such as Florida, Michigan and Texas, is to send personnel to state certified training programs or centers, and to "career development" seminars. Some agencies have also sent personnel to colleges and universities to obtain advanced degrees.   However, in this last option, agencies may encounter high costs typically involved in paying travel, registration and tuition expenses, plus the loss of employee work time.   In addition, the topics offered at colleges or universities may not be relevant to specific agency needs.

Agencies which elect to "do nothing" run a significant risk of serious legal action and liability if a citizen or an offender suffers physical harm because of insufficiently trained personnel.

Traditional agency training approaches often lack a consistent theoretical framework within which to develop employee skills and knowledge.   This has led to new conceptualizations of training and education.

The Criminal Justice Education and Training Continuum

Traditionally, a sharp dichotomy is made between education and training in criminal justice in the United States.   Training is generally regarded as instruction in specific, job-oriented knowledge or skills which is intended to prepare an individual for a given job within a specific criminal justice agency or career specialization.   In contrast, education is concerned with developing the person as a whole, teaching critical thinking and reasoning, developing general knowledge about criminal justice, and preparing that individual for a broad range of academic and professional jobs.   This difference, as stressed by academics, was strengthened by the criteria for funding eligibility of the Law Enforcement Assistance Administration (LEAA) and its LEEP program (Archambeault and Archambeault, 1982, Chapter 12: 320-321.)

In contrast, an alternative view, presented in this and other writings of the authors, is that criminal justice education and training must be viewed as a continuum, ranging from past experience to on-the-job training to college degree work (Archambeault and Archambeault, 1982, Chapter 12: 321-325; see figure 12-1: 321). It is argued that learning in criminal justice is a continuous process which is a lifelong experience and, borrowing from Japanese management, is one which must be addressed by criminal justice organizational management (see, Archambeault, 1982; Archambeault and Weirman, 1983; Archambeault and Fenwick, 1983). Furthermore, learning is often recognized more by qualitative and quantitative degrees, than by the substance itself. Although, college students study criminal law, police enforce it, and courts apply it, the substance of law remains similar. Finally, criminal justice instructional programs can be distinguished along the continuum by the degree of emphasis which is placed on applied occupational knowledge and skills when compared to the emphasis placed on developing individual and professional capabilities.

It is important to remember the criminal justice training-education learning continuum perspective and apply it to the discussions below of CAI, employee training and professional development.

Offender Training – Education

In addition to personnel management training responsibilities, correctional agencies and institutions, particularly those servicing juvenile populations, have moral and legal obligations to provide educational and vocational training to offenders. Cooperative arrangements are often made with local area school systems and colleges to provide educational programs to correctional facilities. In some instances, as in the Federal Bureau of Prisons, the teachers and instructors are employees of the correctional system; in others, they are employees of the local school or college system.

Offender education issues are germane to the focus of this text and to criminal justice administration in three respects. First, computer technology has produced a demand for programmers, technicians and repair personnel. Possession of these skills should increase the employability of released offenders. Second, Computer Assisted Instruction (CAI), provides a structured learning environment which may have great potential for the rehabilitation of offenders. However, research in this area is scarce. Third, the techniques and methods are similar to those utilized in staff development.

Agency Profile 4-1

COMPUTER ASSISTED EDUCATION FOR OFFENDERS

Patuxent Institution is a treatment-oriented maximum security prison located about 15 miles south of Baltimore, Maryland. Inmates volunteer for its program of integrated therapy, education and vocational training. In March of 1986, Patuxent Institution received a $56,720 grant under the Computer Training Initiative of the U. S. Department of Justice, National Institute of Corrections, for the purpose of establishing the Office Automation Program (OATP). OATP offers computer assisted instruction covering microcomputer operations, history of computers, word processing, basic accounting principles, office procedures and career planning. Data Networks, Inc. of Brooklandville, Maryland, developed the course software in consultation with Patuxent. Existing software, including Typing Tutor, WordStar, Microsoft Word, was combined with Data Networks INFORM career planning software. OATP uses an IBM-AT with a 60 Mb hard disk and Novelle network software to link eight IBM-PCs, two ITT workstations, and two printers. Inmates trained in OATP work as clerks in various departments in the institution, using their word processing and office automation skills. OATP graduates have obtained computer related employment upon release to the community. The Education Department of Patuxent Institution made arrangements with Howard Community College to teach introductory computer classes to Patuxent Inmates using a network of 10 Texas Instruments computers (TI-99s) located in the school building. These classes serve as entry level computer instruction for inmates, and also as the training ground for those inmates wishing to advance further. In December of 1986, Frederick Computer Products, Inc. of Frederick, Maryland, donated $75,000 worth of computer hardware and software to the institution. The donated hardware included six AT&T 7300 microcomputers, four Epson printers and the donated software included word processing, spreadsheet, graphics and miscellaneous programs. The donation was initiated by an inmate who requested in writing a donation of equipment from Frederick Computer Products. This hardware and software will be used to provide advanced computer education to inmates, and for joint projects in which inmates will design office automation applications for use by the Patuxent *administrative staff. This participation by the private sector provides Patuxent a unique opportunity to develop quality educational programs for inmates while modernizing its own operation.*

For more information on this institution and its program of computer assisted instruction write Director of Research, Patuxent Institution, P. O. Box 700, Jessup, Maryland 20794-0700.

Picture 4-3 above shows an academic instructor and three inmate assistants reviewing class materials developed in-house for the Office Automation Training Program at Patuxent Institution, Jessup, Maryland. Photo courtesy of Director of Research, Patuxent. Photography by Tommy Foster.

Picture 4-4 shows the classroom of the Office Automation Training Program at Patuxent. In the photo above one inmate is practicing transcription while others work on individual class assignments. Photo courtesy of Director of Research, Patuxent. Photography by Tommy Foster.

Picture 4-5 shows a male inmate of Patuxent Institution who is a graduate of the Office Automation Training program. He is assigned to the Director's office. In this photo he is providing assistance to the Director's Secretary as she learns word processing techniques on an AT&T 7300 microcomputer. Photo courtesy of Director of Research. Photography by Tommy Foster.

Computer Assisted Instruction (CAI):
Theory, Applications and Courseware Evaluation Criteria

Computer Assisted Instruction, also referred to as Computer-Aided Instruction, can be defined as the use of the computer to aid instruction by placing the learner in a conversational or interactive mode with a computer that contains a preprogrammed instructional plan. Through dialog or conversation with the computer, the learner is informed of mistakes. Some programs provide an opportunity to make corrections. Once the learner begins the interaction process, the program selects the next topic or phase of study according to previous responses of the learner, allowing each learner to progress at a pace directly related to his learning capability. In common usage, the term refers to any form of instruction in which students interact in real time or with learning-specific time limits with materials presented under the direct control of a computer (Wang, 1976). The term "real time" distinguishes other meanings of time associated with computers (e.g., microseconds, computer-use time, on-line time). CAI can interface with telecommunications to provide multiple site conference or instructional presentations which allow participant interaction. It can also be used to teach courses ranging from basic education to highly sophisticated technical subjects. CAI programs can integrate video tape and laser disk technology with computer simulation graphics. The end product can be a coordinated video-computer presentation which places the learner in a multi-dimensional instructional setting where pictures of real world events, similar to those which come across a normal TV screen, are presented. The learner is placed in a simulated real-life environment where decisions can be translated into video events. Consider the following two examples which are representative of the technological sophistication.

In the first CAI example, a participant sits at a small microcomputer in front of a large color video monitor in a small desk-cubicle, isolating the participant's field of vision from the rest of the room. After activating the program, the viewer is presented with a TV scene in which he is patrolling in a squad car. The audio portion of the program simulates a radio message about an alleged bomb incident. The presentation then takes the officer to the scene where he receives additional facts. He is then asked to select one of several possible actions. Note that up to this point the presentation is similar to the "Shoot or No Shoot" exercises which require the participant to analyze facts and make decisions. The difference in the CAI program is that the officer will see the consequences of the decision. Among the alternatives from which the officer can choose is "D. Load the suspected bomb into the trunk of the car and carry it away." If the participant entered "D," the program would show the officer placing the bomb in the trunk, driving away, then a sudden loud bang and a computer graphic generated mushroom cloud. In addition, the following message is shown on the screen "Incorrect response. Reconsider the information presented and choose another response." The program then returns to the bomb scene and the participant can enter another response, after which the microcomputer-video interactive program shows the participant the appropriate consequences.

In the second CAI example of video-computer interaction technology, the criminal justice faculty of Dyersburg Community College in Dyersburg, Tennessee, developed a self-paced *Introduction to Criminal Justice* course. This process involved a three steps. First, a conventional classroom lecture was videotaped. Scenes of lecture and class discussions were included. In addition, each topic was illustrated with actual scenes from a courtroom, an officer on patrol, or a jail admitting desk. Second, the course instructors developed overhead transparencies, test and review questions, and other supplemental materials. Third, the video tape and supplemental materials were converted into a CAI software program. The final product was a good quality, non-commercial software package, developed on an Apple IIe system. It allowed a student to sit at a computer, complete a lesson and pass a test on the material before receiving credit for it. The student could start or stop the lesson at any point and review past lesson segments. If the student failed to pass the test, the lesson was repeated and another set of test questions was presented. The system also scored the student's answers and maintained records for each student indicating the number of lessons completed and the final test scores for each.

The first example above is an expensive, commercially developed, recently marketed training program for police officers which applied Hollywood-type motion picture color video and stereo sound techniques to achieve its effects.

The second example above illustrates a low budget, non-commercial, CAI-video application which was prepared by a small community college using Title I Federal Education Grant money to buy computers and a sophisticated video-recorder and player. While there are other more sophisticated criminal justice related CAI available, the Dyersburg example is cited as an alternative to the commercially marketed products. The resources used to produce this particular CAI program are readily available in many agencies. Similar CAI programs could be used for agency-specific training lessons for police, correctional officers, counselors and other employees. Performance records for employees in training could be obtained, validated and used for personnel management decisions, including promotion, dismissal and performance evaluations.

Although CAI programs such as the two described above are only now developing, computers have been used as aids to instruction for over thirty years.

CAI History:
The Educational-Training Interface

Main frame computers were used for instructional purposes as early as 1950 at Florida State University, Dartmouth College and Stanford University. These programs were developed from extensive efforts to design "teaching machines" which could be used for drill and practice. It was believed that this technique would bridge the gap between traditional classroom learning and permit students to practice actual applications of concepts learned through lecture and discussion (Walker and Flammang, 1981). In addition, these devices provided automatic feedback to students and were expected to be more effective than traditional classroom methods (Galanter, 1959; Lumsdaine and Glaser, 1960; Stolurow, 1961). Main frame computers were used on a time share basis to provide this instruction. This appeared to be a relatively inexpensive and practical solution to achieving the "teaching machine" goals (Walker and Flammang, 1981:225).

Patrick Suppes of the Institute for Mathematical Studies in the Social Sciences at Stanford University is considered by some to be the father of CAI (Chambers and Sprecher, 1980; Coburn, et. al. 1982). When Suppes began to work with educational applications for computers, his goal was to turn the computer into a personal, individualized tutor for specific courses or subjects. His efforts have been directed specifically toward those segments of the learner population which he felt could most benefit by individualized learning experiences. The target population originally served by Suppes included gifted high school students whose needs could not be met by their own high schools, college students taking courses with low enrollments, physically handicapped students and low-achieving students who needed drill and reinforcement in basic skills (Coburn, et. al. 1982).

The PLATO Computer-Based Education system was developed at the University of Illinois, beginning in the 1960s. It combined the production of independent instructional software with equipment capable of providing sophisticated simulations and elaborate graphic displays. PLATO, which stands for Programmed Logic for Automatic Teaching Operations, has produced more CAI materials in more subject areas than any other single production center (Walker and Flammang, 1981). Research by the Educational Testing Service involving the effectiveness of PLATO materials as compared to traditional classroom approaches indicates a significant positive achievement effect in favor of PLATO (Alderman, 1978; Murphy and Appel, 1977). CAI materials produced by the PLATO Project usually include tests and records of student performance. Some materials are designed to supplement traditional instruction, while others are intended to be self-contained tutorials.

PLATO utilized equipment manufactured by Control Data Corporation. Some CDC terminals are heat sensitive so that students can simply touch the screen to indicate a response, thus eliminating the need for keyboarding skills. Traditional terminals are also available. Educators using PLATO can prepare their own instructional units using COURSEWRITER, a simplified programming language. Current cost of the PLATO system is approximately $2 per student contact hour (Stern and Stern, 1983).

PLATO illustrates the educational-training interface. Although the system was originally developed for "educational purposes," it has been modified to fit the needs of police training (Walker and Flammang, 1981; 1982). Researchers at the Police Training Institute, University of Illinois, developed police training instructional programs (e.g., juvenile procedures, criminal law, report writing) which interfaced with other basic educational programs already part of PLATO (e.g., spelling drills, grammar, math). Students were placed in an interactive, individualized mode under the supervision of an instructor. PLATO has also been used in firearms training, especially for Computer Assisted Target Analysis, at the Police Training Institute (Palumbo and Connor, 1983). In the firearm training program, diagnostic scoring allows an individual to analyze specific elements of his/her performance.

With the advent of microcomputer technology, some PLATO programs have been modified and are available for use on micros. With telecommunications linkage, microcomputers can also interface with the main frame PLATO program. Currently, according to the authors' information, negotiations are being concluded between the University of Illinois and the Turner Broadcasting Company of Atlanta to make PLATO available to cable customers who would have to subscribe for this special service as they would other special cable services. The plan, if implemented, would require a customer to have a small microcomputer; the specific type has not been determined. There are many implications for criminal justice training and education. For example, a police agency thousands of miles away could utilize the programs of the Police Training Institute. Correctional institutions could utilize the basic education courses of PLATO for both staff and offender education. If successful, other main frame programs, perhaps produced by the National Institute of Justice or the National Institute of Corrections could also be accessed.

Although acceptance and use of CAI is rapidly increasing, it must be regarded as an experimental instructional technology which has not reached full potential or standardization. Long-term research studies concerning the use of CAI have not been undertaken. The few short-term studies of CAI which have been completed are narrow in the scope of topics studied and somewhat limited in generalizability due to the populations selected for testing. Existing software is marked by inconsistent quality in design and documentation. Hardware incompatibility often frustrates educational and training institutions when software, selected by the teaching staff, will not run on previously purchased equipment. Nevertheless, because of advances in microcomputer technology, CAI offers great potential for criminal justice training and education. CAI can provide truly individualized instruction which allows the learner to work with the specific information necessary to perform a designated job or task. In addition, it provides an alternative to large group instruction. Since training programs can be tailored to agency requirements, it allows large and small agencies to efficiently train personnel for specific tasks. To understand how CAI can be applied it is necessary to distinguish the three general categories of CAI courseware or software: 1)tutorial; 2)drill and practice; and 3)simulation.

Tutorial Program Courseware

Tutorial programs are designed to provide initial instruction. They are self-contained and can stand alone for instructional purposes. Tutorial CAI courseware is completely self-explanatory once loaded into the computer. It requires no interaction between the learner and human teacher, and it provides the learner with directions, activities, test questions and reinforcement. Material taught through a tutorial CAI is generally presented to the learner in a series of frames each containing text, questions or feedback. The learner is expected to respond to each frame in some way. Incorrect responses cause the computer to provide review and remediation until the learner can respond correctly. When correct responses are entered, the computer continues to present new information. The individualized approach, which permits the learner to move rapidly or slowly through the material, is ideally suited for job training. New employees, entering all phases of criminal justice, possess a wide range of life experiences and knowledge. Some may be able to move through selected aspects of training more rapidly than others. Test questions can measure judgment and knowledge as they relate to the specific work of the agency. The training performance of all employees can be objectively documented and recorded; this is especially useful if the adequacy of training is ever questioned.

Tutorial programs are available through commercial, educational and entertainment software distributors. Software currently available includes topics such as self-taught programming, GRE and SAT review courses, foreign language, mathematics, geography, logic and reasoning, music and graphic design. In a controlled computer lab environment and networking arrangement, one instructor can supervise up to fifty different learning stations. The instructor can monitor and document the performance of each student because this type of program allows individualized, self-paced instruction. Additionally, the wide variety of basic educational software makes this type of CAI affordable both to individuals and agencies.

Drill and Practice Courseware

Drill and practice CAI courseware is designed to supplement human instruction. The format for this type of CAI is the presentation of questions requiring learner responses and appropriate feedback based on the correctness of the responses. Drill and practice courseware is most often used in programs designed to reinforce basic skills. Much maligned by some educators as "electronic worksheets," drill and practice courseware has specific uses in remedial classrooms and with learning disabled students because of motivational factors. Drill and practice courseware is usually preprogrammed to keep a record of the learner's correct and incorrect responses.   If the learner's knowledge about a subject is not sufficient to answer most the questions presented, then a drill and practice program may become "trial and error" which is an inefficient learning procedure.

This type of software is primarily used in educational and vocational classroom instruction. It requires that a teacher present material and closely supervise individual student performance. Simple, relatively inexpensive programs are available to drill a learner on math skills, spelling, vocabulary or any other content area.

Simulation CAI Courseware

Simulation CAI courseware is designed as supplemental material. Its purpose is to follow-up or reinforce human instruction. The learner is provided with an opportunity to apply previously learned problem solving skills to a specific "real-life" situation. In this manner, the components of a total system are examined in interaction, rather than as individual segments. The learner has no control over the elements of the situation, but must make decisions based on his or her training, perception and interpretation. Feedback is preprogrammed to permit the learner to "see" the consequences of decision making. Simulation CAI has the unique advantage of providing "real-life" experience without the expense or danger of a full-scale mock-up.

Simulation courseware has immense potential in criminal justice training. Bomb-squad trainees can test their knowledge of defusing bombs. Correctional officers can practice procedures for controlling prison riots and police officers can practice surveillance techniques. Some police agencies are employing computer simulations in firearms training utilizing light beams, fired from an officer's pistol at a computer controlled target. After firing, the computer is able to analyze the officer's shooting proficiency and provide the officer and training staff with information concerning performance, including the angle and speed of each simulated shot, time between target cue and firing, accuracy of fire, even whether an individual flinches when pulling the trigger. Pursuit driving techniques can be practiced and driver responses analyzed so that even the most naive rookie can gain experience without endangering persons or property. Simulation courseware can be developed for personnel testing and promotions; assessment center situations using video scenes, which require an individual to apply agency policy and procedure in decision making, can be computer generated and subject responses objectively assessed. It should be noted here that the state-of-the-art CAI simulation courseware technology currently available for main frame and microcomputers, was developed to its present high level of sophistication, in part, because of flight training programs developed by NASA and the U.S. Air Force.

Simulation courseware has several different potential applications for offender populations. Currently available public domain software (e.g., Lemonade, Oregon Trail, Graphic Geometry) and commercially available software in a "game" format (e.g., ZORK, Dungeons and Dragons, Starcross, and other adventure type games) teach reading for specific information, reasoning and decision making with consequences. Other simulation software places the user in decision making situations ranging from environmental management, to personal finance, to animal dissection, to managing a small business. Simulation programs can be written to help subjects better understand themselves and their reactions to different situations.

CAI Response Modes

Several response modes are typical of computer assisted instructional programs. The first response mode is usually called "the locked keyboard" because the student is not allowed to type any answer other than the correct one. All the "wrong" answer keys on the keyboard are frozen. This response mode is generally not desirable because it is very tempting for students to touch all the keys until the only unfrozen key is located. Using this technique for answering questions in the locked keyboard response mode, students can answer every questions correctly without even reading the question. The locked keyboard response mode is most often found in drill and practice software.

The second response mode is direct refusal. In this mode, the program informs the student that the answer selected is incorrect by sounding a "beep" or "buzzer." Students respond to this response mode in a variety of ways. Most students simply listen for the sound to indicate whether an answer was correct or incorrect. Other students however, especially remedial and learning disabled students, may interpret the noise as a personal rejection and become emotionally involved in the number of right and wrong answers they accumulate. Some CAI programs allow the student or instructor to temporarily inactivate the audio part of the program. This response mode is found in drill and practice, tutorial and simulation courseware.

The third response mode is called hints and clues because if a student has selected the wrong answer, the program displays on the screen information which should assist in the selection of the correct answer. Sometimes the "hint" is simply a repeat of the previous statement. Other programs may recycle a student through a whole series of frames for review before asking the same question again. Still other programs personalize the "hint" by using the student's name, and suggesting that the student reconsider the response and try again. This response mode is often preferred by students at all levels, especially adults and other students with well developed reading and logic skills. This response mode is most typically found in tutorial and simulation courseware.

The fourth response mode is best called "three strikes, you're out" because the program allows a certain number of attempts to select the correct answer, usually three. After using all of these attempts, the computer displays the correct answer and immediately proceeds to the next question. Students of all ages and ability levels often find this response mode very frustrating because correct answers are never explained. This response mode is often found in drill and practice software. Several points need to be stressed about the potential use of CAI courseware with offender populations. Most simulation courseware, even the "game-adventure" type develops reading, reasoning and self- discipline which most offenders lack. To enter responses, the user must spell words correctly and learn the computer keyboard. All of these functions can generate frustration. Correct responses in a simulation program are not easy to determine and simulated failure (e.g., from getting lost in a maze, to getting "killed," to losing money) will be experienced by the player. Yet, with effort, even the most perplexing situation is capable of solution because they have been conceived and programmed by some person. The structure of computer programming forces the program's author(s) to account for all finite logical possibilities; thus, somewhere in the program are clues which lead to a solution. In addition, many of the simulation programs can be used in either an individual or group learning situation. With only one machine and program (i.e., Lemonade, Starcross) a group of three to five can be involved in the reading and analysis of the information presented on the monitor, and in the decision making necessary to continue the game. Thus, high user interest is combined with interaction with high technology. The potential of these programs for youthful offenders in a group treatment context has not been thoroughly explored.

The design of CAI courseware suggests several unique conditions which may contribute to the effectiveness of CAI as an instructional technique. Some of these unique features are discussed below.

Advantages of CAI as an Instructional Technique

One of the more obvious of the unique features of CAI is the high level of motivation experienced by most learners when working with computers. As detailed later in this chapter, research studies of CAI indicate that learners report a positive attitude toward CAI programs. A second unique feature, is that the nature of learner interaction with CAI courseware requires that the learner assume almost total self-responsibility for his own instruction. This amount of control over the learning situation is vastly different from traditional instructional techniques in which the learner assumes an essentially passive role, absorbing information provided by an instructor. A third unique feature of CAI is the immediate feedback provided the learner concerning correct and incorrect responses. Some CAI programs produce various sounds to indicate correct or incorrect answers; some programs provide visual responses to answers in the form of star bursts or flashing lights. A fourth unique feature is the complete individualization of the learning process. No two individuals will work through a CAI program in exactly the same way. Each student's responses will cause the computer program to respond in a particular fashion.

Research Concerning the Effectiveness of CAI with Adult Learners and Other Offender Populations

Despite the apparent advantages of CAI described above, several factors have contributed to the relatively slow rate of implementation. Chief among these factors is the nature of research concerning the effectiveness of CAI as an instructional technique in comparison to more traditional instructional methods. Existing research is summarized below.

Any discussion of research findings concerning the effectiveness of CAI would be incomplete without a description of the "John Henry Effect," first identified by Campbell in 1980 as a result of her studies of CAI in Mississippi. Campbell's study compared the test results of two similar groups of students who had received instruction on a particular topic. One group received instruction from human instructors; one group received CAI. In observing the human instructors, Campbell noticed that they all seemed to be especially careful to be certain that all students understood the material thoroughly and had plenty of opportunity for questions. Later, the instructors volunteered that they were not going to allow themselves, or their students, to be "beaten" by the computer. While the well known Hawthorn Effect may have influenced the outcome of some studies concerning CAI, it is probable that the John Henry Effect has influenced others.

Although the number of CAI research projects is rapidly increasing, many of these projects use elementary and secondary school students as subjects. Since the discussion of CAI presented in this text is primarily concerned with employees of criminal justice organizations and offender populations, only those research studies using adult learners or offender populations as subjects will be included.

Most instructors, regardless of the subject matter, will readily admit that a student's attitude toward the instructor and the learning situation is an important factor in the effectiveness of the instructional process. In this area, research findings for CAI are consistently positive. Learners who participated in CAI activities report having strong positive attitudes toward CAI (Diamond, 1969; Chandler, 1984; and Kulik, Bangert and Williams, 1983). A study by Rushinek, Rushinek and Stutz (1985) of adult learners indicates that the positive attitude toward CAI spilled over to include a positive attitude toward the class, the instructor and the subject matter. A study of police officers who used CAI to increase their knowledge of the exclusionary rule (Wilkinson and Chattin-McNichols, 1985) reports positive attitudes toward the CAI experience and a willingness to participate in additional CAI activities.

Less uniformity exists for the findings of research studies concerning the effectiveness of CAI in comparison to traditional instructional techniques in terms of long-term retention of material. The Wilkinson and Chattin-McNichols (1985) study of police officers who used CAI to increase their knowledge of the exclusionary rule, indicated that although pre-test scores for all officers were not significantly different, post-test scores for the group receiving CAI were significantly higher than for the group receiving traditional instruction.

The military has used CAI for some time in various training programs. Poblam and Edwards (1983) report that Air Force student pilots who received CAI make significantly fewer errors on actual aircraft systems than student pilots who received non-computerized training. But this finding is not reported by all researchers of CAI projects used in military training. In a review of 30 research projects covering 18 years of CAI use in military training, Orlansky and String (1979) concluded that CAI "saved time, caused greater attrition among instructors, and produced no learning differences." In contrast, a review of 59 CAI projects involving college students indicates significant gains in achievement in comparison to traditional instructional methods (Kulik, Kulik, and Cohen, 1980). An explanation of the differences in findings is offered by Kulik, Bangert and Williams, (1983). They suggest that more positive findings are found in later studies of CAI projects because of technological improvements in the CAI delivery systems and in the software itself.

CAI has been implemented in several offender education programs. Siegel and Simutis (1979) report that in Menard Prison in Illinois a higher percentage of inmates who reviewed using CAI passed the GED than inmates who did not use CAI materials to review. Dowling (1982) reports that the use of CAI increased reading levels for adjudicated delinquents at the Neeles School in California. Residents of the Adult Detention Center in Bexar County, Texas, used CAI to study reading and math; Diew and Fairweather (1980) report that residents made greater gains in math than reading.

Findings of the research studies cited above can be summarized as follows. First, CAI appears to have a positive effect on student attitude toward the course of study, the instructor and computers in general. Second, CAI seems to be at the least, as effective as traditional instructional techniques in terms of long-term retention of information.

Problems Associated
with Implementation of CAI

Agencies and institutions planning CAI programs for employee training or for offender education need to consider several potential problems inherent in the implementation and support of such programs. A brief discussion of some of these problems follows.

The high cost of hardware and software is a major problem for many agencies and institutions as they plan to implement CAI for employee training or for offender educational programs. Some limited Federal Grants have been available in the past to assist in the purchase of equipment. Some agencies have been the recipients of donations of used equipment from local businesses which are in the process of upgrading equipment. Although the cost of many computer systems is declining, cost of implementation will continue to remain a problem.

Allocating appropriate space to house the equipment and to provide the necessary electrical connections may prove to be a problem for some agencies, particularly if construction or remodeling must occur.

Locating appropriate software for use in educational settings is a continuing problem for educators. Public domain software is available, but locating a source is often the most difficult part of obtaining a copy. Commercially prepared courseware, or software, is available from numerous suppliers. However, courseware must be carefully evaluated prior to purchase to determine if it meets the needs of the particular group of students. The task of screening software before purchase is time consuming.

Appropriate storage for software must be planned ahead. Software is easily damaged by heat, humidity, extreme temperature fluctuation and dust. Storage containers, as well as a place to store the containers, must be available for immediate use as soon as the software has been purchased.

Coordinating the purchase of hardware and software is essential to avoid problems of incompatibility. Generally, in a new situation, it is best to select software first, then obtain compatible hardware. Funding priorities may not make this possible.

Integrating software with current classroom materials is a problem instructors will face even if they have successfully located software appropriate for the course. Few training materials or classroom textbooks have drill and practice software coordinated with each chapter or section of the text. Planning the most feasible way to include CAI will require careful consideration on the part of instructors.

All computers, no matter how well constructed and maintained, have periodic down times. This is particularly true if the computer has multiple users, and even more true, if those users are generally unfamiliar with the equipment. Keyboard keys can break; disks drives can become misaligned; circuit boards may require replacement. It is a normal procedure of many large computer labs to keep some equipment in reserve, so that when down time does occur, the computer in need of repair can be set aside, and the reserved equipment put to use. Any agency or institution planning top implement CAI must plan for periodic down times and allocate sufficient funds for repair.

Lack of keyboarding skills may be a problem especially for institutions planning offender education programs. This is one problem that generally solves itself as learners work with the equipment for a period of time. There are specific software programs available for teaching the rudiments of typing. These programs are relatively inexpensive and may be a worthwhile investment in some situations.

Despite the high motivation rating most learners give CAI, some learners initially hesitate to become involved with the equipment. They may believe that the computer is easily broken, or that the computer is smarter than they are, or that they will appear "stupid" as they work through the CAI program. If instructors anticipate these problems, and plan a strategy for assisting these reluctant learners, this problem will remain a minor one. However, to ignore the problem, or expect these learners to adjust on their own, is usually not productive.

Some instructors are reluctant to become involved with new technologies, even though other instructors in the same program are very interested in utilizing computers in their instructional program. An agency planning to implement CAI will achieve more satisfactory results if administrators express their interest in the program and provide time for instructors to learn the equipment and plan classroom implementation strategies. CAI will not be successfully implemented simply because an administrator believes it to be a good idea. Implementation is a grass roots project; administrators must allow those interested instructors to take the lead.

The last problem discussed in this short section is probably the most important. Ensuring security for hardware and software is time consuming and requires detailed planning at all stages of implementation. Any security plan must be constantly evaluated to determine weaknesses. Keys to the computer room will instantly become valuable possessions for employees, many of whom may be keenly interested in the equipment, but have no legitimate reason to use it. Arrangements for cleaning the computer room may have to be adjusted from time to time to avoid a predictable pattern. If telecommunication equipment is purchased, special security problems arise involving use of long distance telephone lines.

Advance planning can eliminate many of these potential problems. Although not all problems can be avoided, and each agency or institution will experience unique problems, most can be managed simply by planning for contingencies.

Evaluating CAI Courseware

One of the key factors in the success of a CAI program is the quality of the courseware. Courseware quality is highly variable, due partly to the large amount of time required to prepare such programs. Approximately 100 man hours of programming time are required to produce one student hour of computer interaction courseware. Numerous other factors, many of them directly related to the educational process, affect the quality of CAI courseware. Instructors selecting commercially prepared courseware can use evaluation criteria suggested by several educational theorists; some of these evaluation criteria are discussed below.

Quality CAI courseware is educationally sound. It makes use of the principles of learning derived from research. One method for evaluating the educational value of CAI courseware is to identify the "learning outcomes" as defined by Gagne (1977) and then assess the courseware regarding how each outcome is achieved. Gagne identified the following learning outcomes, or expected behaviors, that might result from any learning experience.

1. Verbal information

2. Intellectual skills (including: discrimination, concrete concept, defined concept, rule, problem solving)

3. Cognitive strategies

4. Motor skills

5. Attitudes

The first step in evaluating CAI courseware is to identify the learning outcome expected. Only some of the learning outcomes listed above can be expected as a result of learner interaction with CAI courseware (Gagne, Wager, and Rojas, 1981). Outcomes which can be expected include:

1. *Verbal information.* This refers to meaningful knowledge which is recalled and expressed as words, sentences and names. The word "state" or "recall" is most often used in questions of this type. For example, state the First Amendment; recall the steps in booking suspects.

2. *Concrete concepts.* This outcome refers to the learner's ability to identify the properties of a concept. A measure of this kind of learning is that the properties used by the learner for identification must be original with the learner and must not have been used during instruction. Concepts of this sort are identified by marking them in some way, rather than by definition. For example, identify the shape of a square.

3. *Defined concept.* Learners can identify a concept by defining it. For example, the concept "surveillance" can be identified by writing a definition, possibly including examples.

4. *Rule.* The learner demonstrates understanding of a rule by applying it to a "new" situation. For example, the learner applies the rules of evidence to a specific situation.

5. *Problem solving.* Learners presented with unfamiliar situations can apply known rules to correctly resolve the problem stated. These situations are most like "real-life" problems and require the application of known rules to simulated activities.

Once the specific learning outcomes, expected as a result of learner interaction with the content of the CAI courseware, have been identified, the instructional support system used to achieve these ends should be examined. CAI courseware is highly dependent upon the way material is presented and the instructions provided to the learner as the program progresses. The support system provided to the learner within the CAI courseware itself is an essential part of the program and contributes in many ways to the success or failure of the program as an instructional device. This support system, sometimes called instructional events, can be assessed by using nine evaluation criteria (Estes 1978; Klatzky, 1977; Gagne, 1977; Gagne and Briggs, 1979). These nine criteria are listed below.

1. *Gaining attention.* Do the instructions gain the user's attention quickly, or are instructions given in a manner which can be easily missed or ignored by a user?

2. *Informing learner of lesson objectives.* Do instructions clearly state the lesson objectives? Is the user informed of changes in these objectives as the lesson progresses?

3. *Stimulating recall of prior learning.* Do instructions encourage the user to recall information from previous lessons or program segments?

4. *Presenting stimuli with distinctive features.* Are instructions presented with clearly defined video output characteristics? Are instructions distinctive from the text of the courseware, or

is it difficult to tell where instructions end and informative text begins?

5. *Guiding learning.* Do instructions positively guide and enhance learning? Do instructions distract the learner from meeting objectives because of disorganization?

6. *Eliciting performance.* Do the instructions encourage high performance or detract from it? Does the question format encourage random guessing? Is a sufficient amount of time provided to allow for thoughtful responses?

7. *Providing informative feedback.* Do the instructions periodically give the user the necessary feedback to assess performance? Do they encourage active user interaction? Do they encourage passive learning?

8. *Assessing performance.* Do the instructions give sufficient performance information for the learner to assess performance? Does the program provide frequent assessment? Does the program keep the learner guessing concerning the correctness or responses?

9. *Enhancing attention and learning transfer.* Do the instructions continue to maintain the user's attention? Do they encourage the user to consider alternative situations or circumstances where learning principles or material could be applied? Does the program encourage application of the information to situations separate from the CAI program?

In most instances, each of the nine events of instruction are necessary to properly guide a learner through a CAI software program. One characteristic of quality CAI instructional courseware is that each display frame, or set of frames, contains text or diagrams to reflect all nine events of instruction. Occasionally, events of instruction are purposely omitted to avoid unnecessary repetition. However, the reasons for this omission should be obvious to evaluators. One mark of quality CAI courseware is the number of different instructional events which are included in the total program. Different types of CAI apply some, but not all, events of instruction.

Tutorial CAI almost always includes at least two events of instruction: (1) eliciting performance through questions, and (2) feedback. It may or may not include specific frames to gain the learner's attention, state objectives or assess performance. Tutorial CAI seldom includes the stimulation of prior learning except between frames within the program itself or learning transfer to situations separate from the program. As a result, tutorial CAI is not the best method of ensuring mastery of new material. Nevertheless, it is often effective in introducing new material and as remediation for individual learners. Drill and practice CAI usually includes only two events of instruction which elicit performance through questions and feedback. Other events of instruction may or may not be included. This is not considered a significant drawback in drill and practice courseware since it is intended to supplement traditional instruction rather than present new material. Simulation CAI tends to include more events of instruction. An objective is usually stated, followed by new information, questions and feedback which often includes the presentation of a new stimulus related to the learner's response to the initial situation. Learning transfer is emphasized, and the learner can assess performance throughout the program.

CAI Telecommunications Links

Telecommunication technology makes microcomputer linkage with main frame CAI courseware a realistic alternative. The following examples illustrate this point.

The concept of the "electronic university" has expanded the limitations of some classroom and school campuses. Pioneered by Robert Gordon and marketed as Telelearning System, Inc., of San Francisco, the electronic university uses an inexpensive modem, communication software and credit for long-distance calls. Essentially a variation of correspondence courses, students purchase textbooks and follow a course outline, but have direct contact with professors at distant universities via microcomputer (Hopper and Mandell, 1987). Course fees range from $185 to $400. Students have access twenty-four hours a day to transfer lectures, assignments, questions, answers and exams.

The National Education Corporation of Newport Beach, California, has recently announced that independent-study courses will be available on its new EdNET system to individuals who own IBM, Apple, Radio Shack, Commodore and Timex/Sinclair personal computers (Wierzbicki, 1984). Approximately forty home-study courses will be offered, including computer programming, computer literacy, small business management and bookkeeping. Students in the program will interface directly with instructional specialists as well as take tests via their home computer. EdNET will provide a 300-baud modem and the necessary communications software to study, using the computer. The extra expense will be added to the regular student fee and will average $150.

Another recent development in computer learning systems is Dial-A-Drill, developed by Patrick Suppes, president and founder of Computer Curriculum Corporation of Palo Alto, California. Operating over regular phone lines, Dial-A-Drill allows students to listen to a talking computer and ask drill and practice questions. Students answer by using standard touch-tone telephone keys. Dial-A-Drill currently offers supplemental work designed to increase basic skills in mental arithmetic, spelling and reading. The computer's synthesized speech offers verbal reinforcement for correct responses, and encouragement and explanations for incorrect responses. Each session lasts six to ten minutes. The computer provides parents with a monthly report of student progress. A demonstration of Dial-A-Drill can be heard by dialing (415) 856-3631 (Mace, 1983). The Dial-A-Drill concept has been implemented by school systems in various parts of the United States and Canada.

Computer Assisted Diagnosis
of Learning Disabilities

One of the newest developments in the area of computers and education is the development of expert systems to diagnose learning disabilities. Based on a series of "if-then" programming statements, expert systems combine information supplied by the user with information concerning various characteristics of learning disabilities stored in the computer. Diagnostic expert systems usually have a question and answer format, with provisions in the program for "incomplete" or "unknown" responses to questions. The diagnosis offered will normally be qualified with a "certainty factor" expressed in terms of a percent. For example, the diagnosis offered by the computer for the subject under consideration would be qualified with a statement that the correctness of the diagnosis had a probability factor of 90%. Diagnostic expert systems presently in use are designed to require confirmation of the computer derived diagnosis by a human expert (Hofmeister and Lubke, 1986). Similar expert systems have been developed to assist in the diagnosis of psychiatric disorders (Griest, et. al, 1984) and medical problems (Averill, 1985).

Expert systems for the diagnosis of learning disabilities have a great deal of potential in the area of offender education. Any educational program operating within an institution has a responsibility to identify those offenders whose progress in the program may be hindered by previously existing learning disabilities. Learning disabled students are frequently misclassified; a major problem is overclassification (Hofmeister and Lubke, 1986). Expert systems can provide a readily available second opinion allowing educational specialists who make such diagnoses to check their reasoning against decision guidelines programmed into the computer. Undoubtedly, the use of such expert systems will become routine in the future.

SUMMARY AND CONCLUSIONS

Computer Assisted Instruction (CAI) is a technology which is rapidly changing American education. It is also one which offers great potential for criminal justice agencies in both meeting their responsibilities to train employees and in providing educational services for offender populations. This chapter has provided a general understanding of CAI technology, its potential and limitations. Like other facets of microcomputer technology the potential impact of CAI on criminal justice has not been realized. Tremendous opportunities for research and human creativity exist for persons who can master CAI technology and apply it to the critical problems facing American criminal justice.

REVIEW AND DISCUSSION QUESTIONS

1. Define CAI and discuss the development of CAI in relationship to education and training.

2. Differentiate between education and training in criminal justice. Explain what is meant by the term education-training continuum.

3. Discuss the current and potential applications of CAI to criminal justice training and education.

4. Explain the potential applications of CAI in offender treatment and rehabilitation.

5. Discuss the results of research concerning CAI.

6. List and discuss the advantages and disadvantages of CAI as applied to criminal justice training and education.

7. Discuss criteria for evaluating CAI courseware.

8. Define diagnostic expert systems and explain their potential application in offender education programs.

Chapter 5

COMPUTER ASSISTED MONITORING
OF OFFENDERS

CHAPTER PREVIEW

One of the newest areas of microcomputer applications in criminal justice is that of computer assisted or aided monitoring of offenders. The *Computer Assisted Monitoring of Offenders*, or CAMO, as it is referred to in this text, is an issue of much controversy, both in the real world of criminal justice practice and in the cognate world of academia (see, e.g., Berry, 1985; Bolin and Hartke, 1985; Ford and Schmidt, 1985; Ball and Lilly, 1986; Gable, 1986; Flynn, 1986; Schmidt, 1986; Petersilia, 1986; Byrne, 1986; del Carmen and Vaughn, 1986; Erwin, 1986). Debated under the headings of "electronic monitoring" and the "electronic jail," CAMO appears to have a growing acceptance among some justice practitioners and judges, although others condemn it as the first step toward an Orwellian "1984 Big Brother" society.

STUDY QUESTIONS

The following study questions may be used as a guide to reading Chapter 5. Key terms and concepts related to these questions are printed in italics throughout the chapter.

1. What is CAMO?

2. What are the various types of CAMO? What technological developments are used in each type?

3. What legal and social issues are associated with CAMO?

BACKGROUND TO COMPUTER ASSISTED MONITORING OF OFFENDERS

CAMO and the debates related to its use are not new in the United States. In the early 1960s a portable radio monitoring device with very limited capabilities was tested on parolees, mental patients and research volunteers (Gable, 1986). Also in the 1960s medical science began experimenting with the use of small transmitter implants to monitor blood pressure, temperature and other biological data. Research in the use of telemetric monitoring and stimulation of brain activity was also conducted on animals. By the early 1970s advocates of telemetric monitoring, such as Delgardo of the Yale School of Medicine, argued that the combination of telemetric monitoring and behavior modification could be used to control, as well as monitor, human behavior (see, e.g., Schwitzgebel, et. al., 1964; Schwitzgebel, 1967; Schwitzgebel, 1969; Rorvik, 1974; Ingraham and Smith, 1974). Others argued that "telemetric monitoring," a term which preceded CAMO, could replace prisons. Prototype telemetric projects were submitted to LEAA for funding in the early 1970s. One project would have required parolees to wear transponders as a condition of parole. Monitoring facilities in police stations could monitor parolees in terms of identity, location and body functioning. Condemned as being an invasion of privacy and concern for potential abuse caused the project to be rejected, but the basic idea of computer assisted monitoring has persisted. Experimentation on human prisoners under any form of "behavior modification" label was banned by the mid-1970s. Many believed that the idea had met its demise with the rise of the Justice Model and the emphasis on protection of offender rights. Nevertheless, some argued that the technology would be used extensively by the 1990s (Archambeault and Archambeault, 1982: 152-154).

Two unique concepts differentiate CAMO from other correctional approaches. First, is the notion that a computer, through some form of sensory input and with minimum human intervention, can systematically assimilate, store, analyze and retrieve information about individual offenders. Second, is the notion that the computer assisted monitoring system has the ability to directly or indirectly influence or control the behavior of the offender. CAMO, as it has generally been applied in the 1980s, has been restricted in scope to information gathering about selected aspects of the offender's life and behavior and indirect control of the offender's location. Emerging and existing technology offers many other potential applications.

As we move into the 1990s and into the twenty-first century, to what extent will American Criminal Justice apply this emerging technology? This chapter will explore the rapidly developing technology related to computer assisted monitoring of offenders. This chapter is divided into two parts. The first presents a typology of CAMO applications. The second analyzes some of the criminal justice issues and debates associated with this emerging technology.

TYPOLOGY OF COMPUTER ASSISTED MONITORING OF OFFENDERS: CURRENT CLASSIFICATION SYSTEMS

Current classification systems of computer assisted monitoring devices usually apply a simplistic two category system based on whether or not the devices work with a telephone or employ radio signals. These are divided into "continuous signaling" and "programmed-contact" systems, also called "passive" monitors. The continuous signal monitoring system consists of a transmitter unit worn by the offender, a home receiver unit which relays transmissions to a central office computer, housed in some criminal justice agency. If the offender physically goes beyond the range of the receiver, the signal is broken and the event is reported. Applying a different technology, a programmed-contact or passive system is based on a central computer which calls an offender's location. When the call is received, the offender, who wears some sort of device, must attach the device to a sensing unit which verifies to the calling computer that the offender is in the assigned location. Most of these devices employ a telephone link, although some use radio wave technology. One such system which uses radio frequencies to transmit information allows a supervising probation or corrections officer to patrol in a car or on foot and check on the location of an offender who is wearing a radio transponder.

The problem with this two category typology is that it is static and does not provide for the conceptualization of future developments. Neither does it allow a clear understanding for the degree of control which is being exerted on the offender. To address these problems, another more dynamic typology of computer assisted monitoring devices is employed in this chapter.

The CAMO Typology

CAMO may be conceptualized as seven types of computer based information gathering and behavior altering applications which exist along a continuum. Arranged incrementally, each of the seven classes provides criminal justice decision makers with increasing amounts of information about the offender and increasing levels of influence or control over the offender's actions.

CAMO TYPE 1:
COMPUTER ASSISTED DIAGNOSIS AND INSTRUCTION SYSTEMS

The first type of CAMO is one partially discussed in the previous chapter and elsewhere under the headings of "computer aided diagnosis" and "computer assisted instruction" of offenders (see Waldron, Archambeault, et. al, 1987; Archambeault, 1984). It may not, at first, be clear why these approaches should be regarded as classes of computer assisted monitoring. However, both approaches meet the CAMO definition; namely, computers used to assimilate information on offenders and influence offender behavior.

Standardized personality assessment tests, such as the MMPI, and personal information instruments, such as social histories, have been adapted to allow subject-computer interaction. Diagnostic and social history information collected in this manner often has greater accuracy than interviewing and testing techniques conducted by human evaluators. Computer assisted instruction (CAI) is gaining acceptance as a means of addressing the divergent educational backgrounds (Alessi, et. al, 1982; Chambers and Sprecher, 1980) and problems of various offender populations. The advent of a nationally validated curriculum designed to be delivered via CAI has provided correctional institutions with an educational program ideally suited to the individualized nature of offender educational programs. Another advantage offered by many of these pre-written curriculum programs is that they can be corre-

lated to various state educational minimum standards and state adopted textbooks, thereby enabling correctional institutions to meet state educational
standards (see Archambeault, 1987: 87-96; 1984).

Of all the CAMO applications, computer diagnosis and computer assisted instruction are the least controversial. There are many reasons for
this. First, CAI is frequently found in classrooms around the United States,
and the public perception of CAI is generally positive. Second, both CAI and
diagnostic testing are performed by qualified personnel and the information
collected is viewed by only a small group of professionals who use this information in programs which directly benefit the offender. None of this information becomes public. Yet, it is information which can be used to monitor
both the offender's progress and to influence the offender's behavior.

CAMO TYPE 2:
COMPUTERIZED OFFENDER TRANSACTION DATA BASES

The second type of CAMO has also been discussed. While more controversial than CAMO TYPE 1, computerized offender transaction data
bases are less objectionable than some other CAMO types discussed below.

Criminal justice agencies and institutions are part of an information dependent society. Over the past decade computers have dramatically altered
the normal process of justice agency information collection, storage and retrieval. Emerging computer technology will further change the normal operation of justice agencies (see, Archambeault, 1987: 99-112). The massive
amount of information which must be kept on offenders as they pass through
the criminal justice system makes dependency on computer technology a necessity. As the offender moves through the system from arrest to hearing or
trial and then to incarceration or community control, volumes of facts must
be collected, stored and retrieved for decision-making purposes ranging from
what charge to bring to what date to schedule the offender for post-institu-
tional release.

In the next decade the use of artificial intelligence will become increasingly common in criminal data base management. When combined with fifth
generation computer languages, or native language inquiry, this technology
will permit a much greater range of justice personnel to have easier access to
information about offenders. Artificial intelligence will also allow the integration of multiple data bases which are currently unable to share information. Thus, over the next decade it will become possible to more accurately
and completely track offenders over multiple jurisdictions and integrate information about individual offenders from multiple data bases, thereby im-

proving the monitoring of the individual offender's formal history of contacts with criminal justice agencies.

As this trend continues the issues of computer security and access will become increasingly more critical (see, Conser and Carsone, 1987: 1-14). In addition, the issues of confidentiality will become more important.

Picture 5-1 shows an example of CAMO TYPE 2. The satellite terminal in the picture is at Patuxent Institution, Jessup, Maryland. It is connected to an IBM main frame housed at the Division of Data Services, Maryland State Department of Corrections. It provides access to the Offender Based State Corrections Information System (OBSCIS) which contains a large variety of different types of data related to inmates of state correctional officials. It also provides access to statistical software for research purposes. Photo courtesy of Director of Research, Patuxent. Photography by Tommy Foster.

CAMO TYPE 3:
FIXED LOCATION DETECTOR DEVICES

Commercially marketed *fixed location detector devices* were first used in association with home confinement in 1984 and tend to be the most widely used today (see, Schmidt, 1986). The first to gain notoriety was the "Gosslink," which is currently marketed under the name "BI Home Escort

System." It should be noted that home confinement existed before the use of computer monitoring and continues to be used separately even today. However, these two concepts are becoming increasingly associated with each other and computer monitoring is often assumed to be part of home confinement in much of the recent literature.

CAMO TYPE 3 devices employ a variety of specific techniques. Most involve the wearing of an ankle or wrist telemetric device which sends out a positive or continuous signal similar to the signal transmitted by a wireless portable phone. The signal is received by a unit which is usually secured in the home or other fixed location, and is connected to the telephone through which it is able to communicate with a central monitoring computer. In simple terms, when the offender leaves the positive transmission range, usually from 50 to 200 feet depending on equipment and setting, the receiving unit, which contains a programmed chip, dials the main monitoring computer and reports the time and date that the subject left the monitored range. When the offender returns to the monitored range the same process is repeated (Schmidt, 1986). Other systems employ radio wave transmitters which relay signals to a central computer without using a phone line. Another approach involves a system in which a computer calls an offender's home and then requires the offender to place the wrist band in a verifier box. Some systems even include a voice recognizer which matches the offender's voice pattern with one stored on the computer (Schmidt, 1986).

Specifically, TYPE 3 monitors employ one of several types of computerized telecommunication technologies:

1. *Continuous Signaling Devices* use miniaturized transmitters strapped to the offender, which broadcast an encoded signal at regular intervals over a designated range. A receiver-dialer is located in the offender's home or place of work that detects signals from the transmitter and reports to a central computer any interruption in the signal. Most of the units can be programmed to make periodic checks on the offender's location. The receiver-dialer calls a central computer and makes preprogrammed reports on the offender's location and alerts officials to unauthorized absences. Among the devices currently available which fall into this category are those manufactured by the following:

    BI Home Escort, BI Incorporated of Boulder, Colorado
    Supervisor, CONTRAC, Controlled Activities Corp.,
        Tavernier, Florida
    Home Detention Network, Innovative Security Systems,

West Palm Beach, Florida
In-House Arrest System, Correctional Services, Inc., West
   Palm Beach, Florida
ASC IIb, Advanced Signal Concepts, Clewiston, Florida
Prison Monitoring System, Controlec, Inc., Niles, Illinois

2.   *Central Computer Programmed Contact Devices* involve the
random calling by a central computer to an offender's location
and require the offender to follow some form of procedure to
identify himself. A wide range of products is presently available.

One product involves the wearing of a wristband identifier by
the offender. A central computer dials the offender's location.
A verifier box is at the monitored location. The offender
places his wrist band in the verifier box. In this manner, the
offender verifies his presence at the designated location. The
manufacturer of this product, called "On Guard System," is
Digital Products Corporation, Ft. Lauderdale, Florida.

Another product simply requires the offender to answer the
telephone and an identification is made through voice patterns
stored in the computer memory.   This device is called
"Provotron" and is marketed by VoxTron Systems, Inc., of New
Braunfels, Texas.

Still another product requires the offender to wear a special
wristwatch which contains a unique identification number that
changes as the time changes on the watch. The number is entered into a touch-tone telephone in response to a computer
generated call.

Reminiscent of Orwell's *1984* technology, the "Crypto Tele-
monitor System" of Western Comsec, Lafayette, California,
uses a video/audio camera placed in the offender's location to
identify the subject. When the central computer calls, the offender must stand in front of the camera and identify himself.
A visual image and voice pattern of the offender is stored in
the computer and compared to the image on the screen. This
system may also be used to monitor the offender's activities
without the offender's knowledge.

The Luma "Telecom" is another device which uses a simple snapshot camera. The system looks like a modern desk top phone, with a small video screen and an indented opening on one side. This opening contains a mini camera which takes a picture of the person at the telephone. This photograph is sent across the phone line to an optical video printer. This permits a positive identification to be made. A central computer calls the offender at random intervals and stores the image of the offender as it is received by the system.

Finally, the common pager has been employed to monitor offenders. A product called "Protective Sentry Pager Program," manufactured by Gray and Henry, Inc., Miami, Florida, requires the offender to carry a digital read-out pager which displays the number to be called to verify the presence of the offender. It is claimed that this system includes voice identification, location identification, and does not require the offender to have a telephone at the location, only access to one.

3. *Cellular Telephone Devices* are similar to "continuous signaling" devices but use cellular telephone technology. One product, the "SCAN System" of Life Science Research Group, Thousand Oaks, California, requires the offender to wear a small transmitter, called a "link," and uses a locator unit at the offender's designated location. The system uses a network of 15 to 20 people monitored by a supervisor. It combines group community control concepts in reinforcing acceptable behavior in members of the network. The system allows the establishment of a remote management center which can coordinate and monitor several different networks.

Fixed location monitors can be networked in tandem. For example, a TYPE 3 monitor receiver may be installed in an offender's home and another at the work location. Time logs are generated to record when the offender left home and when the offender arrived at work. The distance and projected travel time can be programmed into some systems. If established norms are violated the computer will record that information for future reference and may automatically notify the supervising agency. At any time, authorized agents can retrieve log data on any offender subject to CAMO monitoring.

Essentially all that is being reported by CAMO TYPE 3 monitoring systems is a log of the offender's fixed location relative to some time framework.

CAMO TYPE 4:
MOBILE LOCATION DETECTORS

Mobile Location Detectors are extensions of TYPE 3 technology in that the reported information includes identification of offender and location. However, the equipment involved is more sophisticated, ranging from signals sent via cellular or radio phone to signals transmitted via communication satellites. While specific technologies vary from product to product, the offender's location is constantly monitored. With some systems the offender's route of travel or movement can be mapped in addition to location and time.

One product which illustrates this type is the "Cost Effective Monitoring System" of Dr. Walter McMahon, Urbana, Illinois. This system requires the offender to wear a transmitter device which sends out radio waves. Supervising correctional personnel have a portable receiver in their automobile which is tuned to the specific frequencies of the transmitters. Location is confirmed when the portable receiver is within one block of the offender. The supervising officer has the option of using either a magnetic rooftop antenna or a hand-held directional antenna. Other products using similar technology are currently under development and have not yet entered the market.

CAMO TYPE 5:
MOBILE LOCATION AND BIOPHYSICAL DATA TRANSMISSION

CAMO TYPE 5 systems combine the elements of mobile location transmitters and add information about the offender's body (e.g., heart beat, respiration, blood pressure). This type requires a very high level of biomedical technology comparable to that employed by NASA in monitoring the biological systems of astronauts. Prototype devices which could be adapted to criminal justice monitoring have been developed in the area of bio-medical research. In fact, this was the general type of system envisioned in a 1971 LEAA proposal. However, standards developed in the mid-1970s still apply to criminal justice applications today. Namely, there is a prevailing legal and philosophical presumption that the transmission of biological data is an invasion of an individual's right to privacy. Most of the products in this category and all later types, are currently experimental and under development. However, one product is on the market which illustrates the current direction of product development.

The "Guardian Home Arrest System" of Guardian Home Arrest Technologies, Denver, Colorado, should actually be classified as a "fixed location" monitor with bio-physiological capabilities. The system adds a breath alcohol analyzer to a continuous signaling monitoring system. In addition to location and identification, the breath alcohol content of the offender is transmitted over telephone lines to a central computer.

It is reasonable to expect that other products able to monitor biological functions will enter the market in the next few years. Devices exist in bio-medical monitoring that can measure alcohol and even drug toxicity-based skin surface perspiration. For example, bio-sensor technologies allow external monitoring of respiration, electro-chemical activity, hormone levels among other data. These inputs are converted into electronic signals which can be read by external monitors. (See Lampe, 1987; *Futurist*, 1988; Erlechman, 1984). This technology can easily be adapted for CAMO applications.

CAMO TYPE 6:
EXTERNAL BEHAVIOR ALTERING AND MONITORING SYSTEMS

CAMO TYPE 6 systems have the characteristics of biological monitoring TYPE 5 systems and, in addition, have an external behavior altering capability. Prototypes are not currently available on the market, although key components are presently available. To operate this system some sort of external stimuli must occur to reinforce acceptable behavior or to extinguish unacceptable behavior. The external stimuli could range from the sound of a buzzer or mild electrical shock to the automatic injection of a chemical substance into the blood. On the conservative side, a buzzer or bell could be made to sound any time the offender left the range of home confinement. On the more radical side, biophysical detection of alcohol or drugs in the blood could trigger the injecting of a substance bringing on nausea or other unpleasant physical symptoms. On the extreme side, biophysical detection of accelerated heartbeat or respiration in combination with other symptoms could trigger the injection of a tranquilizing substance into the bloodstream. Engaging in prohibited behavior could result in a low voltage electric shock.

CAMO TYPE 7:
INTRACRANIAL STIMULATION AND CONTROL SYSTEMS

As a logical extension of TYPE 6 technology, the potential exists for brain implants of electrodes. Currently, experimental implant devices are being used to monitor electro-chemical balances in patients suffering from extreme depression, diabetes, heart disease and liver disease. Operating as miniaturized computers, these devices not only monitor and telemetrically transmit data relative to the patient's physical condition, but also regulate blood electro-chemical balances either by artificially stimulating the patient's own body components or by injecting predetermined amounts of appropriate chemicals into the blood.

New electrical techniques are being developed to "eavesdrop" on the brain. These employ integrated circuits on silicon chips that can be implanted in the brain and can transmit signals from nerves and record these. One device, called "PRONG" (Parallel Recording of Neural Groups), monitors brain activity involved in memory and emotions. Such technology could be used not only to monitor "thought" and "emotion," but could be used to direct thinking and influence other aspects of human logic. Other research technologies in brainwave monitoring could also be employed. (See Miller, 1986; Office of Technology Assessment, 1987.)

This same space age medical technology offers the potential for monitoring and controlling offenders. It has the potential to alter or modify offender behavior and attitude without requiring the exercise of human choice. Its use, however, would far exceed the power of the state envisioned by Orwell.

ANALYSIS OF ISSUES

General Issues

Despite rejection of the concept of computer monitoring during the middle 1970s, computer assisted monitoring of offenders is a reality of present twentieth century American criminal justice and will become even more important during the twenty-first century. Two particular aspects of present day criminal justice have kindled the current level of interest in CAMO.

The first aspect is the growing recognition that the United States is an increasingly information-dependent society. This has been accompanied by a growing acceptance of computers as a normal part of every day life. In contrast to the 1970s when only a few people interacted with computers on a daily basis, computers today have become a way of life for millions of people. Computers are used in virtually every facet of routine activities from classroom instruction to personal banking, from word processing to recreation. Computer assisted instruction is an integral part of American education from teaching pre-school children to read, to teaching graduate level astrophysics, to teaching police officers how to make decisions about when to shoot or not. Every major industry, governmental department and justice agency has become dependent on automated data base information systems. TYPES 1 and

2 CAMO applications seem so normal that they are barely noticed, except when the "systems are down."

Computer based telecommunication information systems are used to monitor everything from patient conditions in hospitals, to the location of endangered species of wildlife, to probing the earth's weather and geological characteristics from space.   In the world of the 1980s the fearful image of "Big Brother" envisioned by Orwell in *1984* has largely disappeared.   It only seems logical, therefore, that CAMO TYPE 3 and TYPE 4 applications, or fixed and mobile location detectors, should be used to monitor an offender's location in compliance with legal court orders.

The second aspect of contemporary criminal justice which has encouraged interest in CAMO, is the growing acceptance of the feasibility of computer monitoring of offenders in combination with home confinement as an alternative solution for nonviolent offenders.   The problem of prison overcrowding and the prohibitive cost of prison construction has forced American criminal justice to seek other less expensive alternatives.   Although CAMO TYPES 3 and 4 equipment are overpriced under present market conditions, they offer a realistic alternative which will become increasingly more cost effective in the future as demand increases and technology improves.

In less than one decade computer assisted instruction, computer aided diagnostic evaluation and fixed and mobile location monitoring of offenders have moved from abstract philosophical and theoretical concepts to operational realities.   What impact does the acceptance of CAMO TYPES 1 through 4 have on the acceptance and use of CAMO TYPES 5 through 7?

CAMO TYPE 5 applications transmit bio-medical information about an offender, in addition to verifying identification and location. CAMO TYPE 5 applications may be useful in the supervision of offenders convicted of nonviolent drug use or sex crimes, and other offenders who exhibit a biological or medical component to the pattern of criminality. Advocates might argue that such monitoring would deter illegal activities by making the offender immediately accountable for any change in normal blood chemistry or the normal biophysical profile. Date and time records of changes could be linked with dates and times of alleged illegal acts and used as evidence. Critics, on the other hand, might argue that such monitoring is a violation of the offender's right to privacy, and that such usage could lead to a police state in which all citizens, not just offenders, would be required to submit to such monitoring. Currently, legal and ethical standards support the view that such monitoring is an invasion of privacy, and as a consequence, CAMO TYPE 5 applications exist only in philosophical argument and theoretical planning. Nevertheless, as computer technology continues to become more generally accepted as part of normal living, how much time will pass before these standards also change? Given the present thrust and speed with which CAMO

TYPES 3 and 4 applications are currently being applied, it is within reason to expect that these standards will be modified by the mid-1990s or perhaps even sooner in the case of monitoring drug abusers. The current level of acceptance for mandatory drug testing as a condition of employment may become generalized to CAMO TYPE 5 applications. If this materializes, CAMO TYPE 5 applications may be in use within the next three to five years.

What about CAMO TYPE 6 and 7 applications? The nature of CAMO TYPES 6 and 7 applications attack fundamental assumptions about the role of free will and human choice. Under U.S. criminal law an individual offender cannot by held liable unless free will or "mens rea" has been exercised. One lasting effect of the late 1970s Justice Model may be the recognition that offenders must have the right to choose whether or not to engage in illegal behavior. CAMO TYPES 6 and 7 applications have the potential of altering attitudes and behavior without concern for an offender's freedom of choice. Consequently, it may be the twenty-first century before these applications become acceptable. Even before the more complex issues associated with CAMO TYPES 5 through 7 are resolved, there remain many fundamental questions concerning CAMO TYPES 3 and 4 which must be answered. One set of issues revolves around the question of which jurisdictions should use CAMO? Should CAMO be coordinated by the state at the department of corrections level, or should local correctional agencies and institutions be free to use CAMO as they see fit? Should CAMO be used in jails and prisons to house higher risk offenders under less costly, lower security housing? Or should CAMO applications be limited to probation and parole supervision, halfway houses and community work release programs? Another issue concerns what types of offenders should be eligible for CAMO. For example, should fixed or mobile location detectors be used in lieu of holding subjects in jail to await trial? Should non-violent offenders, such as those arrested for drunk driving, or for illegal use of a controlled substance, be considered? Should CAMO be used with juveniles?

Related to these concerns is the issue of parity in punishment. How does a day in a jail compare with a day in home confinement with electronic monitoring? Addressing this issue, one county judge in Palm Beach County, Florida, uses the following equation in sentencing: 10 days in jail equals 20 days of weekend jail time or 30 days of home confinement. Only future experience will indicate if this is an equitable sentence.

Legal Issues

The single most important guiding factor in the development and deployment of CAMO technology is the issue of legality. The use of CAMO raises a large number of constitutional and legal questions. Some of these have been addressed, but others remain. Below is a sampling of a few of these issues.

The current view of CAMO is that it is not prohibited by Federal law. Under Title III of the 1968 Omnibus Crime and Safe Streets Act, criminal justice officials, including police, corrections officers and probation agents, at both the federal and state levels are prohibited from tapping or intercepting wire communications or using electronic devices to intercept private communications except with a court order or with the consent of one of the parties. The transmission of information about location is not considered "contents" of oral or wire communications, and most CAMO applications seem to meet this criteria. On the other hand, CAMO technologies which transmit picture data, voice data or biophysical information may not meet the approved criteria, particularly if this information is obtained covertly. That is, if the offender has advance warning that his/her actions or conversations are about to be recorded, as is the case when a phone rings or an instrument "beeps" signaling that the offender must identify him/herself, then the offender's response to the signal (e.g., answering the telephone, placing a wrist band in a monitoring box, or walking to a video camera and pushing a button) may constitute consent. The question of legality arises if the monitoring is done without his/her knowledge and tacit consent.

Another line of legal reasoning holds that a person in a convicted status (e.g., probationer, house arrestee) has been granted leniency by the court and has agreed, as a part of a legal contract, to submit to reasonable monitoring. This agreement constitutes consent. After all, the offender's right to privacy is certainly greater under computer monitored conditions of house arrest than it would be in prison. But does this mean that it is legal to monitor an offender's activities in a bedroom or bathroom without warning? What about the rights of other members of the offender's household?

Still another line of reasoning holds that monitoring does not violate fourth amendment protections against unreasonable search and seizure because in reality it is not "searching" or "seizing." Nor is it a violation of the right against self-incrimination. While location monitoring may not violate fourth or fifth amendment standards, what about video camera monitoring, breath or skin analysis for alcohol or drugs or voice monitoring?

What about the use of CAMO in prisons or jails? What about the use of CAMO with non-convicted prisoners? In general, existing standards would tend to approve the use of CAMO under those conditions as long as the monitoring was for purposes of achieving legitimate objectives of a custody institution, namely safety and protection, and provided that the same restrictions applied to all prisoners in custody.

So far, all of the discussions have focused on adults. Can CAMO be used with juveniles? Because of very limited experience in this area, case law is also limited. In general, all prohibitions affecting the use of CAMO would also apply to programs involving juveniles. Programs affecting juveniles must meet the criteria set for the processing of juvenile offenders in given states and must meet federal standards. For example, the use of CAMO with non-adjudicated offenders or status offenders may be viewed as being too restrictive or "criminalizing." On the other hand, the use of CAMO with routine in-community supervision may be beneficial both in teaching young offenders responsibility and consequences of behavior. Experience with CAMO in dealing with juvenile populations is mixed. The Marion County, Indiana, juvenile authorities use CAMO with generally good success. While the experience of the Louisiana Department of Corrections has been mostly a failure because of technical difficulties with equipment. It is reasonable to expect many other new developments in this area over the next few years as the children of the "baby-boomer" generation start to place renewed strains on the juvenile justice system.

Administrative Issues

In addition to legal issues, there are many justice administration matters which surround CAMO. Perhaps the most frequently articulated concern is the "net widening" effect of CAMO. Essentially, this is the concern that judges may impose CAMO related controls on offenders which might otherwise be diverted from the justice system. Critics, with some justification, argue that historically the creation of any new sentencing alternative has resulted in large numbers of individuals over whom the justice system would not have exerted control if the new development had not become an option. Indeed, there is some merit to the concern that CAMO should be used only in situations where individual offenders would have been sentenced to a custody institution, had CAMO not been available. In developing a rationale for cost savings involving the use of CAMO, a number of factors must be considered. Among these are: 1) cost, as measured in human terms, 2) cost, as measured by the loss of tax revenues which occur because those in custody do not work, 3) the additional tax costs incurred through incarceration, 4) cost, as measured in terms of savings in building construction, maintenance and personnel, and 5) cost, in terms of CAMO equipment purchased and maintenance. Each of these will be discussed separately.

A discussion of CAMO costs, in human terms, returns attention to the offender as a human being. CAMO technology offers the potential for the criminal justice system to force an offender to face the consequence of illegal actions while leaving the offender attached to the family unit of which he/she is a part. For a wide variety of offenders, CAMO offers the means of adequate control over the offender and requiring the offender to be accountable for personal actions, while continuing to be part of the community. CAMO has been successfully used with selected cases of DWI and petty theft, offenders serving weekends in jail, pre-trial diversion and even slum landlords, but it cannot be used with violent or dangerous offenders. Limited data suggests that the application of CAMO may strengthen family ties, improve work habits and increase an individual's sense of responsibility. However, data is too limited to conclusively argue that the application of CAMO technology will routinely produce positive results. It can be argued, on the other hand, that an offender's chances of learning how to live with others in society are better under CAMO control than in prison control. CAMO costs, associated with taxes, are certainly less than the costs that are associated with imprisonment. In all community-based programs the offender is required to obtain or continue employment, and as a consequence, the offender contributes to the local and federal tax bases. Additionally, the offender is expected, in most cases, to pay for a portion of CAMO control costs. At the same time, added costs to the community are avoided. Unlike prison or jail confinement, the offender pays for all of his own expenses and does not put a cost burden on the community's welfare resources.

CAMO costs savings to a community, associated with building construction, maintenance and personnel, are measured in terms of the new cells that do not have to be constructed for persons under CAMO control in the community. One rationale for the expanded use of CAMO is as a less expensive sentencing alternative to imprisonment which still offers a degree of control greater than that possible through in-community supervision. Arguments for cost savings are premised on the assumption that "net widening" does not occur; if it does, no savings are realized.

CAMO cost savings, associated with equipment refers to the funding of the program by fees assessed to the person under CAMO control. After a period of time positive revenue generation can result, meaning that funds are collected beyond the initial purchase cost of the equipment. These funds could be used to buy additional equipment or defer other operating costs. Further, as more and more vendors enter the market, competition will drive equipment costs down. Currently, the cost of a central monitoring system and 20 offender monitoring devices ranges from about $25,000 to $100,000.

Another set of cost-related concerns involves the issue of who should pay for the development of CAMO technology. Historically, the federal government has led the way in providing seed money for technology development, but this trend has changed since 1980. Most of the products currently on the market have been developed by private corporations. Research, development and marketing costs have caused end-user costs to escalate. Consequently, most CAMO systems are over priced, given the comparable state of technology in other areas. A related issue is the question "Who should pay for the CAMO services when they are administered to offenders?" Payment cannot be the sole responsibility of the offender under supervision, otherwise only those who were wealthy enough to afford it would be considered. Such a class bias in sentencing alternatives would be unconstitutional (see, Berry, 1986). Sliding scales have been adapted to address this issue. Based on the number of people in the household and the amount of total monthly income, in-house offenders in Kenton County, Kentucky, pay from $2 per day to $7 per day. There is also a provision for complete waiver of the fee if a defendant has no ability to pay. Similar provisions are made by the Baton Rouge City Courts, Baton Rouge, Louisiana, which uses CAMO as an alternative to incarceration for connected 2nd and 3rd time DWI offenders and is planning a similar program involving CAMO and probationers. Evaluation results should be ready by 1990.

How effective is CAMO and what are the effects on offenders? Limited research into the effectiveness of CAMO have produced some interesting findings. Among these are the following (Friel, et. al, 1987: 21-23):

1. Electronic monitoring was perceived by both offenders and supervising officers as being more "punishing" than originally thought. Restrictions on freedom of movement when combined with home incarceration forced offenders to order their lives in ways which they had never previously been required to do. In some instances, electronically confined offenders became more domesticated and learned homemaking and home repair skills.

2. Offenders on home incarceration with electronic monitoring found that their patterns of social relationships were altered. In some instances, friends, who were interested in "good times," grew tired of monitored subjects and stopped visiting. On the other hand, family and true friends continued to visit the confined offender, thus strengthening these bonds. However, in some instances, the confinement also posed additional strains on marital relationships because of the forced confinement. Because of the small number of cases involved, these behavioral effects must continue to be studied before any con-

clusions can be drawn. Preliminary indications are that substantial changes in behavior occur.

3. The monitor became a symbol to offenders with a variety of meanings associated with it. To some of the offenders it was a "crutch," which they used to get out of social situations that they knew might lead to trouble. In many instances, it was used as an excuse to do what the offender knew he/she should do in the first place. Not measured in this study, however, were differences in racial attitudes toward monitoring. There is some indication that monitoring among some groups of blacks is perceived as a throw back to days of slavery and chains. How prevalent this attitude is remains to be investigated by future research.

Obtaining Information on CAMO

Obtaining information on CAMO is difficult because of the diversity of products and projects which have been undertaken throughout the United States and the lack of a centralized clearinghouse for information. This has been worsened because the vast majority of programs in existence today have no evaluation design and, hence, no evaluation data. For several years, Ann Schmit, NIJ, functioned as the primary source of information on projects and products, but NIJ has reallocated her time to other projects. There is, however, a new publication called *Offender Monitoring* which has recently appeared and claims to be a clearinghouse for information. This publication can be obtained by writing to P.O. Box 88, Maxatawny, PA 19538. Finally, in 1988, the U.S. Parole Commission initiated a CAMO project with parolees involving an eighteen month follow-up. Results should be available in late 1989 or early 1990.

SUMMARY AND CONCLUSIONS

American criminal justice is responding to intensifying pressures from an information dependent society by adapting computer technology to various facets of justice operations. Recent trends indicate that some forms of CAMO have already become integral components of criminal justice, particularly CAI, computerized offender data base management, and fixed location monitors. Other forms of CAMO may play important roles in twenty-first century justice. The extent of application of various CAMO TYPES by American criminal justice remains to be seen.

Dramatic changes will occur during the 1990s. In less than one decade computer applications and limitations, as they exist today, will be radically altered with the wide-spread use of artificial intelligence. When combined with other emerging technologies, such as voice synthesizer and voice recognizer capabilities, CAMO of the mid-1990s may be able to verbally communicate with offenders under supervision. CAMO systems may be able to answer offender questions concerning acceptable and unacceptable actions.

As further miniaturization of computer technology occurs, CAMO devices will become increasingly smaller and less noticeable. Wrist and ankle bands of today weigh only ounces, compared to the early prototypes of the 1960s which weighed over two pounds. Along with miniaturization comes increased capabilities. It may become cost-effective to monitor body functions and blood chemistry with external devices which never invade the body.

By the mid-1990s, prototype CAMO community jails or prisons may be in full operation. A staff of community control officers may be able to adequately supervise and control prison size offender populations at a fraction of present cost and with a great deal more humanity. On the other hand, the same technology may produce an Orwellian nightmare which exceeds the worst fears of *1984*. Only time will tell. In any case, CAMO is here to stay.

Do we really want to take the person centered

REVIEW QUESTIONS AND ACTIVITIES *approach*

out of questioning
a computer
1. What is CAMO? What are the key issues surrounding its present and future use in criminal justice? *Can't read emotions*

2. Explain and give illustrations of each of the seven types of CAMO devices discussed in this chapter. Which types are currently being used and which are purely experimental?

3. Contact local and state corrections agencies to see if they are using some form of CAMO. Find out what types of products are currently being used or are in the planning stages. What experiences have these agencies had with CAMO?

4. Explain the major legal and social issues related to CAMO use.

Chapter 6

EMERGING JUSTICE ISSUES IN
COMPUTER TECHNOLOGY

CHAPTER PREVIEW

This text has presented a brief overview of the use and growth of computers in criminal justice organizational management. Chapter 1 introduced the history, the basic concepts of "computerese" and an overview of the use of computers. Chapter 2 centered on computerized mainframe and microcomputer data based management applications used to meet the information requirements needed for planning, budgeting, fiscal control and other purposes. Chapter 3 discussed the applications of computers in communications with particular emphasis on computer assisted writing (CAW) and information networking. Chapter 4 discussed the applications of computer assisted instruction (CAI) in criminal justice education and training. Chapter 5 presented a discussion of computer assisted monitoring of offenders (CAMO) and related issues. In presenting these topics every effort was made to cite current and still evolving examples of computer technology. Yet, computer technology itself is changing at such a rapid rate that by the time this book is in print some of its content will be obsolete. All these subjects should be regarded as potential areas for both field application and future research.

Chapter 6 is both a conclusion and a beginning. It concludes the text by reviewing key points presented in the previous chapters. It is a beginning in that it introduces several new criminal justice issues involving computer technology which have not been mentioned in the earlier chapters. It identifies areas of theoretical, administrative and research import to criminal justice. Among the issues presented are labor-management concerns associated with the computer use, lack of theory and research information about computer related crime, questions of law enforcement competency to investigate computer crime, computer law related issues and potential computer-robotic applications. Suggestions for future research are also made. More questions than answers are intentionally presented.

STUDY QUESTIONS

The following study questions may be used as a guide to reading Chapter 6. Key terms and concepts related to these questions are printed in italics throughout the chapter.

1. What is the socio-economic impact of the computer revolution?

2. What will be the impact of this computer revolution on criminal justice administration and management?

3. What is the impact of computer related crime?

4. What are the phenomenological, epidemiological, and etiological issues involved in computer crime?

SOCIO-ECONOMIC IMPACT
OF THE COMPUTER REVOLUTION

In the 1950s emerging computer technology began to slowly transform the United States from an industrial to an information based society and economy. This process of change intensified in the 1960s and became a socio-economic revolution by the 1970s with the introduction of microcomputers and telecommunications. By the 1980s both society and the economy had become *information dependent* and were in the throes of a computer generated, information revolution whose theoretical parameters, according to the futurist rationale, made the critical Marxist critique obsolete. Futurists (e.g., Naisbitt, Dervin, Smith, Molitor) asserted that power within society had shifted from "those who control industrial production," as argued by Marx, to "those who control information and its flow" (refer to previous discussion on pages 87-95), and a new theory of socio-economic politics was needed.

Not all agree, however. Perrolle (1987, 69), arguing from a critical sociological perspective, maintains that the computer is "a tool both for making new forms of property and for exercising power which will challenge democratic institutions." Conflicting demands will be placed on the law to protect information as both property and privacy." New forms of social control will be used by law enforcement, government and the military, as well as by business. According to this scenario "The transformation of industrial time and space will shift attention from the social conditions of work to the physiological and psychological conditions of the human/computer interface." The work place as we know it today will be transformed into "workspace." Society will experience a declining middle class because most of the new jobs created will be in the service area. There will also be a growing distinction between "knowledge elite" and "information workers, and the growth of an impoverished under class" without the technical skills to compete in an information society. In this context, the Marxist critique explains that the transformation of society from an industrial base to an information base is but a continuation of the transformation from an agricultural to an industrial base. The same capitalistic forces which create inequality within an industrial society will continue to do so in an information society. In short, "Those groups who own and control information will be able to define the nature of social reality and will influence social norms and values" (Perrolle, 1987: 233). This may be the real meaning of information as power.

Regardless of the assumed validity of the Marxist perspective, the inescapable reality is that information as a commodity has begun to replace industrial production as the controlling factor in the world and national economy (Smith, 1983: 27-29). Power in American society is shifting from those who control industrial production to those who control information and its flow (Molitor, 1981: 24). The significance of this shift is illustrated by an economic battle currently being waged between IBM and ITT in the courts for control of the telecommunications market, a market which experts describe as being comparatively small in the 1980s, but which will be a major source of international economic power by the year 2000. The expected result from this information revolution is a restructuring of American society which will be as significant as the earlier shift from an agricultural to an industrial society (Naisbitt, 1982:18).

Computerized information technology in combination with changes in worker attitudes, educational level and personal job expectations is dramatically changing American management practices and approaches. *Information acquisition*, a key factor to the survivability of any business and industry today, requires the exercise, by those involved, of a high level of autonomy of action and decision making which has the consequence of eroding established patterns of bureaucratic communications and control. New, more flexible organizational management structures and approaches are being forced on the American business and industrial organization (Ouchi, 1982; Athos and Pascale, 1981). In addition, the same computerized information technology is causing computer-related stress and physical ailments among workers (e.g., eye strain, potential radiation hazard, tension) which are becoming increasingly important labor-management negotiating issues. Computers allow management to more closely monitor individual worker performance and productivity rates. With this increased control over workers, management must learn to apply "high touch" as well as high technology. Without a balance between "high touch" and "high tech" management will be cast into an Orwellian "Big Brother" role which could produce unnecessary and unhealthy worker stress and negative management- labor relations.

Computerization and information dependency contribute to the paradox that when people are presented with more information and more ability to analyze that information than ever before in mankind's history, those same people are more distant from direct physical contact with the sources of information and from each other. It is difficult for the analyst working with data involving millions of people, or the social welfare worker processing hundreds of applications for assistance or corrections policy researcher investigating thousands of offender case records, to relate to one case or one human being. Individuality and humanity are lost in categorical classifications. Yet, ironically the adroitness of society to anticipate future trends and changes and the ability to adapt to change may be enhanced. This contradiction may tend to destabilize social institutions and economic structures. This contradiction may lead to new forms of social resistance to the established political order as well.

Implications of these changes for American criminal justice administration and management are described next.

IMPACT ON CRIMINAL JUSTICE ADMINISTRATION AND MANAGEMENT

Computer technology has substantially changed criminal justice management in regard to information processing. There are many examples of this change. In the St. Louis Police Department, a 53% reduction in time spent by investigators in writing and typing reports with a net effective 14% increase in available time for each of the 72 investigators occurred through computer assisted writing (CAW) systems (Boehm, 1983: 128). In San Diego, computerized criminal investigative information systems (i.e., SHER-LOC) have resulted in over 3,000 arrests and case cancellations and have assisted in 3,700 investigations since 1978 (Timm, 1983:124). Administrative costs in St. Louis were reduced by $50,000 through the effective application of computer technology (Jauer, 1983:126). In St. Petersburg, all emergency dispatching is computerized (*Law and Order*, 1981). In Chicago, computers coordinate field command communications (Rodriguez, 1982). In Orlando, the Orange County Sheriff's Department uses computers to coordinate inmate court appearances, and to ensure that inmates appear in court on time. In Baton Rouge, drug investigators for the Louisiana State Police employ microcomputers to search out abusers and unethical doctors from among mountains of pharmaceutical prescriptions. At the University of Illinois, *PLATO* and other forms of Computer Assisted Instruction (CAI) are used to more effectively and efficiently train police officers. In Dallas, courts use computers to transmit subpoenas via electronic mail (McClain, 1982). Computers are used to manage inmate data files in most state departments of correction. MMPI and other psychological testing is done by computers with increased efficiency and effectiveness (Waldron, Sutton, and Buss, 1983: 42). On the other hand, critical issues are raised as to whether computers actually save time or whether time, previously spent in handling files manually, is now being spent in computer support activities. (See, Sykes, 1986). In any event, computer technology continues to challenge the American criminal justice system in ways that it has never before been challenged. Some of these challenges are identified below.

Improving computer technology continues to bring increasing pressures to bear on the American criminal justice system and on the organizational structures through which police, courts, corrections and juvenile authorities deliver their services. Like other types of American organizations the criminal justice organization of the 1980-90s is becoming increasingly more information dependent. Rapid collection and dissemination of accurate information can have life and death meanings, especially in police work. Information demands, when combined with changes in criminal justice employee characteristics of the 1970s, are forcing changes in the traditional Weberian-Fayolian bureaucratic management style characteristic of most police, court and corrections agencies and institutions (Archambeault, 1983; Archambeault and Weirman, 1983; Archambeault and Fenwick, 1983). Younger, better educated, racially and sexually diverse employees demand more independence of action, thought and self-actualization. Thus, new models of criminal justice organizational management theories are emerging which integrate information networking and the Z-dimension of management. This Z-dimension is the basis of Z Theory Management and refers to the reality that workers are part of a larger matrix of social, family, economic and cultural concerns. Effective management must address what Ouchi (1982) terms the "holistic concerns of its workers" (Archambeault and Weirman, 1983). Other approaches, such as Quality-Control Circles or techniques from the "In Search of Excellence Movement," and MBWA (management by walking around), are designed to reduce the distance between management and worker and to create a team atmosphere. With the increased use of high technology to solve contemporary organizational information problems, other human-related management problems remain to be resolved. Consider the following.

One new strain on management-employee relationships has come from the widespread use of mainframe and microcomputer video display terminals (VDT), also called cathode ray tubes (CRT). Environmental conditions surrounding the use of VDTs and CRTs are becoming important labor-management negotiating issues. Associated with this new technology are several new sources of worker stress. Although medical evidence remains inconclusive, workers question the safety of radiation emitted from the terminals. They complain that long-term exposure to VDTs and CRTs causes eye strain and irritations, neck and back pains, dizziness, anxiety and other symptoms of job stress. Stress is further accentuated by the degree of management control which is exercised over the CRT and VDT worker. Since most large systems require operators to log on and off, a permanent record is made of every coffee and bathroom break. Production rates among individual workers can be monitored; thus, the VDT operator is accountable in ways that do not apply to other workers. "High Touch" management approaches are needed in criminal justice organizations as they are in other types of organizations.

Indicative of the importance which workers attach to the VDT issue is "Resolution 12 Video Display Terminals" passed by the NAGE/IBPO (National Association of Government Employees/International Brotherhood of Police Officers) National Convention, October 27-30. This resolution [as printed in the THE POLICE CHRONICLE 11 (December 10, 1983): 7] is presented below in its entirety.

RESOLUTION 12

Video Display Terminals

WHEREAS, *An increasingly utilized new technology already en-trenched in hundreds of thousands of offices and plants across the continent is bringing with it a new kind of job health problem; and*

WHEREAS, *The apparent advantages of the system have led to the installation of an estimated five million of the machines in work-places across the nation, changing the daily routine for countless workers; and*

WHEREAS, *Accompanying the good some workers see in the technology has been a countervailing evil. Continuous exposure to the devices has caused noticeable health problems for some. Among the ailments cited by video display terminal or cathode ray tube operators in government studies are:*

1. *Soreness, redness, stinging, itching, irritation and general discomfort of the eyes.*
2. *Pains in the neck and back.*
3. *Loss of visual acuity, dizziness, nausea.*
4. *Problems with eyeglasses and contact lens.*
5. *Mood disturbances, greater anxiety, anger and confusion, now therefore be it*

RESOLVED, *That this NAGE convention express its deep concern about the health problems that are inherent in the operation of VDTs and CRTs; and be it further*

RESOLVED, *That the NAGE and its affiliates take every action to establish and support programs to provide a continuous and on-going study for the monitoring of the video display terminals and for obtaining adequate occupational safety and health protection for personnel operating these machines; and be it further* RESOLVED, *That the NAGE and its affiliates whose members operate this equipment insist on these minimal safeguards in their collective bargaining agreements:*

1. *Regular rest breaks for 15 minutes each hour worked for each person working on VDTs; a maximum of 4 hours per day to be worked on the machines.*

2. *Eye examinations for persons before they first go to work on VDTs and periodically (yearly) thereafter.*
3. *Detached and adjustable keyboards and screens on the machines.*
4. *Room lighting adjusted and controlled, the machines and their operators' positions arranged and other steps taken to minimize glare and associated visual acuity problems.*
5. *Careful attention to operators' chairs, with the height of the seat and backrest adjustable, and they should have armrests, if requested.*
6. *VDTs should be tested for radiation emissions and proper functioning at regular intervals.*
7. *Transfer of pregnant workers, upon their request, to non-VDT working during their period of pregnancy with no loss in pay; and be it finally*

RESOLVED, That the NAGE and its affiliates work strenuously for federal and state legislation embodying this same health protection, since no member should be required to trade wages and fringes in bargaining for a   safe and healthy work environment.

Computer related organizational management issues remain promising areas for future research, particularly as computers continue to impact justice administration and the delivery of police, court, corrections and juvenile justice services. Little systematic evidence exists which focuses on the impact of automation and computerization on organizational structures, norms and policies of criminal justice organizations. For decades "professionalism," with its many and varied meanings, has consistently been associated with an emphasis on efficiency and technological competency in criminal justice management. The 1970s LEAA perspective on criminal justice as a "system" implicitly assumed that reform meant centralization and systemization of information facilities and functions. Computerization was assumed a necessary requirement for supervision, control and administration of police, corrections and court services.

Computerization and automation were embraced as means through which justice organizations could survive in an information dependent society; this is a position frequently stated through out this text. But in the final analysis, what evidence is there to support these conclusions? Several fundamental questions must be addressed. Does computerization actually reduce the workload with criminal justice agencies or does it merely transfer the load from one area to another? For example, in a police organization does automation of report writing actually decrease the amount of work historically associated with preparing reports, filing and storing them, or has the workload shifted to inputting data into the computer? In any criminal justice organization, what is the consequence of automation on the distribution of power and influence on decision making?

Does computerization decrease bureaucracy and increase the flow of information within an organization or does it simply create another layer of bureaucracy surrounding information management? How does computerization impact on personnel? What happens when the justice employee develops a dependency on the computer? For example, police officers who depend on computers in their vehicles sometimes forget how to take complaints from citizens directly and become so frustrated with their computers that they shoot them with their service revolvers. What is the impact on the quality of justice? Does efficiency and productivity necessarily mean a fairer justice system? Does computerization actually save money in the long run or does it increase costs? These are but a few of the unanswered questions which must be addressed in the next decade. In short, there is no historical basis for answering any of these questions because the information society is a late twentieth century phenomenon and man's earlier history gives no clues in assessing the impact of computers on society, and on society's system of administering criminal justice with the assistance of computers.

Beyond management issues, computer technology has generated other problems for criminal justice. One related group of problems concerns the phenomenology, etiology and epidemiology of computer related crime and the ability of law enforcement to detect, investigate and prosecute this category of crime.

COMPUTER RELATED CRIME: OVERVIEW OF ISSUES

No revolution is orderly, even if it is bloodless. It is not surprising, then, to find that the knowledge base about computer related crime is incomplete. There is a lack of theory and research about the phenomena. Epidemiological (demographic) data is limited. Etiological (theory), beyond the scope of white collar crime, is non-existent. Law enforcement capabilities are questionable. Substantive civil and criminal law on computer abuse is only now emerging. Further, in an information society the distinction between criminal and civil law may be less significant. As computer related crime grows the illegal copying of electronic mediums, especially software, and the gaining of access to unauthorized data bases may be treated more as criminal matters than as civil concerns which govern their handling today. These issues are discussed below.

Phenomenological and Epidemiological Issues

In 1962 the U.S. government prosecuted the first computer crime. It involved a programmer who was charged with grand fraud for changing deposits to eliminate overdrafts from his checking account (Sharma, 1985: 28). Since then the proliferation of computers in American businesses, industries, homes and universities, has created a frequent, multi-dimensional crime phenomenon loosely called computer related crime. Consensus on definition, however, is non-existent. Parker (1979) defines *computer crime* as:

> [A]ny illegal act for which knowledge of computer technology is essential for successful prosecution, [which includes] crimes and alleged crimes (which) may involve computers not actively but also passively, when usable evidence of the acts in computer stored form" (as quoted in *Computer Crime: Expert Witness Manual*, 1980:4).

Bequai (1978) defines it as:

> ...use of a computer to perpetuate acts of deceit, concealment and guile that have as their objective the obtaining of property, money, services and political and business advantages, including threats of force directed against the computer itself...in the form of sabotage or ransom cases, all of which acts have one commonalty--the computer is either the tool or the target of the felon (as quoted in *Computer Crime: Expert Witness Manual*, 1980:4).

According to the first definition, theft of computer hardware or software through conventional means may not be classified as *computer related crime*; however, it would be by the second definition (*Computer Crime: Expert Witness Manual*, 1980:4). But would either definition cover what may be called the "Wargames" actions of the young computer enthusiasts, or "hackers," who recently broke into classified security files of governmental agencies simply because of the "challenge"? Would either definition cover the illegal copying of copyrighted software via a telecommunications link between two home computers where the "personal gain issue" is obscured? Would either definition cover circumstances of "software piracy" in which copyright protected programs are electronically transferred to other disks and then sold for a profit? Would either definition fit the illegal practice of producing outside the United States "exact electronic replicates" of specific brands of high priced, popular personal computers (e.g., Apple, IBM) which are then marketed in the United States either under the name brand or some other name? What about the unauthorized access by personal computer users to data base information networks or services (described in Chapter 2)? The answer to many of these questions is "NO." Conventional specifications of *computer related crime* appear to be primarily oriented to mainframe computer technology. While conventional definitions cover matters such as the illegal use of computer stored information, fraud, embezzlement of funds, and related violations, these do not account for the extensive potential abuses which microcomputer technology may allow.

There appears to be a need for a more comprehensive definition of computer related crime which would include microcomputer related crime. Or, perhaps computer related crime should be applied only to acts committed with a mainframe computer system, and a new term, microcomputer related crime, should be used to refer to a broader class of illegal acts committed with a personal or home computer. In any event, there are numerous definition and phenomenological issues to be addressed by criminology.

Complicating an understanding of the issue even more, a search of the computer crime related literature suggests that there are more than two dozen terms currently used to refer to computer related crime. Among the most common are the terms computer crime, computer fraud, computer abuse, computer theft, stealing by computer and computer managed fraud (see, Bequai, 1978:32). No phenomenon can be understood or properly researched until there is some agreement concerning what it should be called.

Extensive research has been done on "conventional computer crime," or the use of computers to commit fraud or to embezzle funds. Existing data suggests that computer crime costs an estimated $100 million per year in the United States and $300 million per year worldwide (Parker, 1976; Bequai, 1978). Computer crime is big business in which corporate crime losses average $621,000 per incident (Colvin,1979:1). Research into microcomputer related crime is virtually non-existent. The estimated dollar loss due to computer related crime is overly conservative, because these figures do not reflect the multi-billion dollars per year lost to companies because of software piracy, or illegal reproduction of copyright protected software, and hardware piracy which involves the reproduction of hardware, usually outside the United States, and then sale under the original manufacturer's name.

According to Mandell (1984:157) there are five key areas of computer operations which are subject to abuse.

a.   Input operations may be manipulated to avoid legitimate charges to a user or to cause the computer to print a check in payment for nonexistent services. Fictitious accounts, and even whole companies, have been created in this way.

b.   A program controls the computer's operations and if tampered with can benefit the criminal at the expense of the entity that owns the computer. Also, programs themselves are valuable items that are subject to theft.

c.   The central processing unit may be exposed to vandalism or destruction. A user's exclusive reliance on it for vital functions makes it a prime target for vandalism or ransom demands.

d.   Output, though the least likely target for criminal attack, can still present serious criminal problems. Valuable data, such as mailing lists, can be stolen. Computer output, particularly printed checks, is usually the goal of the criminal who manipulates the system.

e.   The communication process is vital to all information flowing in and out of the computer. This data can be intercepted from the lines of communications through wiretapping, or the communications facilities themselves can be destroyed.

An interesting paradox appears to be evolving. On one hand, computer technology appears to be improving in the safe-guarding of electronically stored governmental and industrial data (see Parker, 1983). Yet, detection and prosecution rates suggest that computer related crime is a growing problem. It is estimated that only 1% of all computer crime is detected, only 14% of this is reported, and only 3% of reported crime ends in conviction; furthermore, FBI data indicate that only one out of twenty-two thousand computer criminals will serve any prison time (Becker, 1980:6). These statistics may reflect the expanding involvement of organized crime influences (see, Peterson, 1983). They may indicate the complexities of detecting computer crimes or the reluctance of victims, usually large corporations, to prosecute. The answer is not clear and more research is needed.

Some realities, however, are recognized. Victims often do not want the publicity attached to the prosecution of offenders for fear that it would reflect negatively on the corporation's management and overall security. Computer fraud investigations are time consuming and may cost "victims" thousands of dollars and hundreds of work hours to document; it is often easier and less costly to accept the thief's resignation rather than to prosecute. Electronic evidence can be destroyed in seconds and with it critical information needed by the victim. Criminal investigators may seize hundreds of reels of data tape for evidence, again costing the victim more money. Additionally, investigators may require more information from a victim corporation than it wants to reveal. Another irony is that often those persons in positions to detect computer crime may be the actual perpetrators; hence, they can negate external audits. Another factor behind the low prosecution rate is that both civil and criminal computer law is just now developing.

Computer Law

Computer law is used here as a broad term to include criminal and civil law, court decisions, federal and state statutes and opinion pertaining to computer related matters. It is an emerging area of law whose present level of development is similar to that of correctional law in the early 1960s. As this body of law emerges, extremes and contradictions in court decisions can be expected. The issues of computer related law are complex and opinions diversified. In 1984 Mandell published one of the first texts on the subject, *Computers, Data Processing and the Law*. It covers a number of broad topics including the acquisition of computer hardware and software, computer systems failures, personnel, consulting services, facilities management, writing computer programs for sale, computer crime and privacy, systems design consideration, computer records in court and computer tax considerations. The following discussions outline some of the current issues in computer law affecting criminal justice agencies.

Civil Damages and Copyright Issues

Where possible, victimized corporations try to protect their interests and recover losses through civil mechanisms, mainly through copyright lawsuits.

The Computer Software Act of 1980, used with increasing frequency, [17 U.S.C. Section 102(a)] states:

...original works of authorship fixed in any tangible medium of expression, now known or later developed, from which they can be perceived, reproduced, or otherwise communicated, either directly or with the aid of a machine or device.

The question of whether this statute applied to computer hardware, or whether it was confined only to software, was answered in 1983 in an affirmative judgment for Apple Computer Corporation, Inc., against Franklin Computer Corporation, Inc. At issue was whether the physical configuration of microchips in the Franklin violated copyright laws, since the Franklin appeared to be configured identically to the Apple and Apple copyright protected software could "boot up" to the Franklin. In ruling against Franklin, the court held that 1) a computer program is legally considered to be a "literary work" within the meaning of the statute and therefore protected by copyright law and 2) that this protection extends to "object codes embedded in a ROM chip" which allow one brand of computer to use programs specifically designed for another. Franklin agreed to pay Apple 2.5 million dollars in damages (see Chin, 1984:10).

Privacy and Security Issues

In Chapter 2 the micro-mainframe computer link and its potential for field reporting was discussed and the privacy issue was raised. Privacy, or the protection of individual rights concerning personal anonymity, became matters of national concern in the late 1960s and early 1970s. In criminal justice matters, the individual privacy matter clashed with the state's "right to know" (Trubow, 1978:1). One consequence was the 1969 Freedom of Information Act, which governs all criminal justice agencies and limits the types of information which can be collected, specifies access to agency collected information, and provides an individual the right to demand copies of all information concerning him. Additional liability specifications are reflected in Section 524(b) of the 1973 Crime Control Act:

> All criminal history information collected, stored or disseminated through, or sent therein; the administration shall assure that the security and privacy of all information is adequately provided for and that information shall only be used for law enforcement and criminal justice and shall take place under procedures reasonably designed to ensure that all such information is kept current therein; the administration shall assure that the security and privacy of all information is adequately provided for and that information shall only be used for law enforcement and criminal justice and other lawful purposes. In addition, an individual who believes that criminal history information concerning him contained in an automated system is inaccurate, incomplete, or maintained in violation of the title, shall, upon satisfactory verification of his identity, be entitled

to review such information and to obtain a copy of it for the purpose of challenge or correction.

These obligations were also reflected in the 1976 National Advisory Committee Standards and Goals:

Data obtained by criminal justice researchers under explicit or implicit pledges of confidentiality require protection against improper or unauthorized use. In particular, when researchers assemble a data file that would be subject to the provisions of the Privacy Act if held by a Federal agency, they incur an implicit obligation to protect its confidentiality. When confidentiality of such data is unlikely to be protected, as in research conducted on behalf of a party in litigation, informed consent should include acknowledgment of the circumstances under which the data will be released (NAC, 1976:41-42).

Microcomputer technology has the potential of either enhancing or subverting these protections. An example of a microcomputer used to protect these rights is the practice of some law enforcement agencies of maintaining two data bases. One, using a microcomputer, is used to store and retrieve raw or unconfirmed field intelligence about subjects currently under investigation; this system is closed in the sense that only agency investigators currently working a case have access to this information. Once the raw field information has been has been verified, collaborated or corrected, it is then fed into another microcomputer system which interfaces with a mainframe computer and is available to other agencies sharing the same criminal investigation data base system (e.g., CIS). Individual rights are protected since it prevents uncollaborated, and perhaps incorrect, evidence from being disseminated to other law enforcement agencies.

The same technology can also be used to subvert individual rights. Protected by First Amendment Rights, one investigator, owning a personal computer with telecommunication capabilities, and working at home, can exchange case information with a public or private investigator of another agency thousands of miles away. Only if this material becomes relevant in a court case or is brought to the attention of the court can the files of such transactions be examined. Another example is unauthorized access to confidential criminal justice agency data files through the use of telecommunications links and microcomputers. Although extensive safeguards are employed in most agencies, the rapidly evolving technology in combination with human "hacker" incentive can be capable of breaking any security code.

The issues surrounding the use of mainframe computers by the government and the military is seen as being more odious. Burnaham (1983), in his book *The Rise of the Computer State*, presents a shocking chronology of the use of computerized information by government, military, and special interest groups in the United States and around the world. He documents the use of census tract data by the government during World War II to round up persons of Japanese extraction in the U.S. and ship them to holding camps where many spent the war years. Beginning under the Carter administration and expanded under Reagan, he traces the federal government's systematic use of computers to detect fraud of all types for possible prosecution. He documents the manipulation of the National Security Agency records to undermine the credibility of members of the Carter administration. He describes the vulnerability of ordinary citizens to government and credit bureau inquiry of personal credit card, check writing and telephone transactions. He describes how the technology of an information society can be used to manipulate elections, voter attitudes toward specific issues and substantially violate the rights of personal privacy, involving fundamental issues such as voting choices and sexual preferences.

Statutory and Evidentiary Issues

Because of the relatively brief history of computer related crime, criminal law defining computer crime has yet to be clearly written by the U.S. Congress or by many states. The exception is those laws which relate to the use of computers to achieve more conventional ends, such as embezzlement, theft and misappropriation of funds. However, matters such as the selling of "pirate made" software or hardware for profit, or even the selling of an "illegally made and sub-standard copy of a brand name computer" may be federally prosecuted under more general statutes, such as fraud, electronic mail fraud, conspiracy to commit fraud because more specific criminal statutes are often non-existent. Furthermore, issues of jurisdiction are often complex and state and federal statutes may conflict.

In 1984 the Computer Fraud and Abuse Act was passed which made it illegal to gain unauthorized access to government data bases or to financial institutions protected by the federal government. However, this law fell short of providing the type of enforcement powers many experts feel are necessary to prevent or combat computer fraud or abuse. The problem may not be due to a lack of laws so much as to how white collar crime in general is treated by American justice and viewed by society as a whole.

Beyond these deliberations, however, are other issues relating to the use of computer generated evidence. Computer generated evidence is not only difficult to obtain, but it is also difficult to verify and present in a court of law. According to the best evidence rule, the best evidence is original evidence. However, in the case of computer stored information, the "original" information is the computer binary language code which is virtually incomprehensible to humans unfamiliar with its complexities. Courts will therefore accept data storage mediums, such as data tapes or disks, and upon verification of authenticity, will accept as "original" evidence printouts of the information stored on this medium. In Federal cases, the 1975 Federal Rules of Evidence, Rule 1001(3) provides that "[I]f data are stored in a computer or similar device, any printout or other output readable by sight, shown to reflect the data accurately, is an original."

In cases where the original medium has been destroyed or is otherwise "outside the jurisdiction of the court," printout data can be admissible providing that "...it is established that the primary evidence is in the possession of the adverse party, who, after proper notice to produce it, fails to do so." (*American Jurisprudence*, Second Edition, 29:513). Convictions without "original" evidence are few and difficult to achieve.

Thus, the legal basis for the prosecution of computer related crimes, other than for the obvious instances of theft or embezzlement, is a complex and nebulous process for the investigator, the prosecutor and the "victim" alike. Exact information on the numbers of cases "purposefully" not prosecuted because of legal issues is not available and would be a worthwhile topic for future research, as would the study of state laws and the incidence of computer crime in each state.

The quality of any case, however, is directly related to the competency of law enforcement investigators which in some instances is questionable. This subject is examined next.

Competency to Investigate

Some victims of computer related crime do not prosecute because they do not believe that the law enforcement agencies involved possess the expertise to properly investigate such crimes (Parker,1979). This perception, however, is challenged by computer crime investigators who maintain that...

Law enforcement officers can be trained to investigate competently, professionally, and successfully 93 percent of all computer crimes, and to recognize the level of technical expertise required in a consultant to solve the remaining 7 percent...(Colvin, 1979: 1).

Computer crime experts identify six areas of vulnerability where computer crime schemes originate:

1) input/output alterations of data;
2) computer operations;
3) computer programs;
4) auxiliary storage manipulations;
5) systems penetrations; and
6) computer communications.

Investigators need to be trained on three levels of competency:

1) awareness level, five days of formalized training which prepares an investigator to handle roughly 58% of cases which mostly involve crime schemes 1 and 2 (input/output alterations, and computer operations);
2) comprehensive level, four months of training which prepares an investigator to handle up to 93% of the cases, including schemes 3 and 4 or computer program and auxiliary storage manipulations;
3) specialist level, requires persons with advanced degrees and/or expertise in systems design in order to investigate schemes 4 and 5 or systems penetration and communications manipulation, which account for roughly 7% of computer crimes. [See, Colvin, 1979: 1-4 or contact the Federal Bureau of Investigation, Economic and Financial Crimes Unit, FBI Academy, Quantico, Va., for information.]

Although there is some evidence to support these impressive claims of investigator training and competency (La Palme, 1983), there remains a dearth of hard quantitative research evidence. These issues also present new subject matter to be examined in terms of deterrence research.

ETIOLOGY OF COMPUTER RELATED CRIME

In addition to a lack of consistent terminology, epidemiology and demographic information on computer related crime, there is a void of theory as to the cause of computer crime and a lack of research on offender characteristics, motivation, background and modus operandi. It is assumed that computer crime is a specialized area of white collar crime, that law violators are in their twenties, educated, middle or upper class, and reasonably intelligent (Parker, 1976; Bequai, 1980.) These characteristics are present in many instances of fraud and theft involving computers because they are almost prerequisites for anyone seeking employment in computer jobs. However, with the widespread use of personal microcomputers, these assumptions concerning offender characteristics may not be valid. For a few thousand dollars, one can purchase the technology which would enable the knowledgeable user to steal millions of dollars through electronic transfers or through the pirating of software. In the latter instance, pirate copies of software originally sold for as much as $500, can be made at a cost of $5-10, and sold for $99 to unsuspecting individuals. Bogus computer mail order houses can open, advertise, take in huge profits, close and disappear in a matter of a few months leaving few, if any, tracks. Although copyright laws protect American computer manufacturers from American made clone competition, it cannot protect against foreign made clone competition. The international profit potential in the rapidly growing area of software and hardware piracy makes such illegal trade second only to the illegal sale of drugs in terms of dollar value. Given that the etiology of computer crime remains a virtually undeveloped area of criminology, the growth potential for future research is also significant.

The U.S. Department of Justice identifies twelve basic types of computer crime. Each can be used individually or in combination with others. While many of these are primarily mainframe techniques, some can be used with mini and microcomputers as well. Each of these basic types has been described below.

1.   *Data diddling* involves altering information or data before or at the time of input into the computer. Forging documents, falsifying dates and substituting numerical data are examples of data diddling. This obviously can be performed on any type of computer.

2.   *Trojan horse* involves the inclusion of a sub-routine within a larger computer program which allows the user access to the program or allows the performance of some unauthorized function. The main program will be able to perform its intended purpose, often without any hint of the hidden program. Fairly sophisticated computer programming skills are needed to facilitate this type of crime. For example, the overdraft of a particular account being ignored or the billing of a particular location being ignored are typical trojan horses. Trojan horses

tend to be mainframe and minicomputer problems, but may also be problems for microcomputer users.

3. *Salami techniques* involve the theft of small amounts of assets by a computer. Sometimes the technique involves many different sources, and sometimes it comprises a few sources but many small thefts. This is usually a mainframe problem.

4. *Superzapping* is an approach which uses a program to bypass security controls in a system. Once accessed, the data base can be manipulated or examined. This tends to be primarily a mainframe or minicomputer problem.

5. *Trap door* is a technique used by programmers to regain access to security programs after they have been written and turned over to the user. These provide a hidden password code, known only to the programmer, which allows access to the system or data base, even though the programmer is no longer authorized. Trap doors can be placed in any type of software for any type of computer.

6. *Logic bomb* is a program within a program which is designed to cause the larger program to crash if certain conditions occur (e.g., time, event). Logic bombs are sometimes used individually and sometimes in combination with other techniques. When used individually the offender is often trying to get revenge on an employer or make the purchaser of the program return for an expensive consultation. When used with other techniques, it is often designed to conceal the other technique. For example, a programmer may be using a salami technique. If detected by another programmer or by the computer, any attempt to alter or remove the salami will trigger the conditions for the bomb to go off and the larger program to crash. It should also be noted that software manufacturers use logic bombs in combination with copyright protections; any attempt to bypass the copy protection will set off the bomb and render the program inoperative. Logic bombs can be placed in any type of software and can become problems for any type of computer system.

7. *Asynchronous attack* is a highly sophisticated programming technique which is designed to confuse the operating system.

Computer systems often run programs in batch mode, setting priorities and ordering the sequence in which the programs will run and the amount of computer resources which can be devoted to running a particular job. Jobs with lower priorities are held in queue until those with high rank are run. Lower priority jobs also set limits on the amounts of memory and computer time which are devoted to them. Asynchronous attack manipulates the ordering process, allowing lower priority or unauthorized programs to consume computer resources to a higher degree than officially approved. Only the foremost programmers are capable of performing this technique. This is a problem primarily associated with mainframe computers.

8. *Scavenging* is a technique of searching for information through files and storage devices for something of value, much like sorting through a trash container. This is done by either a programmer or a program. Like the previous technique, a high degree of expertise is required. It should be noted that there are numerous utility programs which allow partial recovery of erased data, this is because erasing is rarely complete and fragments of information can be recovered and pieced together. Scavenging can occur with any type of computer.

9. *Data leakage* is a term referring to a range of possible actions, all of which involve stealing information from a computer or from around a computer. All computers, even microcomputers, can be monitored electronically through radio waves unless special shielding is installed; the obtaining of information via radio "bugging" would be an example of data leakage. Obtaining discarded printouts from the trash or recovering information from an erased disk are also examples.

10. *Piggybacking and impersonation* include the acts of physically impersonating someone else to obtain information, using another person's authorization code, or other similar methods to gain access to the system. These techniques could involve any type of computer.

11. *Wire tapping* is one of the least likely ways of obtaining illegal information, but it can be accomplished. This differs from data leakage in that transmission lines becomes the primary

focus of the activity. This could be a problem for any type of computer.

12. *Simulation and modeling* is involved when a computer is used to plan a crime or as a source of information on which crime planning activities are based. For example, a team of professional burglars could use a computer generated diagram and task planning program to finalize the details of a complex crime and its escape routes. This could be conducted on any type of computer system.

Mandell (1984: 157-162) offers a simplified fourfold classification system. These classes are:

1. *Sabotage.* This is an act which is usually carried out for personal vengeance or political reasons and involves destroying computer hardware, software, or physical plant facilities. Mandell notes that "Computers are targets of sabotage and vandalism especially during times of political activism" and also during times of employee unrest.

2. *Theft of Services.* This refers to a wide range of acts, all of which involve the stealing of on-line computer time.

3. *Property Crimes.* This refers to another wide range of acts, all of which involve the stealing of computer equipment or software or the unauthorized copying of software.

4. *Financial Crimes.* This refers to acts which involve the intentional theft of monetary assets from the government or a business through the use of a computer.

Most computer criminals who are caught tend to be male, between 16-29 years old, conventional in most ways. Yet, a noteworthy number tend to be hackers who are brilliant in dealing with computer related issues, but who neglect other aspects of their lives such as schoolwork, appearance and sometimes even the basics of eating and sleeping (Perrolle, 1987:97). Some are students, while others hold responsible positions of trust within corporations or government. News media attention given to either hackers, those amateurs who gain authorized access to data bases by bypassing security systems, or to professional computer experts who violate the law through fraud or manipulation of systems, often paint the offender as a folk hero. The seriousness of the offense is often glossed over by the attention given the intrepid intellectual sophistication required to commit the act. Hence, society sends a double message; it condemns the act while saluting the technological sophistication of the actor. Often the hacker and the professional alike are cast in the role of Robin Hood, stealing from the rich companies, or at least violating their expensive security systems, in pursuit of intellectual curiosity as much as for personal gain. In an information society traditional sex role differences tend to be reduced. Power is derived from access to information and the use of information. The ability to perform these functions through a computer does not favor one sex or the other, although entry into positions of access and authority within established organizations is still affected by sex role discrimination. However, as more women enter power positions within organizations even these differences may diminish. Unlike the industrial revolution which favored male muscle power, the information revolution places emphasis on intellectual prowess in which both sexes can compete on an equal basis.

The fact that most computer offenders of the 1970s and 1980s tend to be male reflects the residual biases of child-rearing of decades past. As changes in child-rearing occur toward encouraging greater equality in career preparation and opportunities, proportionately more women will likely show up in computer crime statistics. Social and psychological characteristics, excluding gender and sex role distinctions, may provide insight into the growing phenomenon of computer related crime.

ROBOTIC COMPUTER APPLICATIONS

The same technology which is utilized in computers is applied in robotics. This technology began to have practical industrial applications in the 1950s, growing out of digital controlled industrial production technology. Japan's success in the automobile market and its rise to international dominance in the 1970s was primarily due to the combination of computerized robotic production techniques, made possible by mainframe computer control, and the application of newer organizational management techniques, such as Management Theory Z.

Today, computerized robots have the same flexibility of application as do microcomputers; in some senses, the robot is a self-propelled microcomputer which is capable of duplicating human motion, performing manual human tasks, equipped with video sight, and audio speech. Robots have been employed in bomb and toxic waste disposal and in other activities dangerous to humans. Recently, a robotic "corrections officer" was developed for use in riot control and supervision of prison security parameters. Costing $30,000, the four foot tall, two-hundred pound robot looks like R2D2 of *Star Wars*. Although the robot will have no weapons, its 32-bit microprocessor "brain" is enclosed in a bulletproof case. It is equipped with infrared and ultrasonic sensors that can detect human odors, and has two-way video and audio communication capabilities (Wierzbicki, 1984: 17). Personal robots designed for home use are now currently coming onto the consumer market; the level of sophistication is comparable to that of personal computers seven years ago.

Computerized robots have many different criminal justice applications. They can serve multiple functions. For example, "Officer Friendly" of the Orlando, Florida, Police Department is not only capable of functioning in dangerous bomb disposal situations, but is routinely employed in community relations as an educational machine children responds to immediately. "Officer Friendly," who also looks like *Star Wars'* R2D2, is programmed to give kids safety instructions on topics ranging from bicycle safety, to the danger of accepting rides with strangers, to instructing home owners on anti-burglary tips. The beauty of this generation of small, personal robots is that they can be programmed to do a wide range of tasks. Changing programs is as easy as slipping a floppy disk or cassette tape into a drive unit or recorder which is a built-in part of the robot. These may have great potential in dealing with educationally disadvantaged or learning disabled children who comprise a portion of any juvenile offender population. They may be used to relieve humans in many different capacities from guard functions to teacher's aides. Although initial purchase price of $1500-$30,000 seems high, robot maintenance is moderate, and robots draw no salary, no fringe benefits and do not go on strike.

SUMMARY, CONCLUSIONS AND SOME FINAL THOUGHTS

The technology of today has far exceeded that envisioned by George Orwell in *1984*. Helicopters fly faster and carry more weapons and sophisticated monitoring devices than even Orwell foresaw; movies and TV shows like "Blue Thunder" demonstrate only some of the computerized scanning technology now in existence. Computer and telecommunications capabilities also far exceed anything suggested by Orwell. Centralized control centers use TV cameras and computers to monitor prisoner activities, traffic flow on highways, protect businesses from burglary sometimes from hundreds of mile away. Although the technology exists for two-way communications via the home television, cost factors have not yet made this technology affordable for consumers. Furthermore, constitutional protections prohibit governmental use of such devices for routine surveillance of citizens. Thus, although the technology for creating a totalitarian "Big Brother" state exists, the constitutional basis for protecting individual human rights remains intact. Nevertheless, computer technology is changing American society, economy and justice.

Changes are not clearly perceptible on a day-to-day basis, but they become readily apparent when periods of time are considered. For example, when man first walked on the moon in 1969, most police and corrections departments still maintained manual data files, although new mainframe computers were starting to be installed in some departments. When the Watergate hearings were being televised, personal microcomputers were just beginning to enter the consumer market. By the late 1990s, robots may be as common as personal computers are today in homes and businesses.

As with all advances in technology, questions of human ethics and morality are raised. No one really knows the consequences of an information dependent and computerized society; none has ever existed in history before. We do not know the long-term effects on American justice due to the increasing dependency of criminal justice agencies on computers. Perhaps it may come to pass that individual rights in America will be preserved and that Orwell's visions of "goodthink" will be prevented from taking root in America because so many individuals had access to so much information through personal microcomputers. Or, perhaps computer abuse will undermine constitutional foundations.

DISCUSSION AND REVIEW QUESTIONS

1. Explain the socio-economic impact of computers on labor management in criminal justice.

2. Summarize the points included in Resolution 12 of the National Association of Government Employees/International Brotherhood of Police Officers.

3. Define computer related crime. Discuss types of crimes associated with computer hardware and software.

4. Discuss the privacy and security issues related to computer use and criminal justice investigations.

5. Explain why some law enforcement departments may not be competent to investigate computer related crime. Describe the training levels suggested for officers to become competent.

6. Discuss the reasons why some computer related crime is never reported.

7. Discuss the provisions of the Computer Software Act of 1980. How was this law applied to the case involving Franklin and Apple Computers?

8. Explain the problems concerning evidence and computer related crime.

9. Prepare a list of ten suggestions for using robots in criminal justice.

10. Identify and discuss areas for future research concerning computers.

11. Select one of the brands of new "lap size" portable computers. Collect all available evaluation information on the product selected. Write a paper on the applications and limitations of such computers in criminal justice work (e.g., police work, corrections work, court work). Be sure to evaluate at least these aspects:

    a) performance evaluations of the equipment,
    b) use and limitations in basic word processing,
    c) use and limitations in communicating with mainframe computers and other microcomputer systems, and
    d) creative uses for the equipment.

CUMULATIVE BIBLIOGRAPHY AND SUGGESTED REFERENCES

BOOKS, CHAPTERS, GOVERNMENT DOCUMENTS

Abernathy, William J., Kim B. Clark, Alan M. Kantrow. 1983. *INDUSTRIAL RENAISSANCE: PRODUCING A COMPETITIVE FUTURE FOR AMERICA*. New York: Basic Books, Inc.

Alderman, D. L. 1978. *EVALUATION OF THE TICCIT COMPUTER-ASSISTED INSTRUCTION SYSTEM IN THE COMMUNITY COLLEGE*. Princeton, NJ: Educational Testing Serv.

Agelhoff, Robert and Richard Mojena. 1981. *APPLIED FORTRAN 77 FOR STRUCTURED PROGRAMMING*. Belmont, CA.: Wadsworth, Inc.

American Jurisprudence. 1975. *FEDERAL RULES OF EVIDENCE*. Second edition. New York: The Lawyers Co-operative Publishing Company, New Topic Service.

Archambeault, William G. and Betty J. Archambeault. 1982. *CORRECTIONAL SUPERVISORY MANAGEMENT: PRINCIPLES OF ORGANIZATION, POLICY, AND LAW*. Englewood Cliffs, NJ: Prentice-Hall, Inc.

Baehr, Melany E. 1979. "Impact of Civil Rights Legislation and Court Actions on Personnel Procedures and Practices." in Charles D. Speilberger, ed., *PO-*

LICE SELECTION AND EVALUATION: ISSUES AND TECHNIQUES.
New York: Praeger.

Baehr, Melany E. and Arnold B. Oppeinheim. 1979. "Job Analysis in Police
Selection Research." in Charles D. Speilberger, ed., *POLICE SELECTION
AND EVALUATION: ISSUES AND TECHNIQUES.* New York: Praeger.

Becker, Jay. 1980. *THE INVESTIGATION OF COMPUTER CRIME.* U.S.
Department of Justice, Washington, D.C.: Government Printing Office.

Bequai, August. 1978. *COMPUTER CRIME.* Lexington, MA: D. C. Heath
and Company. Borgerson, Mark. 1982. *A BASIC PROGRAMMER'S GUIDE
TO PASCAL.* New York: McGraw-Hill, Inc.

Bork, Alfred. 1984. "Production Systems for Computer-Based Learning." in
Decker F. Walker and Robert D. Hess (editors) *INSTRUCTIONAL
SOFTWARE: PRINCIPLES FOR PERSPECTIVES FOR DESIGN AND
USE.* Belmont, CA: Wadsworth, Inc.

Brightman, Richard W. 1971. *COMPUTER ASSISTED INSTRUCTION
PROGRAM FOR POLICE TRAINING.* Washington, D.C.: National Institute of Law Enforcement and Criminal Justice.

Brodie, Leo. 1981. *STARTING FORTH.* Englewood Cliffs, NJ: Prentice-
Hall, Inc.

Brown, Anthony C. 1976. *BODYGUARD OF LIES.* New York: Bantam
Books.

Burnham, David, 1983. *THE RISE OF THE COMPUTER STATE.* New
York, NY: Vintage Books, Random House.

Campbell, Patricia B. 1980. "Computer Assisted Instruction in Education:
Past, Present, and Future." in Walter Mathews (editor) *MONSTER OR
MESSIAH? THE COMPUTER'S IMPACT ON SOCIETY* Jackson: Univer-
sity Press of Mississippi.

Chaiken, Jan M. and Bernard Cohen. 1973. *POLICE CIVIL SERVICE SE-
LECTION PROCEDURES IN NEW YORK CITY: COMPARISON OF
ETHNIC GROUPS.* New York: Rand Institute.

Coburn, Peter, Peter Kelman, Nancy Roberts, Thomas Snyder, Daniel Watt, and Cheryl Weiner. 1982. *PRACTICAL GUIDE TO COMPUTERS IN EDUCATION*. Reading, MA: Addison- Wesley Publishing Company.

Davis, Gordon B. and Thomas R. Hoffman. 1978. *FORTRAN: A STRUCTURED DISCIPLINED APPROACH*. New York: McGraw- Hill, Inc.

Diamond, J.J. 1969. *A Report on Project GROW: Philadelphia Experimental Program in Computer Assisted Instruction.* Philadelphia: Philadelphia School District, Office of Research and Evaluation.

Ennis, Miles. 1982. *A GUIDE TO MICROCOMPUTERS FOR CRIMINAL JUSTICE*. Sacramento: Search Group, Inc.

Estes, W. K. 1978. "The Information Processing Approach to Cognition: A Confluence of Metaphors and Methods." in W. K. Estes (editor) *HANDBOOK OF LEARNING AND COGNITIVE PROCESSES, VOLUME 5, HUMAN INFORMATION PROCESSING*. Hillsdale, NJ: Earlbaum.

Equal Employment Opportunity Commission. 1970. *GUIDELINES ON EMPLOYEE SELECTION PROCEDURES*. Washington, D. C.:   Government Printing Office. Feur, Alan. 1982. *THE C PUZZLE BOOK: PUZZLES FOR THE C PROGRAMMING LANGUAGE*. Englewoods Cliffs, NJ: Prentice-Hall, Inc.

Fox, Gene. 1979. "Some Implications of Equal Employment Opportunity Procedures: A Practitioner's Point of View." in *EVALUATION: ISSUES AND TECHNIQUES*. New York: Praeger. Gagne, R. M. 1977.
THE CONDITIONS OF LEARNING. Third edition. New York: Holt, Rinehart and Winston.

Gagne, R.M. and L.J. Briggs. 1979. *PRINCIPLES OF INSTRUCTIONAL DESIGN Second edition*. New York: Holt, Rinehart and Winston.

Galanter, E.H. (editor) 1959. *AUTOMATED TEACHING*. New York: John Wiley and Sons.

Glossbrenner, Alfred. 1983. *THE COMPLETE HANDBOOK OF PERSONAL COMPUTER COMMUNICATIONS: EVERYTHING YOU NEED TO GO ON LINE WITH THE WORLD*. New York: St. Martin's Press.

Graham, Neill. 1986. *The Mind Tool: Computers and Their Impact on Society, 4th edition*. St. Paul, MN: West Publishing.

Hernandez, Ernie, Jr. 1982. *POLICE HANDBOOK FOR APPLYING THE SYSTEMS APPROACH AND COMPUTER TECHNOLOGY*. El Toro, CA: Frontline Publications.

Hopper, Grace Murray and Steven L. Mandell. 1987. *Understanding Computers, 2nd edition*. St. Paul: West Publishing.

Kerningham, Brian and Dennis Ritchi. 1978. *THE C PROGRAMMING LANGUAGE*. Englewoods Cliffs, NJ: Prentice-Hall, Inc.

Klatzky, L. 1979. *HUMAN MEMORY: STRUCTURE AND PROCESSES*. Second edition. San Francisco: W.H. Freeman.

LaPalme, Glen John. 1983. *AN EDUCATIONAL RESOURCE CURRICULUM IN COMPUTER CRIME INVESTIGATION*. Ann Arbor: University Microfilms International.

Larson, Richard C. 1975. *COMPUTER PROGRAM FOR CALCULATING THE PERFORMANCE OF URBAN EMERGENCY SERVICE SYSTEMS: USER'S MANUAL (BATCH PROCESSING) PROGRAM VERSION 75-001 (BATCH)*. Cambridge: Massachusetts Institute of Technology.

Lawless, Michael W. 1976. *IMPLEMENTATION ISSUES IN CRIMINAL JUSTICE MODELING*. Santa Monica: RAND Corporation.

Lenn, Peter D. and Thomas F. Maser. 1971. *COMPUTER ASSISTED/PROGRAMMED INSTRUCTION ON THE LAW*. San Francisco: American Analysis Corp.

Luehrman, Arthur and Herbert Peckham. 1981. *APPLE-PASCAL: A HANDS-ON APPROACH*. New York: McGraw-Hill, Inc.

Lumsdaine, A.A. and R. Glaser (editors). 1960. *TEACHING MACHINES AND PROGRAMMED LEARNING*. Washington, D.C.: National Education Association.

Mandell, Steve L.. 1984. *Computers, Data Processing, and the Law: Text and Cases*. St. Paul, Mn.: West Publishing Co.

Murphy, R.T. and L.R. Appel. 1977. *EVALUATION OF THE PLATO IV COMPUTER-BASED EDUCATION SYSTEM IN THE COMMUNITY COLLEGE.* Princeton, NJ: Educational Testing Service.

Naisbitt, John. 1982. *MEGATRENDS: TEN NEW DIRECTIONS TRANSFORMING OUR LIVES.* New York: Warner Books, Inc.

National Advisory Commission. 1976. *CORRECTIONS.* Washington, D.C.: Government Printing Office.

National Commission on Libraries, Information Science. 1982. *PUBLIC SECTOR/PRIVATE SECTOR INTERACTION IN PROVIDING INFORMATION SERVICES.* Washington, D.C.: Government Printing Office.

National Technical Information Service. 1978. *A DIRECTORY OF COMPUTER SOFTWARE APPLICATIONS--URBAN AND REGIONAL TECHNOLOGY AND DEVELOPMENT.* Springfield, VA: National Technical Information Service.

Orlansky, J. and J. String. 1979. *COST-EFFECTIVENESS OF COMPUTER BASED INSTRUCTION IN MILITARY TRAINING.* IDA paper P-1375. Arlington, VA: Institute for Defense Analysis.

Ouchi, William G. 1981. *THEORY Z: HOW AMERICAN BUSINESS CAN MEET THE JAPANESE CHALLENGE.* New York: Avon Books.

Parker, Donn B. 1983. *FIGHTING COMPUTER CRIME.* New York: Charles Scribner's Sons.

Parker, Donn B. 1979. *COMPUTER CRIME: CRIMINAL JUSTICE RESOURCE MANUAL.* U.S. Department of Justice, Washington, D.C.: Government Printing Office.

Parker, Donn B. 1976. *CRIME BY COMPUTER.* New York: Charles Scribner's Sons.

Parker, Donn B., Susan H. Nycum, and S. Stephen Oura. 1973. *COMPUTER ABUSE.* Menlo Park, CA: SRI International.

Pascale, R.T. and A.G. Athos. 1981. *THE ART OF JAPANESE MANAGEMENT: APPLICATIONS FOR AMERICAN EXECUTIVES.* New York: Warner Books, Inc.

Perrolle, Judith A. 1987. *Computers and Social Change: Information, Property, and Power*. Belmont, CA: Wadswoth Publishing Co.

Peterson, Virgil W. 1983. *THE MOB: 200 YEARS OF ORGANIZED CRIME IN NEW YORK*. Ottawa, IL: Green Hill Publishers.

Raygor, Alton L. 1977. "The Raygor Readability Estimate: A Quick and Easy Way to Determine Difficulty." in P. David Pearson, ed., *READING THEORY, RESEARCH AND PRACTICE*. Twenty-sixth Yearbook of the National Reading Conference. Clemson, S.C.: National Reading Conference.

Resta, Paul Emil and Charles Philip Smith. 1983. *THE USE OF ELECTRONIC DATA PROCESSING IN CORRECTIONS AND LAW ENFORCEMENT*. Santa Monica: System Development Corp.

Rothenberg, Jerome S. 1976. *ASSISTANCE IN PUBLIC ADMINISTRATION DECISIONS: THE PUBLIC SAFETY PROGRAM*. Washington, D.C.: Department of Housing and Urban Development, Office of the Assistant Secretary for Policy Development and Research.

Sippl, Charles J. 1985. *COMPUTER DICTIONARY, Fourth edition*. Indianapolis: Howard W. Sams and Company.

Sippl, Charles J. and Roger J. Sippl. 1982. *COMPUTER DICTIONARY, Third edition*. Indianapolis: Howard W. Sams and Co.

Stern, Nancy and Robert A. Stern. 1983. *COMPUTERS IN SOCIETY*. Englewood Cliffs, N.J.: Prentice-Hall, Inc.

Swanson, Charles R. and Leonard Territo. 1983. *POLICE ADMINISTRATION*. New York: MacMillan.

Tansik, David and James Elliott. 1981. *MANAGING POLICE ORGANIZATIONS*. Belmont, C.A.: Duxbury: Wadsworth, Inc.

Territo, Leonard, C. R. Swanson, Jr., and Neil C. Chamelin. 1977. *THE POLICE PERSONNEL SELECTION PROCESS*. Indianapolis: Bobbs- Merrill.

Waldron, Joseph, Betty Archambeault, William Archambeault, Louis Carsone, James Conser, and Carol Sutton. 1987. *MICROCOMPUTERS IN*

CRIMINAL JUSTICE: CURRENT ISSUES AND APPLICATIONS. Cincinnati: Anderson.

Waldron, Joseph, Carol Sutton, Terry Buss. 1983. *COMPUTERS IN CRIMINAL JUSTICE: AN INTRODUCTION TO SMALL COMPUTERS.* Cincinnati: Pilgrimage, Anderson Publishing Co.

Walker, Decker F. and Robert D. Hess. 1984. *INSTRUCTIONAL SOFTWARE: PRINCIPLES FOR DESIGN AND USE.* Belmont, CA: Wadsworth Publishing Co.

U.S. Department of Justice. 1981. *CRIMINAL JUSTICE PLANNING AND MANAGEMENT SERIES.* Washington, D.C.: Government Printing Office.

U.S. Department of Justice. 1980. *COMPUTER CRIME: LEGISLATURE RESOURCE MANUAL.* Washington, D.C.: Government Printing Office.

U.S. Department of Justice. 1980. *COMPUTER CRIME: EXPERT WITNESS MANUAL.* Washington, D.C.: Government Printing Office.

U.S. Justice Statistics Bureau. 1982. *COMPUTER CRIME: COMPUTER SECURITY TECHNIQUES.* by SRI International. Washington, D.C.: U.S. Government Printing Office.

COMPUTER BUYERS GUIDE AND HANDBOOK. New York: Computer Information Publishing, Inc.

_____. 1983. *DIRECTORY OF AUTOMATED CRIMINAL JUSTICE INFORMATION SYSTEMS.* Bureau of Criminal Justice Statistics. Washington, D.C.: Government Printing Office.

PERIODICALS

Antonellis, Janice. 1983. "Software Solutions for Small Business." LIST. 1(November) 4:78-82.

Archambeault, William G. and Betty J. Archambeault. 1983. "Readability and Reading Comprehension Problems Among Correctional Employees: Implications for Policy Implementation." *THE JOURNAL OF CORRECTIONAL EDUCATION*. 1(March) 34:18-23.

Archambeault, William G. and Charles Fenwick. 1983. "Comparative Analysis of Japanese and American Police Organizational Management Practices." *POLICE STUDIES: INTERNATIONAL REVIEW OF POLICE DEVELOPMENT*. 6 (Fall) 3: 3-12.

Archambeault, William G. and Charles W. Weirman. 1983. "Critically Assessing the Utility of Police Bureaucracies in the 1980's: Implications of Management Theory Z." *JOURNAL OF POLICE SCIENCE AND ADMINISTRATION*. 11 (December) 4: 420-429.

Archambeault, William G. 1982. "Management Theory Z: Implications for Correctional Survival Management." *FEDERAL PROBATION QUARTERLY*. 46 (September) 7-12.

_____. 1983. "Management Theory Z: Its Implications for Managing the Labor Intensive Nature of Work in Prison." *PRISON JOURNAL*. 62 (Autumn-Winter) 2: 58-67.

Ball, Richard A. and J. Robert Lilly. 1986. "The Potential Use of Home Incarceration for Drunk Drivers." *Crime and Delinqency*. Vol 32 (2) p. 224-247.

Bartimo, Jim. 1984. "A Real Computer in Your Lap?." *INFOWORLD*. 6 (May 7). 91-95.

Beck, Allen R. 1984. "Crime Analysis: Can the Process be Computerized?" *POLICENET*. 1(Spring) 12-14.

Beechhold, Henry F. 1984. "Review: Peechtext 5000." *INFOWORLD*. 6 (January 16) 59, 63, 65.

Berry, Bonnie. 1985. "Electronic Jails: A New Criminal Justice Concern." *Justice Quarterly*. Vol 2 p. 1-22.

Boehm, Norman C. 1983. "Using Computers in Crime Fighting, Training, and Administration: A Practical Approach." *THE POLICE CHIEF*. (March) 123-124.

Bolin, Jerry and Kenneth Hartke. 1985. Computerized Corrections: Missouri's Experience. *Corrections Today*. Vol 47 (7) p. 104-106.

Bonner, Paul. 1983. "When You'd Rather Switch Than Swap...The New Integrated Business Packages May Be The Way Out." *PERSONAL COMPUTING.* 7(AUGUST) 8:73-78,158.

Brin, Stan. 1983. "The Evolution of dBASE II." *POPULAR COMPUTING.* 2(February) 4: 74-80, 154.

Bryne, James M. 1986. The Control Controversy: A Preliminary Examination of Intensive Probation Supervision Programs in the United States. Federal Probation. Vol 50 (2) p. 4-15.

Burkhart, Walter R. 1986. Intensive Probation Supervision: An Agenda for Research and Evaluation. *Federal Probation.* (April) p. 75-77.

Carpenter, James, Dennis Deloria, and David Morganstein. 1984. "Statistical Software for Microcomputers: A Comparative Analysis of 24 Packages." *BYTE.* 9(April) 234-236, 238-258, 260, 262, 264.

Casmey, Howard B. 1976. "Computer Based Education: An Approach Toward Adaptive Learning Procedures." Paper presented at the Association for the Development of Computer-Based Instructional Systems.

Chambers, Jack A. and Jerry W. Sprecher. 1980. "Computer-Assisted Instruction: Current Trends and Critical Issues." *COMMUNICATIONS OF THE ACM.* (23) 332-342.

Chandler, Harry N. 1984. "Skinner and CAI." *JOURNAL OF LEARNING DISABILITIES.* 17 (7) 441-442.

Chin, Kathy. 1984. "Franklin to Pay Apple $2.5 Million Settlement." *INFOWORLD.* (January 30) 10.

_____. (b) 1984. "Home Is Where The Job Is: Is Telecommuting the Work Style of the Future or Just Another Fad?" *INFOWORLD.* 6 (April) 30-36.

Cole, Bernard. 1983. "The Family Tree of Computer Languages." *POPULAR COMPUTING.* (September) 82-88.

Colvin, Bill D. 1979. "Computer Crime Investigators: A New Training Field." *FBI Law Enforcement Bulletin.* (July) 1-4.

Damos, James and Zanna Stepanek. 1982. "Sharing Your Computer: More Information More Economically." *THE POLICE CHIEF*. (April) 32-34.

Davis, Thomas. 1981. "Computer Scheduling Optimizes Police Manpower." *LAW AND ORDER*. (September) 84-87.

Dennis, J. Robert. 1983. "Computer Literacy Among Pre-College Students." Symposium presented at Louisiana State University, Oct.

del Carmen, Rolando V. and Joseph B. Vaughn. 1986. Legal Issues in the Use of Electronic Surveilliance in Probation. *Federal Probation*. Vol 50 (2) p. 60-69.

Dervin, Brenda. 1983. "More Will Be Less Unless the Scientific Humanization of Information Systems." *NATIONAL FORUM*. (Summer) 25-26.

Diem, R.A. and P.G. Fairweather. 1980. "An Evaluation of a Computer Assisted Education System in an Untraditional Academic Setting--A County Jail." *AEDS JOURNAL*. 13(3) 204-213.

Dizard, Wilson P., Jr. 1982. "The Coming Information Age." *INFORMATION SOCIETY*. (February) 91-112.

Dowling, Barry. 1982. "Microcomputers Behind Bars: CAI for Juvenile Delinquents." *CLASSROOM COMPUTER NEWS*. 3, 70.

Embrey, Glenn. 1983. "COBOL." *POPULAR COMPUTING*. (September) 90-96.

Erwin, Billie S. 1986. "Turning Up the Heat on Probationers in Georgia." *Federal Probation*. Vol 50 (2) p. 17-24.

Flammang, C.J. and Roy O. Walker. 1982. "Training: A Rationale Supporting Computer-Based Instruction." *THE POLICE CHIEF*. (August) 60-64.

Flynn, Leonard E. 1986. "House Arrest: Florida's Alternative Eases Crowding and Tight Budgets." *Corrections Today*. Vol 48 (5) p.64-68.

Ford, Daniel and Annesley K. Schmidt. 1984. "Electronically Monitored Home Confinement." National Institute of Justice Reports. Vol 194 p. 2-6.

Friel, Charles, Joseph Vaughn, and Rolando del Carmen, 1987. "Electronic Monitoring and Correctional Policy: The Technology and Its Application." National Institute of Justice, U.S. Department of Justice.

Fry, Edward. 1977. "Fry's Readability Graph: Clarifications, Validity, and Extension to Level 17." *JOURNAL OF READING.* (December) 242-252.

Gable, Ralph K. 1986. Application of Personal Telemonitoring to Current Problems in Corrections. *Journal of Criminal Justice.* Vol 14 p. 167- 176.

Gaines, Brian R. 1981. "The Technology of Interaction--Dialogue Programming Rules." *International Journal of Man-Machine Studies.* (14) 133-150.

Gagne, Robert M., Walter Wager, and Alicia Rojas. 1981. "Planning and Authoring Computer-Assisted Instruction Lessons." *EDUCATIONAL TECHNOLOGY*, 21(September) 17-26.

Gaydosh, Dan. 1984. "Revolution for the Masses?" *INFOWORLD.* 6(January 23) 12.

Green, Dough and Dennis. 1983. "EasyWriter II: Word Processor from Information Unlimited Software." *INFOWORLD.* 5(December) 11-12.

Griest, John H., Kenneth S. Mathisen, Marjorie H. Klein, Lorna S. Benjamin, Harold P. Erdman and Frederick J. Evans. 1984. "Psychiatric Diagnosis: What Role for the Computer?" *HOSPITAL AND COMMUNITY PSYCHIATRY.* 35(11) 1089-1093.

Gunning, Robert. 1968. "The Fog Index After Twenty Years." *Journal of Business Communication.* (Winter) 3-13.

Halfhill, Tom R. 1983. "Selecting the Right Word Processor." *COMPUTE.* (April) 24-31.

Hafner, Katherine. 1983. Electronic Ball and Chain Sparks Controversy. *Computerworld.* March 28, p. 23.

Hart, Richard. 1983. "VisiCalc Advanced: Spreadsheet from VisiCorp." *INFORWORLD: Report Card.* 5(December) 48A:40-41.

Hersch, Jack and David Cushing. 1983. "Electronic Spreadsheets: What Are Your Training Options?" *LIST.* 1(October) 3:14-18, 20, 23.

Hixson, Amanda. 1983. "Multiplan: Spreadsheet from Microsoft." *IN-FOWORLD: Report Card.* 5(December) 48A:42-44.

Hofmeister, Alan M. and Margaret M. Lubke. 1986. "Expert Systems: Implications for the Diagnosis and Treatment of Learning Disabilities." *Learning Disability Quarterly* Spring, vol. 9, 133-136.

Hughes, Robert and Joseph Pedroncelli. 1982. "To Catch a Rapist." *The Police Cheif.* (September) 32-34.

Ingraham, Barton L. and Gerald W. Smith. 1974. "The Use of Electronics in the Observation and Control of Human Behavior and Its Possible Use in Rehabilitation and Control." In *Crime and Justice 1970-1971.* Jackwll Susman, ed., New York: AMS Press.

Ioimo, Ralph. 1981. "Computerization of the Small and Medium Size Police Department." *The Police Chief.* (May) 56-57.

Iversen, Wesley R. 1985. High-Tech Leg Irons Put to the Test. *Electronic Week.* March 4, p. 30.

Jadrnicek, Rik. 1983. "SuperCalc: Spreadsheet from Sorcim." *INFOWORLD: Report Card.* 5(December) 48A:45-47.

Jauer, Robert E. 1983. "Using Computers in Crime Fighting, Training and Administration: A Practical Approach." *The Police Chief* (March) 126-130.

Kinnucan, Paul. 1983. "Integrated Software--Single Products for Multiple Tasks." *LIST.* 1(October) 3:50-53, 55.

Kulik, James A., Robert L. Bangert and George W. Williams. 1983. "Effect of Computer-Based Teaching on Secondary School Students." *JOURNAL OF EDUACATIONAL PSYCHOLOGY.* 75 (1) 19-26.

Kulik, James A., Chen-Lin C. Kulik and Peter A. Cohen. 1980. "Effectiveness of Computer Based College Teaching: A Meta-analysis of Findings." *REVIEW OF EDUCATIONAL RESEARCH.* 525-544.

Lachenbruch, Peter. 1983. "Test the Accuracy of Statistical Microcomputer Software with these Tools." *BYTE.* 8(November) 11: 560-563, 566-568, 570.

Latessa, Edward J. 1986. The Cost Effectiveness of Intensive Supervision. *Federal Probation*. April, p. 70-73.

Lehrman, Stevanne R. 1984. "Peachtext 5000." *BYTE*. 9 (April) 186-188, 191, 192, 194, 196, 198, 200-202.

Lehtinen, Marlene. 1984. "CAPE: Using the IBM PC for Personnel Evaluation." *POLICENET Magazine*. 1 (Spring) 1:20-23.

Lipchitz, Joseph W. 1986. "Back to the Future: An Historical View of Intensive Probation Supervision." *Federal Probation*. (April) p. 78-81.

McClain, W. Troy. 1982. "Computer Assisted Subpoena Transmittal." *THE POLICE CHIEF*. (September) 27-30.

McGehee, Lee and Glenn M. Whiteacre. 1983. "Microcomputers in Law Enforcement." *FBI Law Enforcement Bulletin*. (March) 24-26.

McLaughlin, G. Harry. 1969. "SMOG Grading -- A New Readability Formula." *JOURNAL OF READING*. (May) 639-46.

McMullen, Barbara and John. 1983. "The Super Spreadsheets: How DoThey Compare?" *POPULAR COMPUTING*. 2(June) 8:112-115, 118, 120, 122-123.

Mace, Scott. 1983. "Teaching Computer Phones and Drills Students." *INFOWORLD*. 5(July 18) 1, 8.

_____. (b) 1983. "'Electronic University' Opens For Enrollment: Modem-based Network Featured." *INFOWORLD*. 5 (September 26) 1, 6-7.

_____. (c) 1983. "'Computer Literacy' Dominates Fall Education Books." *INFOWORLD*. 5(October 17) 30, 42.

Markoff, John. 1983. "Who's In Front." *INFOWORLD*. 5 (October) 44:32-36.

_____. 1984. "Review: Microsoft Word." *INFOWORLD*. 5 (December 12) 73-74.

Meachum, Larry R. 1984. House Arrest: The Oklahoma Experience. *Corrections Today*. Vol 48 (6) p. 102-110.

Miller, Michael J. 1984. "Wordstar Number One Competitive." *POPULAR COMPUTING*. 3 (January) 121-23, 126-127.

Molitor, Graham T. 1981. "The Information Society: The Path to Post-Industrial Growth." *THE FUTURIST*. (April) 23-30.

Muhlin, Gregory. 1983. "ABSTAT: Statistical Program from Anderson-Bell." *INFOWORLD: Report Card*. 5 (December) 48A:50-52.

Palumbo, Paul A. and Gregory J. Connor. 1983. "Firearms Training: The Computer Assisted Target Analysis System." *THE POLICE CHIEF*. (May) 67-70.

Parker, Donn B. 1976. "A Look at Computer Fraud and Embezzlement in Banking. *THE MAGAZINE OF BANK ADMINISTRATION*. (May) 21-22.

Petersilia, Joan. 1986. Exploring the Option of House Arrest. *Federal Probation*. Vol. 50 (2) p. 50-55.

Perez, Marta Brito. 1982 "IACP Conducts Two Training Programs." *THE POLICE CHIEF*. (August) 35-36.

Ping, Charles J. 1983. "Planning as if People Mattered." *NATIONAL FORUM*. (Summer) 36-37.

Poblam, David L. and Bernell J. Edwards. 1983. "Desk Top Trainer: Transfer of Training of an Aircrew Precedural Task." *JOURNAL OF COMPUTER-BASED INSTRUCTION*. 10 (3-4) 62-65.

Robertson, Gary and Samson Chang. 1980. "Crime Analysis System Support." *THE POLICE CHIEF*. (August) 41-43.

Rodriguez, Matt. 1982. "Computer Applications: Links Field to Records via Mobile Terminal System." *THE POLICE CHIEF*. (September) 19-23.

Rothenberg, Sheribel. 1977. "Minorities' Constitutional Rights to Police Department Employment." *POLICE LAW QUARTERLY*. (June) 22-31.

Rorvik, David. 1974. Behavior Control: Big Brother Comes. *Intellectual Digest*. January, p. 17-20.

Rowe, Neil C. 1981. "Some Rules for Good Simulations." *EDUCATIONAL COMPUTER MAGAZINE.* (November-December) 37-40.

Rushinek, Avi, Sara F. Rushinek, and Joel Stutz. 1985. "Instructor-Course Evaluation and The Use of Interactive Computer Assisted Instruction: An Empirical Investigation." *THE JOURNAL OF COMPUTER INFORMATION.* (Fall) 17-25.

Ryabik, James E. and Kenneth R. Olson. 1985. "Computerized Testing." *PROFESSIONAL PSYCHOLOGY: RESEARCH AND PRACTICE.* Vol. 16, no. 1, 6-7.

Schacter, H.L. 1979. "Job-Related Examinations for Police -- Two Developments." *JOURNAL OF POLICE SCIENCE AND ADMINISTRATION.* (July) 86-89.

Schmidt, Annesley K. 1986. "Electronic Monitors." *Federal Probation.* April Vol. 50 92) p. 56-59.

Schwitzgebel, Ralph. 1967. "Electronic Innovation in the Behavioral Sciences: A Call to Responsibility." *American Psychologist.* Vol. 22 p. 364-370.

Schwitzgebel, Ralph K. 1969. "Issues in the Use of An Electronic Rehabilitation System with Chronic Recidivists." *Law and Society Review.* Vol. 3, p. 597-615.

Schwitzgebel, Ralph, Robert Schwitzgebel, Walter N. Pahnke, and William Sprech Hurd. 1964. "A Program of Research in Behavioral Electronics." *Behavioral Science.* Vol. 9, p. 233-238.

Shaw, William. 1980. "Police Technology." *LAW AND ORDER.* (January) 10-16.

_____. (a) 1979. "Police Technology." *LAW AND ORDER.* (August) 8, 10, 12, 13.

_____. (b) 1979. "They Are Being Called Dream Machines." *LAW AND ORDER.* (August) 9-13.

Siegel, M.A. and Z.M. Simutis. 1979. "CAI for Adult Basic Skill Training: Two Applications." Paper presented to 24th Annual Convention of International Reading Association, Atlanta.

Smith, Kent A. 1983. "Information As A Commodity or Public Good." *NATIONAL FORUM*. (Summer) 27-31.

Sykes, Gary W. 1986. "Automation, Management, and the Police Role: The New Reformers?" *Journal of Police Science and Administration*. (14) 1: 24

Timm, Kimberly. 1983. "Using Computers in Crime Fighting, Training, and Administration: A Practical Approach." *THE POLICE CHIEF*. (March) 124-126.

Thomas, William V. 1981. "Organized Crime: The American Shakedown." *EDITORIAL RESEARCH REPORTS*. (23) 451-468.

Vallee, Jacques. 1983. "Confessions of a Computer Scientist." *POPULAR COMPUTING*. (February) 85-91, 156-159.

Walker, Roy O. and Christopher J. Flammang. 1981. "Instructional Application of Computer-Based Education in Police Training." *JOURNAL OF POLICE SCIENCE AND ADMINISTRATION*. (9) 224-228.

Walker, Roy O. 1983. "Computer Use In Instruction: Central Systems vs. Microsystems." *THE POLICE CHIEF*. (January) 58-60.

Wilkenson, Tom and John Chattin-McNichols. 1985. "The Effectiveness of Computer Assisted Instruction for Police Officers." *JOURNAL OF POLICE SCIENCE AND ADMINISTRATION*. Vol. 13, no.1, 230-235.

Wierzbicki, Barbara. 1984. "EdNET System to Offer Study-At-Home Courses." *INFOWORLD*. (January 23) 20.

_____. (b) 1984. "Mobile Robots Scheduled for Testing as Prison Guard." *INFOWORLD*. 6 (February 20) 17.

_____. 1983. *CRIME CONTROL DIGEST*. (August 15) 1.

_____. 1983. "Demystifying Computer Languages: Special Report." *POPULAR COMPUTING*. 2 (September) 80-152.

_____. 1984. "Electronic Fund Transfer and Crime." Bureau of Justice Statistics: Special Report. February. U.S. Printing Office.

_____. 1982. "Law Enforcement Training Centers: Highlights of Institutions with Law Enforcement Training Programs of National Significance." *POLICE CHIEF*. (49) 30-34.

_____. 1983. "New Problems with Computer Crime: How Computers Help Us." *CRIME CONTROL DIGEST*. (October) 17 3-4.

_____. 1982. "POSSE Fights Crime In Albany." *LAW AND ORDER*. (February) 14-18.

_____. 1983. "Report Card." *INFOWORLD*. 5 (December 1) 39-47.

_____. 1983. "Resolutions Adopted at Convention." *THE POLICE CHRONICLE*. (December) 6-7.

_____. 1981. "St. Petersburg's Computerized Dispatching System." *LAW AND ORDER*. (May) 54-58.

_____. 1983. "Wordstar: The First and Still Most Popular." *LIST*. 1 (November) 52-56.

GLOSSARY OF SELECTED TERMS

The following *Glossary of Selected Terms* is provided for the reader's convenience and quick reference. For more complete definitions and explanations of these terms, readers are referred to the appropriate chapters. This is not a complete listing of all terms and concepts used in this text.

Applications Software Programs. Programs which employ electronic languages to translate keyboard input into messages which can be read by the CPU and then re-translates back into language symbols understandable to the user.

Auxiliary Word Processing Programs. Programs used with a main word processing program (e.g., WordStar, EasyWriter II, Word) and used to check spelling, determine readability levels, check grammar and punctuation, or perform other functions related to editing.

Baud Rates. Unit of measure for modem speed, expressed in bits per second (bps). Baud rate, for a microcomputer modem is typically 300 to 2400 Baud, although some devices are capable of 9600 Baud.

Bernoulli Box. A data storage device capable of 10-40 Mb capacity. These devices can be inserted or removed in a manner similar to that of floppy disks. Advantages include amount of storage available, ease of changing devices, and the ease of establishing physical security procedures for data stored on individual devices.

Binary. A number system based on zeroes and ones. Corresponds to the presence or absence of an electric impulse.

Binary Code. A coding system based on zeroes and ones. Binary code is the basis of all computer operations and logic.

Bit. A simple electrical binary impulse code; the electrical current is *on* (+ = 1) or *off* (- = 0). The basic unit of storage or memory.

Bit Rating. Term used to describe the number of bits or units of information which a given computer system's microprocessor is capable of reading in a single impulse, often expressed as 8-bit, 16-bit, etc.

Bubble Memory. Memory capability unique to certain computers based on magnetic "bubbles" or cylinders of magnetic material that have been polarized. Bubbles can be moved about on metal paths, arranged on the top of bubble chips. Bubble memory does not require power to maintain stored data. Technology not perfected at this time.

Buffer. An auxiliary storage device which temporarily holds data as it is transferred from the CPU to an output device or as it is transferred from an input device to the CPU. Designed to compensate for differences in the rate of flow of data into or out of the CPU. Printers and modems commonly have data buffers.

Bus. A circuit or path over which data is transmitted or received from one or multiple sources. A control bus coordinates memory, input/output, and CPU. A data bus is a bi-directional communications circuit capable of transferring information among peripherals, storage devices and the CPU.

Byte. The smallest number or string of bits (on or off electrical impulses) which a computer system can save, process, or retrieve at any given time. One byte represents one letter, number, symbol, or word. For example, in an 8-bit byte the central processor is capable of reading or understanding an electrical impulse code or string of eight bits (e.g., 00110110); in a 16-bit byte system, a string of sixteen (e.g., 1100111000101110).

CAMO. Computer Assisted Monitoring of Offenders. A computer is used to receive, store, analyze, and retrieve information about individual offenders. CAMO devices can be classified into seven incremental categories, each providing increasing amounts of information about offenders.

Central Processing Unit (CPU). The microchip board which contains the circuits that control the execution of computer processing and creates computer memory. The CPU has three major sections: the arithmetic/logic unit which performs mathematical functions and responds to logic questions, the input/output unit which handles all data transfer into and out of the CPU, and the memory unit which provides the temporary storage for instructions and data. The timing mechanism of the memory unit controls the overall speed of data processing. Often the CPU is contained on a single chip and the memory section is augmented with additional chips.

Chip. An integrated circuit or integration of many circuits consisting of transistors and diodes interconnected by chemical processes on a wafer slice usually made of silicon. Chips utilize large-scale integration (LSI) technology and typically have 18, 24 or 40 pins for mounting on the circuit boards.

Circuit. A system of conductors and related electrical elements through which electric current flows.

Communications Protocol. The link between the terminal and the mainframe CPU which must be established before operations can be executed.

Computer. Device capable of accepting information, applying prescribed processes to the information, and supplying the results of these processes.

Computer Assisted Instruction (CAI). The use of computers to aid instruction in which the learner is placed in interaction with a preprogrammed study or instructional plan. Once begun, the program selects the next topic or phase of study according to previous responses of the learner, allowing progress at the learner's own capability.

Computer Assisted Writing (CAW). The application of computer technology to the preparation, editing, printing, distribution, and electronic storage of written (printed or video) material; to include: prose, charts, graphs or diagrams, numerical data listings and other forms of printed material.

Computer Awareness Level. The notion of general awareness of computers and their functions, including social, economic, and legal issues associated with computers.

Computerese. A coined term which refers to terminology used to describe microcomputers and the technology related to them.

Computer Hardware. The physical components or parts of computers (e.g., CPU, keyboard, disk drives, monitor).

Computer Language. A standardized set of symbols and rules of grammar which are used to communicate meanings, information, directions and understanding between a human user and a computer's CPU. Since computers are actually only able to understand a binary code of electronic impulses (off,on) which have been expressed in arithmetic binary logic (zeroes and ones), all computer languages must bridge the communications gap between the human user and the machine. There are over 400 computer languages written in English (e.g., BASIC, FORTRAN, C). All software programs and operating systems are written in some computer language.

Computer Law. Broad term which includes both criminal and civil law, court decisions, federal and state statutes, and opinion pertaining to computer related matters.

Computer Literacy. Term used in this text to refer to the minimum level of computer competency that an agency or a department within an agency expects from its employees. The meaning of the term differs from setting to setting.

Computer Operator Level. Computer competency or literacy level beyond awareness which involves learning computer specific and program specific skills by those personnel expected to operate data management or word processing or other programs.

Computer Related Crime. Refers to "[A]ny illegal act for which knowledge of computer technology is essential for successful prosecution," or "use of a computer to perpetuate acts of deceit, concealment and guile that have as their objective the obtaining of property, money, services, and political and business advantages," including "threats of force directed against the computer itself...in the form of sabotage or ransom cases."

Computer Software Act of 1980. Refers to 17 U.S.C. Section 102(a) which states: "original works of authorship fixed in any tangible medium of expression, now known or later developed, from which they can be perceived, reproduced, or otherwise communicated, either directly or with the aid of a machine or device."

Data. Individual pieces of information stored for future use. Distinct from "information" which refers to data that has been analyzed or summarized in some manner.

Data Base. Centralized storage of case files or other kinds of information.

Data Base Management (DBM). A systematic approach to storing, updating, and retrieving of information stored as data items, usually in the form of records in a file, where many users, or even many remote installations, will use common data files, sets or banks. In criminal justice, there are many different types of data or information bases (e.g., criminal information files, case investigation files, budgetary information files, and personnel files).

Dedicated Word Processor. A computer system which is specifically designed only for professional word processing. Some systems contain components common to computers (e.g., video screen, floppy disks, microprocessors).

Disk Drive. A random access data storage device which interacts with the CPU to input or output information. Within the device a diskette rotates which contains magnetic sections or "electronic groves" called tracks divided in sectors. Information is electronically stored on these tracks for later processing or retrieval. (*See* Floppy Disk Drive and Hard Disk Drive.)

Diskette. Formal term for a floppy disk which is a thin, flexible, plastic circle coated with a magnetic surface and covered with a protective hard-paper or plastic covering. This is the data recording medium on which programs and data are stored and input/ output through a disk drive to the computer's central processing unit.

Disk Operating System (DOS). A general-purpose program which contains numerous sub-programs or routines called utilities. These provide a logic link between the hardware of a computer (e.g., monitor, disk drive, printer, and keyboard) and application programs (e.g., word processing, accounting, statistical, or instructional program). Among the more common operating systems are: CP/M80, MS-DOS, APPLE DOS, TURBODOS, CP/M86 and UNIX. Operating systems provide such functions as disk formatting, the saving of work onto a disk, the debugging of a program, and the control of printers, disk drives or other peripherals.

Direct Memory Access or DMA. The capability of a computer system to directly input/output data stored on disk or other device, into RAM and back without utilizing CPU circuits. With DMA the user does not have to stop and "save" completed work; neither must the user "load" information from a disk. Once a program, capable of using DMA (e.g., CP/M, WordStar), has been "loaded," DMA automatically transfers information.

Dot Matrix Printer. Device which produces hard or paper output similar to that of a typewriter. Letters are formed electronically by the grouping of dots into patterns or symbols. Dot matrix printers operate at speeds of 60 to 200 characters per second (CPS) and create dots through three different principles: 1) impact transfer, through which small needles strike against a ribbon; 2) thermal transfer, which "burns" dots into paper; and 3) electrosensitive transfer, which requires a special type of paper and operates much like the transfer process in photocopying.

Drill and Practice CAI Courseware. Computer Assisted Instruction software intended to supplement traditional instructional practices in which questions are presented requiring learner responses. Appropriate feedback is supplied to the user.

Electronic Toys. Large class of electronic devices which contain microchips or microprocessors and are capable of limited memory.

Electronic Spreadsheets. A type of business application software which presents the user with an electronic ledger sheet and then provides commands to enable the user to input headings, numbers and to perform mathematical and statistical analyses of entire columns or sections of data. Also allows the generation of multiple and integrated reports from the same basic ledger sheet.

EPROM. Electrically Programmable Read Only Memory. Memory stored in EPROM is not erased when power supply to computer ceases. Information stored here can only be erased through special procedures. EPROM is usually employed by computers which are designed for fast execution of large volumes of identical programs.

Expert Systems. A computer program designed to elicit input from the user and combine that information with data previously stored in the program. The result is a computer generated diagnosis of physical or mental disability, personality profile or learning disorder. Often used as a "second opinion" by the medical profession.

Filtered Communication. A term which describes the fate of information flowing "up" through an organization's bureaucratic channels.

Floppy Disk Drive. Device used to access (use) software, store information, interact with the computer's memory, input/output data, and perform storage-retrieval functions. A floppy disk is a thin, flexible, circular object whose surface is coated with a magnetic material that allows it to retain electronic impulses. Floppy disks are enclosed in a plastic cover to protect the disk surface and within which the disk rotates. These come in several sizes: 3 1/4, 3 1/2, 5 1/4 and 8 inch.

Formatting. Process which informs the computer where to store information, where to obtain information, and how to give the commands necessary for the system to operate. Most systems require that each disk contain certain stored operating system information in order for the disk drive to be used. Sometimes called "initializing."

Game or Home Use Computers. A class of computers which have a standard RAM memory of from 4 to 64K; some can be expanded to 64K. Most of these use an 8-bit processor system, although some may use a 4-bit.

Gigabyte. A unit of measure designating one billion bytes.

Hard Disk Drives. Similar to floppy disks in function but disk storage is ten to fifty times that of the floppy disk. They have the advantages of reliability and durability since they are not as subject to damage by carelessness or dirt as are floppy disks. Sometimes called fixed disks.

High Level Language. A computer language similar to the user's own language and significantly different from binary code. High level computer languages require the use of a "compiler" or "interpreter" program to convert the commands to machine code. BASIC, COBOL and PASCAL are examples of high level languages.

Individual Use Microcomputers. A class of computers which have 8-bit processors with 48 to 64K RAM memory; a few systems come with 16-bit processors and 128K. There are generally limits on system expansion and related costs. That is, regardless of the amount of memory or the bit-rating, all of the systems listed in this class are suitable for many individual or small business applications.

Information Networking Theory. A set of organizational management and structuring principles which maintain that organizations must be flexible, structured around the central flow of information instead of the distribution of power and authority which is typical of bureaucratic management, and capable of rapidly adapting to change.

Information Storage Devices. Input/output devices used to hold information in a form which can later be read or accessed by a computer. In general, there are three types of devices in common use: 1) the floppy disk drive; 2) the hard disk drive; and 3) the tape recorder.

Information Utilities. A type of electronic networking service which provides both information and a variety of services to subscribers. Services range from computerized conferences to banking, to new information, to bulletin boards.

Ink Jet Printers. Typewriter-like output devices which form characters by spraying ink through micro-jets onto paper; the shape of the spray is electronically configured to form letters and symbols. The end product is letter quality.

Input Devices. A variety of devices which allow a user to enter data to the computer. Input devices include: 1) *keyboards*, which are similar in appearance to a typewriter or adding machine keyboard; 2) *mouse (mice)*, a small hand held box used to control the cursor on the screen and allow the user to enter commands with a single push of a button; 3) *joy-sticks*, which are usually associated with games; 4) *light pens*, which allow a user to enter/erase or draw graphic designs electronically on the display screen; 5) *disk drives*, which can either input or output information; 6) *optical scanners or bar graph readers*, which allow specially coded information (and even standard written information) to be entered simply by passing a electronic reader over the information; 7) *voice recognizers-synthesizers*, which allow the user to input verbal instructions and information. Additionally, a link of computers via *networking* using *modems*, and other devices to input instructions and information into the computer.

Integrated Software Package. The commercial packaging of multi-tasking software. That is, within the software package are different programs (e.g., word processing, speller, accounts receivable, or spreadsheet) which are interactive. Interactive in this context means that all the programs interface (e.g., use the same operating system, are compatible with the same computer) and that information from files in one program can be transferred to or combined with another.

K of Memory. The total potential storage of information. Most manufacturers of microcomputers use *K* to mean *Kbytes* or *kilobytes*; this literally represents 1,024 bytes of information (2 to the 10th power).

LANS (Local Area Networking). A special hardware and software configuration which allows individual micro / minicomputers to share common data bases, programs, and memory. LANS are physically connected systems -- as opposed to other forms of networks which are linked via phone lines. LANS have three basic configurations. 1) The *bus* consists of a single line shared by several different computer work stations which are often complete individual microcomputer systems. 2) The *ring* provides a point to point link between micros arranged in a physical circle. Like the bus, the ring does not have a central controlling computer. 3) The *star* links several different work stations with a centralized control unit. The physical configuration may take different shapes, but the routing of all information is through the master computer.

Letter Quality Printers. A general term referring to a group of high volume printers which produce a print type comparable to electric typewriter print, usually without a keyboard. Symbols and letters are formed in a manner similar to a conventional typewriter. Printer based on a daisy wheel or thimble which contain preformed characters which strike a typing ribbon are letter quality. Some dot matrix printers are designated as letter quality printers if the character produced is not visually distinguishable from the output of a traditional typewriter. Laser printers and ink jet printers are also letter quality printers.

Mainframe Computer. Large computers with greater than 1Mb of memory and an operating system greater than 32-bits. They are capable of millions of bytes of RAM.

Management Information Systems (MIS). Data bases used by agencies in management decision making.

Megabyte. A unit of measure indicating one million bytes of data.

Memory. The amount of "electronic space" which is available to process or sort information in a computer, expressed in terms of *K of memory* (e.g., 64K, 128K, 640 K).

Microprocessor. A semiconductor central processing unit or CPU containing the logic capabilities of the modern computer.

Modem. A device which allows the computer to "hear" or receive electronic impulses from other computers as well as to transmit information.

Motherboard. The main CPU circuit board which functions much like the human central nervous system in terms of coordinating and relaying information to other parts of the system.

Multi-Tasking Software. Software package which permits several separate but related tasks to be accomplished with one software operating system program (e.g., word processing and budget computations).

Organizational Management Communication. A general term which includes the collection, assimilation, generation, transmission and dissemination of information.

Organizational Management. The administrative processes of organizing, planning, communications, staffing, training, budgeting, directing and controlling.

Output Device. Used to transfer information from the CPU to some other user medium. Many input devices, such as drives and modems, can also be used for output. Other examples of these include: CRT or video screen displays, printers, modems.

Personal Robots. Computerized robots designed for home use.

Piracy. The illegal reproduction and selling for profit of copyrighted computer hardware (e.g., computers, microchips) or software (e.g., programs, operating systems).

Pixel. The smallest unit on a video screen which can be addressed by a graphics program. Screens with larger numbers of pixels produce higher resolution.

PLATO. Programmed Logic for Automatic Teaching Operations. A computer-based education system developed at the University of Illinois. Combines the production of independent instructional software with equipment capable of providing sophisticated simulations and elaborate graphic displays.

Printers. Similar to a typewriter or teletype machine without a keyboard and used to produce "hard copy" or paper reports.

Printer Memory and Buffers. The built-in storage capacity (usually 1-4K) of a printer. Also, additional peripheral devices to store programs or files awaiting printing, thereby freeing the computer's memory for other activities.

Privacy Act and Personal Security Issues. The protection of individual rights concerning personal anonymity. Includes the 1969 Freedom of Information Act which governs all criminal justice (and other public) agencies and limits the types of information which can be collected, the access to agency collected information, and provides individuals the right to demand that agencies provide copies of all information on the subject.

Professional Application Microcomputers. A class of microcomputers which are flexible and capable of memory expansion to over 640K. Most can operate multiple floppy disk drives or combinations of floppy and hard disk drives, and are capable of networking, and "multi-tasking."

PROM. Programmable Read Only Memory. Contains the program or operating systems instructions. Some can be erased and reprogrammed.

Readability. The level of reading difficulty of printed text, usually expressed in grade level equivalents.

Reading Comprehension. The ability (or inability) of a reader to correctly understand and act upon a written communication.

Response Modes. The manner in which a computer assisted instructional program conveys information to the student concerning the correctness of individual responses. Common response modes include: locked keyboard, direct refusal, hints and strike out.

Robot. A self-propelled microcomputer which is capable of duplicating human motion, performing manual human tasks, video sight, and audio speech. Robots have been employed in bomb and toxic waste disposal and in other activities dangerous to humans in criminal justice. Currently, they are being tested as institutional guards.

RAM. Random Access Memory. The extent of memory which is free for the user to access, store information, or perform processing functions. Information stored in RAM is erased when the power to the computer is turned off.

ROM. Read Only Memory. The memory that contains the computer's operating system. Instructions in ROM are permanently installed during the manufacturing process.

Scalared Communications. The bureaucratic principle of organization which states that all management policies must be in writing; that written policy must be interpreted by someone in a higher position with an organization; and that all instructions and orders must be initiated at upper organizational levels and implemented at lower levels. This results in a "funnel effect."

Simulation CAI Courseware. Supplemental instructional software intended to reinforce human instruction or to serve as a basis for evaluating learner decision making and judgment. The learner is provided with an opportunity to apply previously learned problem solving skills to a specific "real-life" situation.

Single-Tasking Software. The ability of the software to perform one function at a time (e.g., word processing, budget management, or inventory control).

Systems Analysts. The fourth level of computer competency or literacy. In addition to writing programs, systems analysts are capable of determining equipment specifications, planning expansion of existing systems, and are knowledgeable of detailed computer microcircuits.

Software. Programs which are either written by the user or purchased from commercial software manufacturers. There are two main classes of software required to operate most microcomputer systems: applications or source programs which allow the user to perform specific applications (e.g., word processing, accounting, graphics) and operating systems programs which coordinate all the parts of a computer system, allowing the user control over them.

Tracks. Electronic divisions on floppy disks which are subdivided into sectors; the exact location of a piece of stored information is called its address which is essentially the sector/track intersection.

Telecommunications Information Networking. The linking of multiple microcomputers to each other or to mainframe computer systems through the electronic linkage of any communications equipment, including telephones, closed circuit-cable television, microwave-satellite connections, among others. These information networks allow a microcomputer user to access a wide variety of information services (e.g., library literature searches, Dow Jones stock market reports, weather and news information directly from satellites, banking transactions).

Telecommuting. An area of telecommunication networking which allow persons to be physically located in one place (i.e., home, office) and to transmit work to another computer at another location.

Tutorial Programs. CAI software designed to provide initial instruction. Tutorial CAI courseware is self-explanatory once loaded into the computer; requires no interaction between the learner and human teacher; and provides the learner with directions, activities, test questions and reinforcement.

Video Display Terminals (VDT). Computer output device which is similar to a television screen, also called cathode ray tubes (CRT). These allow the user to see displayed information.

Windows. A capability of certain software programs which allows the user to view several different miniature electronic "windows" on the video display terminal.

Weberian-Fayolian Bureaucracy. A more specific name given to the organizational model which other authors have described as "para-military" or "bureaucratic," and which is typical of American-style organizations in general. This model is characterized as creating impersonal, authoritarian, hierarchial work environments where management demonstrates only segmental concern about worker welfare and where management control is implemented through formalized written policy.

Word Processing. The application of computer technology to the preparation and printing of text material through a *printer* or *typesetting device*. The most common form of CAW.

CUMULATIVE AUTHOR
AND TOPIC INDEX

247

B

C

M

P

Z

COMPUTERS IN CRIMINAL JUSTICE ADMINISTRATION AND MANAGEMENT

Introduction to Emerging Issues and Applications
Second Edition

William G. Archambeault, Ph.D.
Department of Criminal Justice
Louisiana State University at Baton Rouge

Betty J. Archambeault, Ph.D.

anderson publishing co.
2035 reading road
cincinnati, ohio 45202
(513) 421-4142

ISBN 0-932930-83-2
Library of Congress Catalog Number 88-70122

Kelly Humble *Managing Editor*

Cover Design by Scott Burchett